A DESCRIPTION OF ACQUAINTANCE

Recencies Series: Research and Recovery in Twentieth-Century American Poetics
Matthew Hofer, Series Editor

This series stands at the intersection of critical investigation, historical documentation, and the preservation of cultural heritage. The series exists to illuminate the innovative poetics achievements of the recent past that remain relevant to the present. In addition to publishing monographs and edited volumes, it is also a venue for previously unpublished manuscripts, expanded reprints, and collections of major essays, letters, and interviews.

Also available in the Recencies Series:

All This Thinking: The Correspondence of Bernadette Mayer and Clark Coolidge edited by Stephanie Anderson and Kristen Tapson
A Serpentine Gesture: John Ashbery's Poetry and Phenomenology by Elisabeth W. Joyce
Evaluations of US Poetry since 1950, Volume 2: Mind, Nation, and Power edited by Robert von Hallberg and Robert Faggen
Evaluations of US Poetry since 1950, Volume 1: Language, Form, and Music edited by Robert von Hallberg and Robert Faggen
Expanding Authorship: Transformations in American Poetry since 1950 by Peter Middleton
Modernist Poetry and the Limitations of Materialist Theory: The Importance of Constructivist Values by Charles Altieri
Momentous Inconclusions: The Life and Work of Larry Eigner edited by Jennifer Bartlett and George Hart
Yours Presently: The Selected Letters of John Wieners edited by Michael Seth Stewart
LEGEND: The Complete Facsimile in Context by Bruce Andrews, Charles Bernstein, Ray DiPalma, Steve McCaffery, and Ron Silliman
Bruce Andrews and Charles Bernstein's L=A=N=G=U=A=G=E: The Complete Facsimile edited by Matthew Hofer and Michael Golston

For additional titles in the Recencies Series, please visit unmpress.com.

A DESCRIPTION

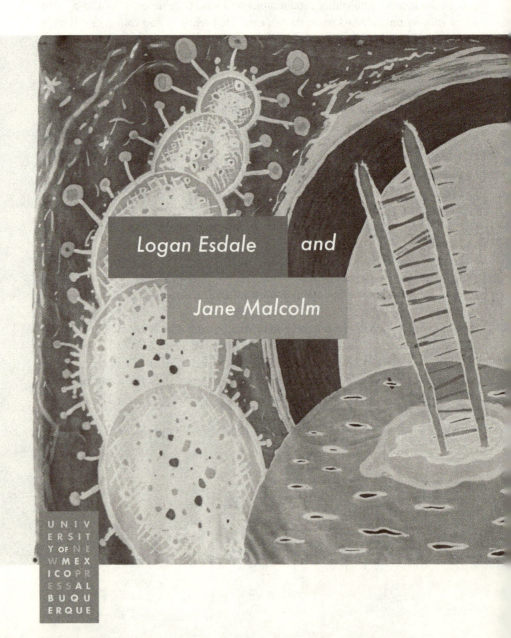

Logan Esdale and Jane Malcolm

UNIVERSITY OF NEW MEXICO PRESS ALBUQUERQUE

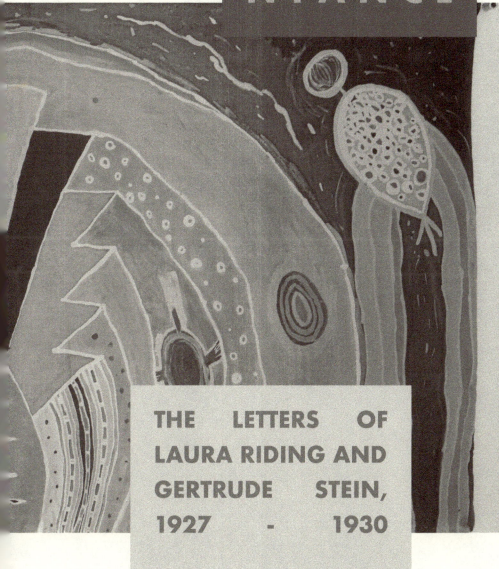

OF ACQUAINTANCE

THE LETTERS OF LAURA RIDING AND GERTRUDE STEIN, 1927 - 1930

© 2023 by University of New Mexico Press
All rights reserved. Published 2023
Printed in the United States of America

First paperback printing 2025

ISBN 978-0-8263-6489-0 (cloth)
ISBN 978-0-8263-6805-8 (paper)
ISBN 978-0-8263-6490-6 (electronic)

Library of Congress Control Number: 2022950974

Founded in 1889, the University of New Mexico sits on the traditional home-lands of the Pueblo of Sandia. The original peoples of New Mexico—Pueblo, Navajo, and Apache—since time immemorial have deep connections to the land and have made significant contributions to the broader community state-wide. We honor the land itself and those who remain stewards of this land throughout the generations and also acknowledge our committed relationship to Indigenous peoples. We gratefully recognize our history.

Cover and title-page illustration adapted from image by Laura Rosselló Gracies. Shawl painted by Len Lye. Use of shawl provided by The Len Lye Foundation. Commission of image and usage permission granted by The Fundación Robert Graves.

Designed by Isaac Morris
Composed in Charter, Averia, and Futura

CONTENTS

List of Illustrations | ix
Acknowledgments | xi
Introduction | 1

The Letters of Laura Riding and Gertrude Stein | 23

Appendix | 109
The New Barbarism, and Gertrude Stein | 121
  Laura Riding
An Acquaintance with Description | 131
  Gertrude Stein
Works Cited | 155
Index | 159

ILLUSTRATIONS

Figure 1. Laura Riding to Gertrude Stein, September 1929. | 17

Figure 2. Contents. *transition* 3, June 1927. | 24

Figure 3. "With Latin Quarter Folk." *The New York Herald*, 2 June 1928. | 28

Figure 4. "With Latin Quarter Folk." *The New York Herald*, 4 July 1928. | 28

Figure 5. "Gertrude Stein: Recent Snapshot." *transition* 14, Fall 1928. | 38

Figure 6. "Laura Riding Shawl, by Len Lye." *transition* 14, Fall 1928. | 38

Figure 7. Laura Riding to Gertrude Stein, November 1928. | 40

Figure 8. Len Lye to Gertrude Stein, November 1928. | 42

Figure 9. Frontispiece. Gertrude Stein, *An Acquaintance with Description*. | 47

Figure 10. Laura Riding to Gertrude Stein, 5 April 1929. | 48

Figure 11. Title page. Gertrude Stein, *An Acquaintance with Description*. | 52

Figure 12. Laura Riding to Gertrude Stein, May 1929. | 58

Figure 13. Laura Riding to Gertrude Stein, July 1929. | 67

Figure 14. Gertrude Stein to Laura Riding, 11 February 1930. | 88

Figure 15. Front cover. Laura Riding, *Twenty Poems Less*. | 93

Figure 16. Laura Riding to Gertrude Stein, 3 April 1930. | 95

Figure 17. Laura Riding to Gertrude Stein, May 1930. | 97

ACKNOWLEDGMENTS

For permission to publish the writing of Laura (Riding) Jackson, Gertrude Stein, Robert Graves, and Len Lye, we very gratefully thank the Division of Rare and Manuscript Collections, Cornell University Library; Stanford G. Gann Jr., literary executor of the estate of Gertrude Stein; the Robert Graves Copyright Trust; and the Len Lye Foundation.

We wish to thank Jack Blackmore, Elizabeth Friedmann, William Graves, Mark Jacobs, Nancy Kuhl, Ruth Ogden, and Lisa Samuels for their assistance with archival materials and biographical details, and Jennifer Ashton and Bob Perelman for their careful readings of our manuscript. We are grateful to the Language poets for teaching Riding and making her work central to a long view of modernism, and especially to Bob Perelman and Charles Bernstein, our mentors, for introducing us to the Riding-Stein nexus and for their support and friendship.

Logan would like to single out Edward Burns for his inimitable scholarship, in particular his editions of Stein's correspondence with Carl Van Vechten (1986) and with Thornton Wilder (1996), the latter coedited with Ulla Dydo. Those editions set a standard that this one can only strive to reach. For their kindnesses, he offers all the ice cream they want to Lara Odell and Ida Esdale, and he would like to dedicate this book to the two people he's lucky to call his parents, Robert Esdale and Patricia Esdale.

Jane would like to thank Laura (R) Heffernan for her support in the beginning of this project and Geneviève Robichaud for her research assistance and enthusiasm. P, L, and M, thank you for being my anchors.

INTRODUCTION

This book tells the story of Laura Riding and Gertrude Stein through their letters to each other. For three years, from 1927 to 1930, their literary friendship was sustained through correspondence—they met just twice—as they lived in cities (London and Paris) and villages (Deyá and Bilignin). They were both Americans who left for Europe in their mid- to late twenties, but Stein was a generation older than Riding. They were women living unconventional lives, and they were writers whose texts challenged the reader's ordinary mode of meaning-making. Both were central modernist figures when they knew each other. After their personal relationship ended, they kept the letters and eventually placed them in university archives.

Now, for the first time, the extant letters have been gathered, ordered, and annotated. They tell the story of the work of writing and publishing, of Riding's personal turmoil and her coming through it with Stein as a much needed interlocutor, of Stein's quite sudden silence and Riding's hurt. But this edition is also about the letters themselves, their material history and the particular narrative created through epistolary contingencies and delays. Most of the letters are undated, and while we have almost all of them, there are missing letters, enclosures, and contexts; they were writing to each other, after all, not for us. While ordering and annotating does create a narrative and brings clarity to our understanding of Riding and Stein's relationship, this is not the smooth narrative of biography. No amount of annotation will tell the whole story. The uneasy thrill of reading other people's letters comes not only from having access to private documents but also from their incompleteness; both the gaps and the annotations invite us to read creatively, to imagine a story from what we have provided here.

The narrative of this book can be read as a romance—one-sided perhaps, as Riding's emotional investment outweighs Stein's. Reading their letters is like reading a novel about two people who have so much in common but are incompatible. Love and loyalty and a sense of possibility defer the end, but eventually the end comes. Framing the letters is a scholarly apparatus, and even if it gets in the way—the contextualizing materials make this a mediated perspective on the letters—it is necessary; we want to promote informed readings of texts that often demand speculation. But the main story is in the words of these two writers, what they say to each other and how they say it. Stein and Riding were surrounded by men equally as ambitious for recognition, and in a world made for men, they could look to each other in the spirit of solidarity as Jewish American women who wrote difficult texts and asserted their voices. They avoided, however, an assumed solidarity, knowing the uncertainty that writers feel in the time between letters, waiting for connection and a reply.

The Riding-Stein letters are the focus of this volume, but there are, of course, other figures around them. Of the ninety-three letters in this collection, forty-six are from Riding

1

and thirty-two are from Stein. Fifteen are from Robert Graves, Riding's writing and life partner at the time. From the beginning, these letters involved Graves; he and Riding ran Seizin Press, which would publish Stein's *An Acquaintance with Description* in April 1929. For the first year and a half of this correspondence, there were updates on the publishing process, so a letter from Riding usually implied Graves's presence, and for a few months in 1929, he writes as a proxy for Riding. Riding is the primary correspondent, but Graves's role must be acknowledged and his letters included. Another secondary figure is artist Len Lye, a close friend of Riding's and Graves's, whose work was gifted to Stein. Lye's four letters to Stein will be found in the notes. Background figures include poet Hart Crane (as an amative force) and composer Virgil Thomson (as a divisive one). Friendships with others nurtured and complicated the Stein-Riding relationship.

    A Description of Acquaintance is for scholars of modernism and of early Riding and mid-career Stein. It is also for poets and general readers interested in topics such as the epistolary genre, Americans abroad, self-publishing, mental health, and women writers in the 1920s. It offers access to the private history of collaboration and exchange between these two influential writers and the affective and intellectual bond between them. It invites us to read Riding and Stein together.

Before

When the correspondence began, in 1927, Stein was fifty-three years old and had published five important books: *Three Lives* (1909), *Tender Buttons* (1914), *Geography and Plays* (1922), *The Making of Americans* (1925), and *Composition as Explanation* (1926). All received significant attention from reviewers, who were either confused and dismissive or enthusiastic and ready to champion her as a paradigmatic radical. Stein (1874–1946) and Alice Toklas (1877–1967) met in 1907 and had lived together for seventeen years. The two women, both Americans from the San Francisco Bay Area, had held a Saturday salon, before World War I, at their Paris apartment—27 rue de Fleurus, where Stein had lived since 1903—and in the 1920s, they were legendary figures for visiting Brits and Americans to meet. On the apartment's walls was her collection of modernist paintings—by Paul Cézanne, Pablo Picasso, and many others—and it was a place to find out the latest. Old friends were not necessarily forgotten, but Stein's visitors were often young, from the new generation. She was generally accessible and affable, while projecting a seriousness about her work. She had her creative principles and liked meeting people who were likewise developing their own and were sustaining the modernist infrastructure (presses, magazines, etc.).

    Riding had moved from America to England a year earlier, in 1926. From a correspondence she had had with the English poet Robert Graves in 1925, she decided to join him and his wife Nancy Nicholson. Riding (1901–1991) had married and was recently divorced, and when she arrived in London, she had unpublished manuscripts and was looking forward to collaborating with Graves (1895–1985), who was already established as a writer.[1] She quickly published two books of poetry, *The Close Chaplet* (1926) and *Voltaire: A Biographical Fantasy* (1927), a French-to-English translation (1926) of Marcel Le Goff's *Anatole France*

2   *Introduction*

at Home (1924), and *A Survey of Modernist Poetry* (1927), a critical book. The last in that list was cowritten with Graves, who had gravitated to Riding emotionally and drifted from his role as husband and father to his four children with Nicholson.[2] Riding's parents, like Stein's, had a background as Jewish immigrants from Europe, and also like Stein, Riding was university educated: she had gone to Cornell (1918–20) while Stein had attended Harvard (1893–1897) and Johns Hopkins (1897–1902). Riding grew up in New York City. When the correspondence with Stein began, she was young—twenty-six years old—but felt herself to be a person of experience and stature.

By 1927, Stein had published only a fraction of what she had written, so she was looking for adventurous publishers who would take her on. The emergence of Seizin Press in the summer of that year was thus welcome news, and Stein was apparently the first person whom Riding and Graves contacted for a manuscript. It was this request that initiated the correspondence and kept it going until April 1929, when Stein's *An Acquaintance with Description* was published. But before we describe, in more detail, the context for Riding and Stein being in correspondence, we need to back up to 1926 and amplify what's already been said. That year was a turning point as, coincidentally, both writers established or secured an audience in England.

After Riding arrived in England at the beginning of 1926 and joined Graves and Nicholson, she immediately went with them to Cairo, Egypt, where Graves took a lucrative teaching position.[3] They returned to England in June, and by the end of that summer she and Graves shared an apartment in London. Nicholson and the children were in Islip, a village just north of Oxford. From September to December 1926, Riding and Graves lived in Vienna, Austria, working primarily on *A Survey of Modernist Poetry*. Leonard and Virginia Woolf had accepted *The Close Chaplet* for their Hogarth Press, and it was published in October 1926. To that point, Riding had published more than forty poems in magazines, many in *The Fugitive*, out of Vanderbilt University in Nashville, Tennessee. Poets associated with that magazine, such as Allen Tate and John Crowe Ransom, had promoted Riding, but *The Close Chaplet* generated a new level of attention. Despite an unflattering review in *The Monthly Criterion* that compared her writing to Stein's, Riding's move to England, an impulsive one, was working out; indeed, to be misunderstood by the British literary establishment, to be compared to Stein, was arguably a point of pride.[4]

When Riding, Graves, and Nicholson returned to Islip in June 1926, they just missed the opportunity to hear and meet Stein, who had lectured at Oxford on 7 June (and at Cambridge on 4 June). They did not attend, but Graves was an Oxford graduate and was well connected with the circle of people around such an event. In London on 1 June, for instance, at a welcome party for Stein hosted by Edith Sitwell, was Siegfried Sassoon, a close friend of Graves. (Also at the party was Virginia Woolf, who wrote in her diary that Stein was "rather formidable" [qtd. in Dydo 104].) As they reached Islip and settled themselves after five months of travel and Cairo life, stories about Stein's visit to England must have been in the air. It is unclear when Riding first read Stein or what she read; whatever her familiarity at that point, this example of an American woman, a modernist, holding center stage in England must have been energizing.

Sitwell had organized the lectures and was a self-elected champion of Stein in England prior to Riding's taking a similar role.[5] Indeed, Stein had many supporters, many of whom

Introduction   3

were women. Mabel Dodge Luhan, Carl Van Vechten, Sherwood Anderson, Ernest Heming-way, Jane Heap, Marianne Moore, and Bryher had helped with publishing, and Moore and Mina Loy had recently praised her writing.[6] On the other hand, as her friend Henry McBride warned her in 1920, "There is a public for you but no publisher" (qtd. in Dydo 62). That is to say, as interesting as her work could be to other writers, it would not be a commercial success. Until *The Autobiography of Alice B. Toklas* (1933), a bestseller, Stein would largely rely on small presses and magazines—on her personal connections with other writers.

This visit to England was an opportunity to promote herself in public, in her own words and with her own presence. The latter aspect was discomfiting: "As a woman, she was sure to be admired less for her work than for her personality" (Dydo 80).[7] Stein wavered on accepting Sitwell's invitation and then took the risk and wrote an essay that "falls into two parts, the first on modernism, the second on [her] own work, which exemplifies the modern impulse" (Dydo 90). Originally titled "An Address," the lecture concluded with four examples of her writing: a poem, "Preciosilla" (1913); a play, *A Saint in Seven* (1922); and two portraits, "Sitwell Edith Sitwell" (1925) and "Jean Cocteau" (1925–26). When Hogarth Press accepted the lecture for publication, Stein changed the title to "Composition as Explanation" and included the four other pieces.[8] It came out a month after *The Close Chaplet*, in November 1926, and it got Riding's attention.[9]

Early in 1927, Riding wrote an essay defending Stein and placing her at the center of the modernist story. She had in mind a review of "Composition as Explanation" by T. S. Eliot:

> There is something precisely ominous about Miss Stein. Her books of "about one thousand pages" may, and will, remain unread; but Miss Stein is going to make trouble for us just the same. In this Hogarth essay of fifty-nine pages the atom is dissociated. . . . [H]er work is not improving, it is not amusing, it is not interesting, it is not good for one's mind. But its rhythms have a peculiar hypnotic power not met with before. It has a kinship with the saxophone. If this is the future, then the future is, as it very likely is, of the barbarians. But this is a future in which we ought not to be interested. ("Charleston" 595)

At stake was influence; if people liked Stein, they might write like her, with an improvisatory style and abandonment of literary referentiality, a future that Eliot claimed was alarming.[10] Modernism would be defined, in part, by alliances, and Riding made her choice; her essay "The New Barbarism, and Gertrude Stein" was published in the third issue of *transition* magazine in June 1927.

Coedited by Eugene Jolas and Elliot Paul, both Americans in Paris, *transition* launched in April 1927 (and ended in 1938). It stood in opposition to magazines such as Eliot's *Criterion*, or at the least it was an alternative. Paul especially wanted to ally the magazine with Stein, and her work appeared regularly, in eleven of the first sixteen issues (April 1927–June 1929). They brought *Tender Buttons* back into print in the fall 1928 issue (no. 14) and in February 1929 (no. 15) included a bibliography of her writing from 1904 to 1929, listing chronologically by year not just publications but most everything she had written—the full scope of her career was hardly yet known. Riding was also a regular in *transition*, having

4   *Introduction*

work in eight of the first fourteen issues, and the two women appeared together six times (nos. 3, 6, 10, 12–14).

On the contents page of the magazine's first issue was a list of contributors to the forthcoming second issue in May 1927, and among the names was Riding's. Although her essay did not appear until the third issue, it is evidence that *transition* had it lined up by early spring. Paul was likely the editor who accepted it, as he alludes to Riding in an article on Stein for the Paris edition of the *Chicago Tribune* (otherwise known as the Paris *Tribune*) on 17 June 1927. Referring to Stein's 1926 Hogarth book, he writes:

> Hasty people are often misled by a title. Mr. Edmund Wilson, the anonymous clerk on *The Dial* who deigned to notice the book at all, and all other American reviewers decided, erroneously, that *Composition as Explanation* was merely an attempt on Miss Stein's part to explain her own work. Nothing could be farther from the point. She uses her own work and development incidentally, as illustrations, but the book is an exposition of certain fundamentals of aesthetics which needed badly to be stated. What she says would apply to Nathaniel Hawthorne or Li Po. . . . It was left for Miss Laura Riding, American poet residing in England, to discover this, and to appreciate it. (266)

Indeed, Riding was an early and enthusiastic defender of Stein's radical poetics. Her audacious essay for *transition* reclaims the pejorative (and racist) term *barbarism* from Eliot's disparaging review.[11] Riding also critiques what she views as modernism's misplaced devotion to criticism, which "assumes all the prerogatives which belong to creation without assuming any of its concrete responsibilities" (121). She faults Eliot especially, calling him an "autocrat of authority" (124), for writing always with the profession of poetry and not "direct communication" in mind (124). She argues that his version of modernism (Ezra Pound and James Joyce are mentioned too) merely produces an "earnest caricature of ordinary language" (124), unlike Stein, who is "divinely inspired in ordinariness" (125). Stein's work, she argues, uses words that "are no older than her use of them" (125) to create "a human mean in language" (127); it is a modernist practice that rejects "sophistication" and "haughty coyness" for the "literal" and the "naive" (123). Stein's emphasis on composition thus embodies a truly avant-garde poetic mode: "The criticism is talking backwards. The composition, because its time is a continuous present, is talking forwards" (129). Riding's stance on Stein was and remains a major paradigm in the context of modernist studies. Her insights locate Stein's work at the beginning of a long genealogy of language-based experimental poetry that extends into the present. Along with writing on Stein, publishing her would likewise promote a modernism "divinely inspired in ordinariness" (125).

Much later, in 1983, Ulla Dydo wrote to (Riding) Jackson to learn more about how Seizin Press came to publish *An Acquaintance with Description*: "There is an (undated) letter to Gertrude Stein from Elliot Paul, who says, 'Laura Riding wants to publish something of yours.' Is this what happened and is this the beginning of that publication?" (Cornell 18.5).[12] Although (Riding) Jackson does not answer Dydo's question, we can try. In May 1927, Riding and Graves moved into an apartment at 34A St. Peter's Square, Hammersmith,

Introduction   5

London, where they would live until September 1929. In June 1927, Riding and Paul published their essays on Stein, and Graves started *Lawrence and the Arabs*, receiving a large advance.[13] With that money, he and Riding started Seizin Press, and Riding wrote to Paul that she wanted to publish something of Stein's. Paul knew Stein and passed on the message. Then the correspondence between Riding and Stein began.

The Letters

The letters begin in November 1927, with Riding acknowledging receipt of the manuscript of Stein's "An Acquaintance with Description," and the publication process is one thread for readers to follow. Through late summer 1928 and into the winter, they handle page proofs for the book (Letters 8–9)[14], Stein signs labels that will be pasted onto the frontispiece (L12–15, 24–25), and in January 1929, Riding reports that the book "is nearly done" (L24). Also at that time, she sends Stein a sample of the binding. Finally, in April 1929, Stein receives the book, and Graves will discuss with her where to send review copies (L33–36). The business of publishing continues in 1930, from Riding's assuring Stein in January that "we are going to send you a cheque some time in settlement of Acquaintance" (L71), to Stein's saying in June that her royalty had arrived (L84). Stein stops writing to Riding shortly after that. When we see this thread all laid out, publishing the book began and clearly fueled the correspondence, and perhaps once it was done, Stein felt she could drop the connection.

As essential as it was to their relationship and as important as it is to recognize the work of small-press publishing, the Seizin Press thread ultimately is not what compels our attention; it was a structural support for the correspondence but not the heart of it. What started for Riding as an interest in Stein's writing became immensely personal. Following that narrative, the move from seeing Stein as an author she admired to needing her as a palliative presence—the move from "Dear Miss Stein" (L1) to "Thinking to Gertrude, tell her, has kept me alive in the worst hours" (L44)—is what we will focus on in this section.

The correspondence has a slow start, with just seven (extant) letters in the first nine months. After a brief exchange in November 1927, they do not write again for five months. In her next letter, Riding is in Paris with Graves, and she would like to meet Stein. Before this May 1928 visit, she drops off a copy of her latest book, *Anarchism Is Not Enough*, and tags a couple of chapters for Stein to read. This may not have been a welcome conversation starter for Stein, and Riding's next step was certainly a miscalculation. Reacting to being referred to as "Mrs. Graves" in a newspaper article, taking it personally as an attack on her, she blamed Virgil Thomson and asked Stein "to destroy him" (L6). The visit, a positive experience for both, had led Riding to believe that Stein would take her side. Stein replies in no uncertain terms: "I don't like controversy and I like to mind my own business" (L6n).

Riding, though, is unwilling to sidestep controversy, particularly when "there is a point at which these things become physical to me" (L7), nor can she look past Stein's frank reply. "It makes me very sad," Riding says, "that you should have felt it necessary to write to me in this way" (L7). After a cooling-off period of a couple of months, the letters resume, and both

6   *Introduction*

seem to recognize their temperamental differences. Riding acknowledges Stein's congenial nature—"pleasure of course is a feeling for other people, and it seems very natural to me that you should say this about *transition*, because you are kind. I should never have thought of saying it myself" (L17)—while Stein will accept Riding's intensity: in a letter to Graves, she will observe that "Laura is so poignant and so upright" (L41).

In fall 1928, the correspondence matures and becomes more personal. Seizin business is one aspect, and there is also a book exchange: Stein sends *Useful Knowledge*, and Riding reciprocates with her book of poems, *Love as Love, Death as Death*. Riding has been doing the labor of proofing and printing Stein's *Acquaintance*, a labor that involves concentration and care—with font in hand, Riding was composing word by word—so even if the texts they share were not about each other, their language and material presence were ingredients for affective bonding. *Love as Love, Death as Death* was the first Seizin book, and Stein knew that hers was next.

They begin addressing each other with first names—Laura and Gertrude—and signing with "always" and "love"; an emotional intimacy (and dependence, for Riding) begins to develop between them. Riding invites Stein into her world, drawing her into the relationships that drive her creativity, particularly with Len Lye—Riding is enthusiastic about his hand-printed shawls and sends some to Stein, who will close 1928 with "the best of the New Years to you and Robert and also Len Lye" (L23)—and of course with Graves, a scenario Stein aptly describes as "the two of you with Len firmly in the background" (L45). Stein, who is less forthcoming about her personal life, nevertheless sends Riding updates on her life with Alice Toklas and notes that she derives a "very lively pleasure" (L21) from the correspondence.

As they move into 1929, the preliminary period—the establishment of their relationship—has concluded, and if it was not apparent before, it is now: Stein the person, as much as the writer, is the object of Riding's love. The second half of the correspondence, from April 1929 to November 1930, is far more intense than the first. Here is a sketch of the final four "chapters": through April there is an outpouring of mail as Riding experiences a crisis in her romantic life—a dysfunctional polyamorous entanglement—and then almost dies after jumping out a third-story window (L27–41); as she slowly recovers from her spinal injuries, she feels that her suicidal jump has brought her even closer to Stein, and she looks forward to leaving England and seeing Stein again in person (L42–57). This happens in October 1929—their second visit—as Riding and Graves are on their way to the island of Mallorca, where they will build new lives (L58–86); then in July 1930, Stein suddenly cancels their imminent visit with her and never replies to the letters that follow from Graves and Riding (L87–93).

Riding's strong attachment to Stein during this crucial period often manifests as experiments with a Steinian compositional mode. Readers will note several instances of stylistic convergence in Riding's letters (see L33, 42, 49, 51, 54, 86, and 92), and we can understand these as moments where she tries on or models Stein's inflections—an unpunctuated, paratactic "Steinese." We can see this style most particularly in the dramatically emotional letters (L49, 51, and 54), when Riding feels palpably close to Stein. But this convergence could also be the result of what Riding, in a 1982 letter to Ulla Dydo, calls their "common preoccupation with word reality" (Cornell 18.5). Riding was seeking alternatives to institutional modernism

Introduction   7

and its "cloud of snobbery" (121), and her discovery of Stein's work, and especially their friendship, may have enabled her to write in a similarly unfettered, open manner.

Even if it is primarily Stein's style manifesting in Riding's letters, both Stein and Riding describe wanting to radically deconstruct the English language. Stein, who during their friendship is working on *How to Write*, explains, "I am saving the sentence, I began preparing to save it last summer but now I am actually saving it and it is a good deal of a job and I was low in my mind but now it is better and I guess the sentence will be saved" (L65), and Riding replies, "We are glad you are saving the sentence. I am busy on the word" (L70).[15] Stein likewise comments on Riding's wordplay, reacting to her poem "Fine Fellow Son of a Poor Fellow" by highlighting what she says are its essential, Riding-esque qualities: "it is what I like you begin play and it becomes literal and you begin literal and it becomes play, and to me that is you" (L19). The phrase "literal and it becomes play" could also describe Stein's own writing. In *An Acquaintance with Description*, for instance, are both literal expressions ("two is the second of two" [133]) and ones that play with equivalence ("Acquainted with description is the same as being acquainted with turkeys" [133]), so that we question if two really is the same as two. Stein's infamous "Rose is a rose is a rose is a rose" motto is another obvious example of the literal becoming play through repetition.

Riding would explicitly address, in a palpably Steinian idiom, the perceived similarity between her writing and Stein's, imagining that readers may already confuse them: "There is always Gertrude and just now there is Laura and it is a very clear or confused thing but it is a thing. It is the same thing that people who know our work but not us and imagine our faces and make mistakes about them make no mistakes but only get us mixed" (L51). Riding's next letter ironically suggests that such similarities, as they emerge in the fruitful exchange of poetic texts and life narratives, are precisely what allow each of them to become more distinctly individual: "Laura's writing is becoming more & more Laura, and Gertrude's writing is becoming more and more writing and . . . and so everything is becoming more and more what it is" (L54). For Riding, convergence promotes stylistic divergence; knowing Stein personally helped her discover how different they were. She sees Steinian experiments as a productive method of artistic self-discovery, and their friendship appears to foster her development as a poet.

Often in her letters, Riding mentions feeling physically or emotionally unwell. Initially, these mentions of ill health fall in line with the epistolary etiquette of explaining lapses in communication or uncompleted tasks, but as the correspondence unfolds, they become a trend that we do not see in Stein's letters. Riding's moments of vulnerability, as in "I have been ill and not-doing" (L10), contrast starkly with Stein's relative vitality and constancy. By April 1929, Stein emerges as a soothing, palliative presence: "Always you [Stein] are there in this sameness," Riding says (L33). Nowhere is this contrast (and her reliance on Stein) more apparent than in the letters written during the months surrounding Riding's April 1929 suicide attempt. From the earliest days of her recovery, writing from the hospital on her behalf, Graves tells of Riding's desire to see Stein, explaining that she wanted only to see "Gertrude." He sends an exigent telegram, part of which reads, "MIND LUCID ASKS FOR YOU" (L39), and in a flurry of letters he urges Stein to respond. In her reply, Stein is obviously upset—"I am altogether heart-broken about her" (L41)—and also implies that

8   *Introduction*

she had worried about Riding's mental health: "I had an unhappy feeling that Laura would have sooner or later a great disillusionment" (L41).

Once Riding recovers enough to write again, she offers an enigmatic description of her actions—"Robert went out of the window with me in bodily spirit. you are always outside" (L42)—implying that the jump out the window constituted not just a rejection of an untenable romantic scenario but a leap (with Graves) *toward* Stein. Her actions, Riding writes, were both a demonstration of her profound attachment to those closest to her and a way to gauge their loyalty. Graves was the only one present that night who chose to come with her (he ran down one flight of stairs and jumped from the floor below): "Anyone else who wants to be here with me as Robert is must discover in herself or himself an out-of-the-windowness. Gertrude does not have to; she was never inside the window" (L44). Riding insists that Stein already understood "out-of-the-windowness" and that their mutual attachment and affection were never in question. Stein was always already with her.

Stein's attentiveness to Riding's frail psychological state during this period remains one of the only instances where she reveals more of herself than her affable side. The moments of tenderness toward Riding in these letters show Stein's vulnerability and suggest that perhaps she understood intimately the kind of emotional pain Riding was experiencing before the jump because she had experienced a similar bout of depression herself, in 1903–4 after her breakup with May Bookstaver. Possibly Stein saw her younger self in Riding and thus was able to comprehend the suicidal impulse, what she obliquely calls the "permanentest cut to liberty" (L50). She shows empathy—"Laura I do hope you are getting better and better spinal columnly speaking" (L50)—and agrees with Riding that the jump will lead to a better life, that it will be possible to thrive again. To Graves she writes, "As soon as the pain is over Laura has such real vitality that she will go on" (L45). Although Stein offers comfort, she avoids acknowledging her role in the story of the jump, as if to suggest that Riding should not ultimately need her.

Riding's long recovery marks an important transition in their correspondence and relationship, as well as a pivot in Riding's own personal circumstances. After a much anticipated second visit with Stein and Toklas in Belley, France, she and Graves move to Mallorca. They will build a new home—including in it the printing press they had purchased for Seizin— and embrace a more private life away from the London pressures and relationships that had led to Riding's suicide attempt. The letters from this period display a comfortable intimacy—Stein can tell anecdotes about Belley, knowing that the references will be familiar, and Riding can likewise describe Mallorca, where Stein and Toklas had lived in 1915–16. They can all celebrate the success of Graves's autobiography, *Good-bye to All That*, and after Lye visits Stein in Paris, at the end of 1929, Riding can update her on Lye's time with them on Mallorca. Yet undercurrents reveal Riding's increasingly unreciprocated, or differently calibrated, investment in the friendship.

There is from Stein the repeated sentiment "we are really very fond of you both" (L84), but we get the sense that by early summer 1930, one of Stein's motivations for writing is to settle the business end of things. She inquires about the promised royalty for *Acquaintance*: "And how did the accounts turn out, you didn't send me the cheque well cheques are a pleasure even when you don't have them" (L80). Conversely, Riding documents a period of creative flourishing and looks to Stein's letters for expressions of affection. When they are

Introduction   9

not forthcoming, she airs her disappointment: "But you must always send love when you send. I couldn't find any anywhere in your letters and it's made me feel different all night and all day different not well" (L69). Like the summer before, Riding's letters from this period anticipate seeing her again—she and Graves plan a third visit for August 1930 in Belley—to affirm Stein's place in Riding's most intimate circle of friends.

Alas, this visit was not to be. In her penultimate letter to Riding in July 1930, Stein writes to cancel the plans: "I am so sorry but we will have to put off your visit to us" (L87). She cites understandable reasons—pressure from a deadline, feeling overwhelmed with visitors—and appears regretful, if somewhat cavalier: "I am sorrier than I can say, it would have been nice seeing you and Robert again and having you here but better luck next time." Then, on the heels of this letter, Stein sends a postcard with "The books have just come thanks so much, / G" (L88), and that is her final word.

It takes Riding a few months to realize or accept that something is wrong. She writes with her usual familiarity in August, and then, in October, Graves writes twice to ask if Stein is alright; the only reason they can think of for her lack of reply is "that you have been ill or something, as we have had no word since early July, and no reply to two notes of Laura's. Please reassure us" (L90). Riding tries again in November, reassuring Stein that there are no hard feelings regarding the canceled visit: "we are very very fond of you, you mustn't overlook it" (L92). Still there is no reply, no explanation.

By late November 1930, a deeply hurt Riding sends her last letter, the tone of which is terse and resentful. But she accepts that, for reasons she does not understand, the friendship has ended: "If you don't care how we feel, to keep it from being unpleasant you ought to say something unpleasant. All right, you won't answer this either, so don't. . . . I promise not to write again not even about the weather <u>certainly</u> not" (L93). The palpable anger in this final letter surely masks Riding's understandable anguish at being so suddenly and definitively rejected by Stein, her friend and confidant, and it is difficult to read.

As break-ups go, theirs is not mutual, and perhaps most frustratingly, it happens *sans mots*. Why does Stein simply stop writing, and how can she ignore Riding's growing concern? We do know that Stein was predisposed to circumscribed relationships and that she may have entered the friendship for transactional reasons related to the publication of *Acquaintance*. Perhaps she could sustain only a minor interest in Riding's poetry and criticism. Perhaps she grew weary of Riding's propensity to experiment with a Steinian idiom or disliked the implication that it was a way of thinking and writing anyone could deploy. It is equally possible that Stein grew tired of the palliative role she played for Riding or that the manifest need expressed by Riding may have made Stein uncomfortable or pushed her toward a false position, promising more than she wanted to give.

Or is this a case of two formidable women who were simply, fundamentally, incompatible? If Riding wished to know and be known by Stein, this may have been a futile endeavor. Perhaps Riding came to understand what Waverley Lewis Root saw in *The Autobiography of Alice B. Toklas* when he read Stein's book in 1933: her approach "permits the writing of an autobiography without self-revelation. After reading this book, one knows the life history of Gertrude Stein, one still does not know Gertrude Stein. She is seen as an outsider, a very intimate outsider but still as an outsider sees her. I do not think she wants to reveal herself" (280).

In the search for answers, we have the letters to pore over, looking for subtle shifts in tone or unregistered, passive moments of annoyance or disaffection that point to fatal dysfunction. We imagine readers will interpret Stein's never responding in quite different ways, with some readers feeling all along that it was inevitable or that Riding was indeed a difficult correspondent, while others will see Stein as hard-hearted and as acting inexcusably. We have enjoyed debating the nature of their attachment and how predictable the end is, and we trust you will as well.

Our title, *A Description of Acquaintance*, is of course a play on Stein's title for her Seizin book. Indeed, each letter in the correspondence describes the nature of their acquaintance. The two key terms in the phrase should not be underestimated—*description* and *acquaintance* should both imply intimacy and connection. Like letter writing, those terms here connote an immersive and mutable state, caught up in the present moment of where you are and what is seen, or as Stein wrote in her *Acquaintance*, "A description refusing to turn away a description" (131).[16] Through describing their lives, Stein and Riding became acquainted with each other, *acquaint* meaning, in its etymology, to get to know. Across a relationship, perceptions and circumstances shift, however, and one can turn away. In May 1929, after her suicidal jump, Riding wrote this to Stein: "Dear Gertrude Dear Robert Robert went out of the window with me in bodily spirit. you are always outside This is a description becoming an undescription" (L42). We can play on words once more and say that at moments of acute flux an acquaintance with description can falter. In late 1930, with the dissolution of their friendship, description became undescription.

Yet the Riding-Stein correspondence, the story it tells, is not to be defined by its abrupt end. The letters offer us a window into their personal and intellectual lives, a view that includes dramatic moments as well as the mundane and the unsaid, all of which helps us imagine the rest of life as it unfolded around and between the letters. We learn a great deal about their personalities from what they choose to share or avoid. The congenial Stein reveals very little of her emotional life; neither does she describe her very active social life during those years, as documented in *The Autobiography of Alice B. Toklas*. Riding, on the other hand, proves to be quite a vulnerable writer and interlocutor, inviting Stein into her most trying experiences. Neither Riding nor Stein appear concerned with the outside world—they do not, in the letters, discuss the literary debates that preoccupy their contemporaries, let alone politics or global events. Rather, their subjects are personal, albeit calibrated differently, as in Riding's "I'm going to reopen a long closed correspondence with my mother. Did I tell you about her?" (L64) and Stein's "I am writing and Alice is tapestrying" (L74). Both share the details of their daily living.

Beyond the dramatic pivots is a subtle narrative of their particular equilibrium, of the negative space that gives the letters depth and emotional resonance. Early on, both Riding and Stein are enamored by Len Lye's hand-painted shawls, and after receiving two, Stein writes: "I like the little one a whole lot but the big one is really quite xtraordinary in its beauty, he makes all his colors very alike and as he says easy to wear it really is rich and not gaudy, exact and warm" (L21). Where are these shawls today and did Stein really wear hers? Riding and Graves collect Mallorcan rocks from the nearby beach: "Pebbles for you and Alice from Deya shore a trial collection" (L79). And Stein responds in kind: "we do use

Introduction   11

the pebbles in tarts really we do and you will see ours, they came from the garden and you'll see" (L80). "We have a vine of pinky-white grapes in front of our house just like yours," writes Graves, "and this is the season of fireflies so much love and what fun in August" (L85). These and many other sweet moments offer us a way to understand their friendship as more than just a transaction or a one-sided affair; they point to a nuanced personal correspondence between two avant-garde women that cannot be unmade by its ambivalent end.

After

Seizin Press brought Riding and Stein together, but after the *Acquaintance* business was complete, it was not enough to hold the connection. In Riding's penultimate letter, she invites Stein to publish again with Seizin and got no response. This was not solely a personal repudiation of Riding's offer. Stein had other publication options: she had published two books with Georges Hugnet and his Éditions de la Montagne (see L80), and earlier in 1930, Stein and Toklas had started their own press, Plain Edition. To Riding, in a June 1930 letter, Stein had mentioned that "Lucy Church Amiably" would be out in August, and she asked Riding for information on the sales of *Acquaintance*: "I am very anxious to know that for other reasons" (L84). Unless Riding knew more from other sources, this reference to the novel *Lucy Church Amiably* and the "for other reasons" may have been puzzling; there is nothing else on this in the correspondence. She could have surmised that Éditions de la Montagne would be publishing *Lucy*, but the novel was instead the first of five books from Plain Edition (see L84).[17]

In writing about the start of Plain Edition—financed through selling some valuable art that Stein owned, chiefly Picasso's *Woman with a Fan* (1905)—Gabrielle Dean has noted Stein's frustration with the publication model typical of modernism: friends publishing friends. "Stein's inability to separate social networks from business arrangements" finally led her to self-publishing (Dean 16). Working with Contact Editions, Hogarth Press, Seizin Press, and Éditions de la Montagne were all gratifying experiences in their way, but in 1930 Toklas initiated their own venture.[18] She and Stein wanted to "take possession" (the meaning of *seizin*) as Riding had (see L8).

Shortly after publishing the fourth Plain Edition book, *Operas and Plays*, in August 1932, Stein wrote *The Autobiography of Alice B. Toklas*, which would be published in September 1933 and become a bestseller (see L48). The book names dozens of people Stein had known, but not Riding or Graves, although Seizin Press is mentioned, briefly, as the publisher of *An Acquaintance with Description* (224).[19] The *Autobiography* had a powerful aura, as if it offered a definitive account of modernism; naming the imprint but not the people who ran it was a significant slight. The story of Stein's association with Riding was struck from the historical record.

For Riding, however, the end of the correspondence was not the end of Stein. Her feelings about Stein and her writing would reverberate over the decades. But first, in the wake of the end, was her book *Experts Are Puzzled*, which came out just after the final letter. Back in June 1929, as Riding was recovering from the injuries inflicted by her jump, Graves may have referred to what

12   *Introduction*

became a chapter in it, "Obsession" (L47). (This chapter is in the appendix.) Riding mentions it in August (L54), using a style that resembles what we can see in "Obsession," and she shared a draft with Stein when visiting her in October 1929 (see L64). In her penultimate letter, she wrote about wanting to send forthcoming books: "Len's book is such a pleasure. I should like to send it to you when it is finished; and <u>Though Gently</u> which is being bound; and <u>Experts Are Puzzled</u> which you liked in manuscript" (L92). Surviving the jump was an opportunity to begin again, and in "Obsession" she meditates on Laura, Robert, and Gertrude, on who they are and who she herself is in relation to the other two. "Sad Laura is glad because of Gertrude and glad Gertrude is sad because of Laura" (116) and perhaps Riding's ideal is "Strong all-together Gertrude, separate strong Laura" (119). Not being in a position to share *Experts* with Stein must have been deeply frustrating and exacerbated the lack of closure for Riding, who after all wrote the book imagining Stein as an ideal reader, as one who would understand.

In 1934, with George Ellidge as coauthor, Riding published *14A*, a fictionalized representation of her London life before and after the jump. Names were changed and there were narrative inventions, but the novel's opening disclaimer, "No character in this story has any existence in fact," belied how close it was to the reality—so close that the book was available for only four months.[20] Riding is "Catherine," Graves is "Eric," Stein is "Amelia," Lye is "Joho," and so on (see Friedmann 210–11). Catherine is somewhat aloof, helping others see who they are. For instance, when Jim says to Catherine, "I think Hugh's not good enough to *look* at you," she replies, "It doesn't matter how good or bad he is. I only want him to get clear *what* he is" (117). Chapter 22 is set in Paris at Amelia's apartment, a version of 27 rue de Fleurus, and is based on the events related to the letters from April 1929 (see L27–33), except that in the novel, the Stein character receives a visit from "Hugh" (Geoffrey Phibbs), a visit that did not occur in real life. Amelia says of Catherine, "What she needs is to be hurt—something to make her let go. Then she'll really be a wonderful person. . . . You go back and make something happen. You'll see. She'll stop being an Influence and become—why, one of us. That's what she needs" (225–26). These remarks compare with what Stein sent to Graves in May 1929, after the jump: "it will make Laura a very wonderful person, in a strange way a destruction and recreation of her purification but all this does not help pain" (L41).

After World War II, Graves reached out to Stein, in part to ask her if she could relay some money to his destitute cousin Hubert von Ranke. She had lived through the war in the Bugey region, in Bilignin and then Culoz, and knew von Ranke.[21] As she said to Graves in a February 1946 letter, his cousin had done "xcellent and courageous work" with the French Resistance, and "anything I can do to help you help him you can count on" (O'Prey 339). They also addressed Riding and the causes for the break in 1930. (Graves and Riding had separated in 1939 when she moved back to the United States, and in 1941 she married Schuyler Jackson.) Graves's version is at odds with what we know from the letters: "I was very sorry when Laura broke with you in a fit of spleen: I think because you always mentioned the weather, and that seemed unworthy. But of course the weather is very important in the short run and the long run consists of short runs" (O'Prey 337; see L93). Although Graves has moved on from Riding, he defends their former relationship, saying first, "I stand still greatly in her debt, though our life together grew more & more painful from 1930 or so onwards" (O'Prey 337), and then, "I don't regret a moment of the life I spent with

Introduction   13

Laura. I was learning all the time and she was a wonderful poet at her best and as good to me as I deserved, I suppose" (O'Prey 341).

Graves also discusses his new book, *King Jesus* (1946), a historical novel that understands Jesus as "no more of a Christian than Isaiah or Ezekiel, or Rabbi Hillel his contemporary, or myself or you: he was pure Jew" (O'Prey 338). In her reply, Stein overlaps Graves's comments on Riding and Jesus: "I was much interested in the Laura story, of course it was terribly important for you to have lived her; for your Jesus book, after all, she was Jew every single bit of her, but and that was really the basis of our break, she was the materialistic jew camouflaging her materialism by intellectualism" (O'Prey 339).[22] She points out what the letters make evident, that Stein had broken with Riding; that is no surprise. What is surprising and striking is Stein's reasoning, which is unsettling in both of its contexts, the historical and the epistolary; she says this right after the Holocaust, which she narrowly escaped, and in between praising von Ranke's Resistance work and telling Graves a story about taking a walk on Easter day in 1944: "I heard the church bells, and of course it was the moment of the worst Jewish persecution, and the most [fervent] Easter emotion of many years, and suddenly it struck me as comical completely comical, and I met a Catholic friend on the road and I said isn't it funny, making such a fuss about Christ and Jews at the same moment and never connecting the two ideas" (O'Prey 339).[23] What is clear is that neither Riding nor Stein offer satisfying or accurate reasons for the break in 1930. Neither Stein mentioning the weather nor Riding's Jewishness can explain why Stein stopped corresponding and why Riding felt that she had in fact initiated the break. Their memories became reductive.

Stein died somewhat suddenly on 27 July 1946, following an operation for abdominal cancer. Although her end came quickly, she had been preparing the afterlife of her papers since 1937, when, with the help of Thornton Wilder, some of them first went to the Yale University Library for safekeeping. Then through the late 1930s and again after the war, Stein sent notebooks, manuscripts, typescripts, photos, newspaper clippings, art, and letters. Yale was enthusiastic about this collection and held exhibitions in 1941 and, to honor the completed Stein archive, in 1947. Among the stacks of letters were those from Riding and Graves, and among the books that were sent from Paris to New Haven were Graves's *Poems (1914-1927)* (see L5), Riding's *Love as Love, Death as Death* (see L18), and Graves's *Good-bye to All That* (see L62 and L71).[24] The curator then overseeing the Stein archive at Yale was Donald Gallup, and after sorting through the letters that Stein received from dozens of people, he edited *The Flowers of Friendship* (1953), covering five decades of Stein's life, from 1895 to 1946. As Gallup collected letters for the book, he contacted Riding, but, as he recalled in a letter to her in 1975, "you refused me permission" (Cornell 31.5). None from Riding or Graves were included.

By the mid-1960s, (Riding) Jackson was working on her own archive, "gathering and sorting correspondence and manuscript material to be deposited at Cornell University" (Friedmann 411). At that time, Graves was married to Beryl (formerly Hodge, née Pritchard)—and since 1946, they had lived on Mallorca in a house called Canellun that Riding and Graves had built. In March 1974, (Riding) Jackson heard from Beryl Graves that "After all these years we have finally got round to sorting out the papers [in the] Canelluñ attic" and among them were "21 letters to you from Gertrude Stein, 2 picture

14   *Introduction*

postcards and 1 p.c" (Cornell 22.2).[25] Seeing these letters again prompted (Riding) Jackson to contact Yale, in December 1974, and ask for copies of her letters to Stein. After rereading the 1927–30 correspondence early in 1975, she wrote a new essay on Stein, a follow up to "The New Barbarism" from 1927. She titled it "The Word-Play of Gertrude Stein" and it was published in *Critical Essays on Gertrude Stein* (1986).[26] At the same time that she wrote the "Word-Play" essay, she also wrote notes on the first twenty-four letters (as we have them numbered here).[27] In the following years, she indicated that more on Stein would be forthcoming, but the essay and notes from 1975 appear to represent her final thoughts. For instance, when Ulla Dydo asked for permission to read the letters at Yale, (Riding) Jackson said in 1983: "my present stand is to keep them restricted until I shall have finished my notes on them, written to accompany them in their presence in my papers at Cornell" (Cornell 18.5). She never finished the notes, and restricting access delayed a full engagement with the Riding-Stein relationship until the twenty-first century.[28]

The notes and essay are complementary. At one point in the latter, (Riding) Jackson refers explicitly to the former, without explaining what the notes are. She says that she will cite "my notes to Gertrude Stein's letters to me" and then offers this: "With likeness to Aristotle, Gertrude Stein made use unhesitantly of the obvious. This has two sure advantages: it enables one not to want for words—of either complimentary or sagacious effect, of the both kinds in combination—and one is likely to be right, or at least safe from dispute" (258). Is this Gertrude Stein the person or the writer? For (Riding) Jackson, it is both, but in 1975, she feels very differently than she once did; what in the late 1920s had made Stein attractive as a writer and person, her "promising ease," now made her repellent. In her notes, (Riding) Jackson laments that Stein's techniques

> were uncriticizable as far as they went – they never went into areas that challenged actual adult mentality, adult techniques of word-use, intellectual canons of good judgement, moral value, taste in the sophisticated sense. Everything was formative, nothing – by prescription – got beyond the initial processes, the formative stages: nothing got formed, determinatively made. This produced an environment of promising ease. . . . all urgency was suspended while she took her time, avoiding anything conclusive. (Cornell 72.1)

When Riding saw this in Stein in the late 1920s, she loved it, as she needed that Steinian steady avoidance of judgement in her life and writing. To then have Stein conclude the correspondence in 1930, with no explanation, must have utterly stunned her.

The story of their relationship has thus far not been a balanced one. The first Stein biography to receive wide approval was James R. Mellow's *Charmed Circle* (1974), and he does not even mention Riding. Linda Wagner-Martin's *"Favored Strangers"* (1995) offers four superficial references. Yet when one turns to the Riding side, Stein is omnipresent. In Deborah Baker's *In Extremis* (1993), the first Riding biography, Stein appears repeatedly across a hundred pages, and in Elizabeth Friedmann's *A Mannered Grace* (2005), five chapters (11–15) are Stein focused. Of course, Riding wrote about Stein at length, but the difference is also in knowing the letters: while Baker does not cite their correspondence, she

Introduction   15

had read it, and Friedmann cites the letters extensively.[29] We trust that knowing the letters will open new lines of inquiry—perhaps especially for readers of Stein—and thereby bring about a greater balance between the two.

Editing the Letters

A Description of Acquaintance includes the letters that comprise the correspondence, some shorter pieces that are referred to in the letters or were enclosed with them, as well as Riding's *transition* essay and Stein's "An Acquaintance with Description."

The letters are held in three collections:

> Gertrude Stein and Alice B. Toklas Papers, Yale Collection of American Literature. Beinecke Rare Book and Manuscript Library, Yale University.
> - Riding to Stein: Box 112, folders 2286–2287 (forty-six letters): 1 3–8 10 12 15 17 18 20 22 24 26–28 32 33 42 49 51 54 56–58 60 64 65 67 69–71 73 76–79 81–83 86 89 92 93
> - Graves to Stein: Box 108, folder 2178 (fifteen letters): 30 31 35 37 39 40 44 46 47 53 62 75 85 90 91
> - Lye to Stein: Box 115, folder 2405 (four letters): 20 (in the notes) and 68 (in the notes)
>
> Laura (Riding) Jackson and Schuyler B. Jackson collection, #4608. Division of Rare and Manuscript Collections, Cornell University Library.
> - Stein to Riding: Box 72, folder 1 (twenty-four letters): 2 9 11 13 14 16 19 21 23 25 29 34 43 48 50 55 59 61 68 72 80 84 87 88
>
> Correspondence of Gertrude Stein, 1929 to 1946, 1952. Papers of Robert Graves: Correspondence (arranged by correspondent). St John's College Library, University of Oxford. GB 473 RG/J/STEIN.
> - Stein to Graves (eight letters): 36 38 41 45 52 63 66 74

Most of the letters are undated, but references and contextual clues, which are detailed in the annotations, establish an order, and a number has been assigned. With the number at the start of each letter is a date and the sender's address. Brackets enclose the date if it is uncertain.

All ninety-three are called "letters," but we acknowledge what is also noted in the correspondence: seven (26–28, 30, 32, 37, 39) are telegrams, and four (72, 79, 81, 88) are postcards.

Because the letters were not written for publication and each letter has a unique visual form, our transcriptions resemble the manuscript. What might appear to be mistakes or inconsistencies are there because the writers exercised an epistolary license. We have not corrected words or punctuation, but we have regularized two elements: the sender's

16   Introduction

address and the dash (we use the en dash). When a word in the manuscript is not sufficiently legible, it is in brackets, usually with a best guess.

But between resemblance and readability or pragmatic considerations, we have compromised. The size and color of the paper, the idiosyncratic handwriting, the squiggly lines, the shape of the lines down the page: these material aspects are not evident in this edition. That last aspect—our decision to translate the letters as prose, even when there are what can look like poetic lines—creates ambiguity for the transcriber. So we close with an example, Riding's postscript in L57 (see fig. 1). A diplomatic transcription would read:

> these are from earlier parts of Len's film
> the hand is accidental not composition
> they are good to show the development
> of the right & left hand sides
> the hand one is the second in
> order of these of course

Except for Len's name, there are no capital letters, and there is no punctuation. But as there appear to be four sentences, we have transcribed the postscript as follows, with a second space between each sentence:

> these are from earlier parts of Len's film the hand is accidental not composition
> they are good to show the development of the right & left hand sides the hand one
> is the second in order of these of course

So when we feel it is appropriate to distinguish sentences—when there is a line break (in the example above) or an extra space between words that indicates a new sentence (or a significant pause)—there are two spaces between the words. We are inconsistent on this issue, however. There are moments when the letter writer is clearly running the words together and has left taking a pause to the reader.

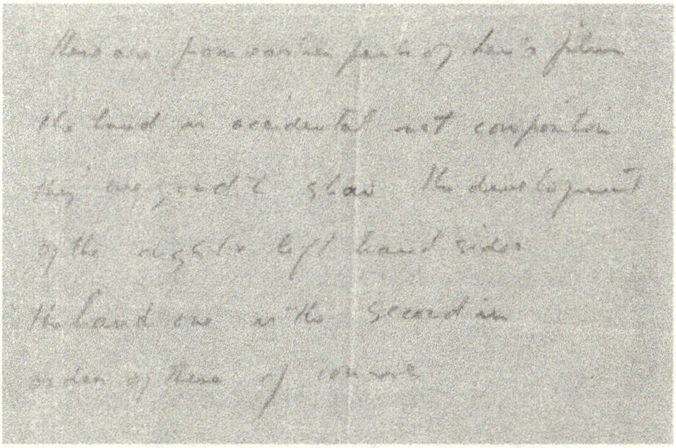

Figure 1. Laura Riding to Gertrude Stein, September 1929. Gertrude Stein and Alice B. Toklas Papers, Yale Collection of American Literature. Beinecke Rare Book and Manuscript Library, Yale University. Box 112, folder 2287.

Notes

1. Riding's name changed over the years. Born Laura Reichenthal, she became Laura Gottschalk in 1920, Laura Riding Gottschalk in 1923, Laura Riding in 1927, and Laura Jackson in 1941. By 1963, her writer's name was Laura (Riding) Jackson. Because we are focused on 1927–30, we will use Laura Riding unless a specific context demands otherwise.

2. To understand Riding's publication history, we have relied on Joyce Piell Wexler's *Laura Riding: A Bibliography*, still an indispensable resource.

3. While this threesome was certainly unusual, there was another well-known (in modernist circles) one at the time: Bryher (born Annie Winifred Ellerman), Kenneth Macpherson, and H. D. (Hilda Doolittle).

4. *The Monthly Criterion* is generally known as *The Criterion*, edited by T. S. Eliot. In its run, the title shifted from *The Criterion* (1922–25) to *The New Criterion* (1926–27) to *The Monthly Criterion* (1927–28), and then back to *The Criterion* (1928–39). In the August 1927 issue, John Gould Fletcher reviewed Riding's *The Close Chaplet* along with five other books, including Graves's *Poems (1914–1926)*. This review led to Graves's breaking with Eliot, who had been a friend. While Fletcher said of Graves that he was "a leader of the modernists" (168) and anyone wishing "to know what English poetry is doing to-day, would be well advised to read" (169) his poems, of Riding he said that a "practised reader can readily distinguish the derivations of her manner," naming Graves, Stein, Marianne Moore, and John Crowe Ransom as Riding's models (170). In October 1927, the magazine published a letter from Graves: "Riding's work is more original and strong," he asserted, "than any first book without a blurb or preface has any right to be" (357). And by "attributing Laura Riding's poem, 'One', to Gertrude Stein's influence he shows that he doesn't understand it, which is precisely why he has mentioned Gertrude Stein whom he does not understand either. The difference in the poetic method between the two writers can perhaps be most clearly seen by reading Miss Riding on the subject of Miss Stein in a recent number of *transition*" (358). Eliot printed Graves's retort, but there "would be no more letters between the two men for nearly 20 years" (Wilson 342).

5. In *Poetry and Criticism*, for example, Sitwell had said that "Miss Stein is bringing back life to our language by what appears, at first, to be an anarchic process. First she breaks down the predestined groups of words, their sleepy family habits; then she rebrightens them, examines their textures, and builds them into new and vital shapes" (qtd. in Liston 67). She said to Stein in a 1 January 1926 letter, "I shall lose no chance of doing propaganda work for you. . . . There are *many* fresh admirers" (Gallup 185).

6. Dodge Luhan published Stein in 1912 and in "Speculations, of Post-Impressionsim in Prose" (1913) wrote one of the first major essays on her writing. Stein met Van Vechten in 1913. He was always a staunch supporter, helping with publication matters in the United States from *Tender Buttons* (1914) on. She met Anderson in 1921, and he supplied an introduction to *Geography and Plays* (1922). Hemingway, whom she met in 1922, helped arrange for *The Making of Americans* to be serialized in *The Transatlantic*

18 *Introduction*

Review in 1924 (the last nine issues of the twelve), before it was published as a book by Robert McAlmon's Contact Editions in 1925. In 1922–24, when Stein published in *The Little Review*, Heap coedited the magazine with Margaret Anderson. Moore was the editor (1925–29) of *The Dial*, and after reviewing Stein's *The Making of Americans* in the February 1926 issue, she solicited Stein for contributions, which appeared in October 1926 and September 1927. Stein appeared in issues 2–4 (August–October 1927) of *Close Up* magazine, coedited by Bryher. Loy wrote a two-part essay on Stein for *The Transatlantic Review*, in the September and October 1924 issues.

7. Let's remember Virginia Woolf's story in *A Room of One's Own* (1929) of visiting "Oxbridge" University, of walking along engrossed in thought when "a man's figure rose to intercept me. . . . His face expressed horror and indignation. . . . He was a Beadle; I was a woman. This was the turf; there was the path. Only the Fellows and Scholars are allowed here; the gravel is the place for me" (6). Then "Mary" (Woolf's persona) was barred from the library, being told that "ladies are only admitted to the library if accompanied by a Fellow of the College or furnished with a letter of introduction" (8). "Oxbridge" is a portmanteau of the two universities Stein was invited to, Cambridge and Oxford, not the most welcoming places for women at that time.

8. The lecture was first published in *The Dial* in October 1926, a month before the Hogarth book.

9. Graves was also connected with Hogarth Press, having published several books with them, starting with *The Feather Bed* (1923) and *Mock Beggar Hall* (1924). The press began a Hogarth Essays series in 1924 and published three by Graves, including *Contemporary Techniques of Poetry* (1925), which discusses Stein. The third, *Impenetrability* (1926), was in a list on the verso page facing the title page of Stein's *Composition as Explanation*, and in 1928, in *The Hogarth Essays*, a selection of already-published titles, Graves and Stein appeared together. Hogarth Press was also a precedent for Seizin Press; the former began a decade earlier, in 1917, when Virginia and Leonard Woolf bought a handpress and printed *Two Stories*, one by each Woolf.

10. In "New Barbarism," Riding observes that Stein's words "contain no references, no meanings, no caricatures, no jokes, no despairs. They are so automatic that it is even inexact to speak of Miss Stein as their author: they create one another" (127). This, along with Stein's "hypnotic" rhythms, works in direct opposition to Eliot's sense of tradition, in which a modernist writes "not merely with his own generation in his bones, but with a feeling that the whole of the literature of Europe from Homer and within it the whole of the literature of his own country has a simultaneous existence and composes a simultaneous order" ("Tradition" 44).

11. Riding will revise and expand "The New Barbarism" into a chapter for her 1928 monograph, *Contemporaries and Snobs*. In their introduction to a 2014 reissue, Laura Heffernan and Jane Malcolm describe Riding's motivations for championing Stein and new modernist poetic modes: "Poets, taking their marching orders from criticism, had begun to churn out deadened, impersonal poetry that gave voice to an imagined 'zeitgeist' rather than individual experience. *Contemporaries* was Riding's attempt to stem this tide—to resist the consolidation of poetic experimentalism into monolithic modernism. . . . As modernism turned self-referentially inward, *Contemporaries* forged a

pathway outward toward newly referential uses of language, toward an unknown and unsanctioned poetry of the person" (x). Riding's preoccupation with the truth value of words will eventually lead to her repudiation of poetry in 1938.

12. References to Cornell are to the Laura (Riding) Jackson and Schuyler B. Jackson collection, #4608, at Cornell University; the numbers refer to box and folder. Likewise, references to Yale (in Letters 20, 34, and 68) are to the Gertrude Stein and Alice B. Toklas Collection at Yale University, and the reference to Oxford (in n. 21) is to the Correspondence of Gertrude Stein in the Papers of Robert Graves at Oxford University.

13. *Lawrence and the Arabs*, a biography of T. E. Lawrence (1888–1935), was published in November 1927 and was a bestseller. The royalties were "by far the highest [he] had so far earned from his writing" and not only financed Seizin Press but provided a general income going into 1928 (Wilson 340). Graves repeated this success again in November 1929 with his autobiography *Good-bye to All That*.

14. Hereafter, Letter will be abbreviated to L.

15. Riding's life-long interest in words as units of truth value culminated in the book *Rational Meaning: A New Foundation for the Definition of Words*, begun as a dictionary and thesaurus in the 1930s and published posthumously in 1997.

16. As Ulla Dydo has noted, Stein took her sense of *acquaintance* from William James's *Principles of Psychology* (1890), which held *acquaintance* as the privileged term in contrast with *knowledge-about*: "[Stein] refused to reduce composition to explanation, which removes objects from direct acquaintance, from the intimate, total knowledge that sensation gives us. It is the opposite of 'knowledge-about,' which does not require the immediate sensation of an object" (122). Our title also acknowledges a common contemporary meaning of *acquaintance*, a person one knows slightly—true for Riding and Stein, perhaps, even after three years of intense exchange.

17. In December 1930, just after ending her correspondence with Riding, Stein broke her friendship with Hugnet, with whom she had experienced the "intimacy of collaboration" since 1928 (Dydo 303). Stein had written thirty poems in response to his "Enfances" poem cycle, and they quarreled over how they should be published, Hugnet wanting Stein to be credited as a (mere) translator. When Stein's poems were first published, as "Poem Pritten on Pfances of George Hugnet," in the magazine *Pagany* (vol. 2, no. 1, winter 1931), Hugnet's French poems were on facing pages. But when in May 1931 Stein republished the poems as *Before the Flowers of Friendship Faded Friendship Faded*, the third book from Plain Edition, Hugnet's poems were absent. The break with Hugnet also led to Stein's suspending her relationship with Thomson, from January 1931 to May 1933 (see Holbrook and Dilworth 187–92).

18. Harry Horwood, a book agent they worked with then, wrote to Stein in February 1930: "there would be a market and real demand for a sort of memoir covering not only the people you have met but the whole history of the literary movement that you stand for and are at the head of. With your sense of proportion and of humor it would be the big book of its season" (qtd. in Dean 17–18). This certainly anticipates Stein's *The Autobiography of Alice B. Toklas*.

19. To follow up on people already mentioned, here are names and pages: Mabel Dodge

20   *Introduction*

Luhan (128–36), Mina Loy (132), Carl Van Vechten (134–38), Sherwood Anderson (196–97), Robert McAlmon (200), Ernest Hemingway (212–20), Virgil Thomson (226–30), Jane Heap (220–21), Georges Hugnet (230–31), Edith Sitwell (231–35), and Elliot Paul (238–41).

20. The novel is little known. It was published in January 1934, received mixed reviews, and was withdrawn in May 1934 because of a threatened libel suit from Norah McGuinness, who appeared in the novel as "Maureen" (Friedmann 226).

21. Three of the letters that Graves and Stein exchanged in 1946 are in Paul O'Prey's *In Broken Images: Selected Letters of Robert Graves, 1914–1946* (1982). O'Prey prefaced them with a note saying that Graves's initiating "letter and Stein's reply have been lost" (336). It turns out that Graves had pasted Stein's reply into a copy of her book *The World Is Round* (1939). Here is that letter, from late 1945 or early 1946:

> My dear Robert, All these years Hubert and I talked about you, it was strange stuck away in a little village that we should meet and talk about you but this has been a war of coincidences and this was a nice coincidence, write to me Robert, the end of the drama your drama was [curious?] some day it would be nice to talk about it, come over and see us and you will find us in the telephone book so telephone and come, / lots of love / Gtrde. (Oxford)

The "drama" is probably a reference to the end of their relationships with Riding. In the *Alice B. Toklas Cook Book* (1954), Toklas noted that during World War II "our most important news came from a friend, Hubert de R., who was in the *Résistance*. He would bicycle over from Savoie and lunch with us" (206). The two Huberts must be the same person.

22. Stein was Jewish, although her immediate family did not consider themselves religious. Moreover, within the Stein family, there were distinctions to be made among Jewish people over the issue of materialism—between being merely a consumer of culture (as Gertrude saw her cousin Bird Stein) or a creator (as she saw herself) of it—and over where in Europe one's family came from. These remarks about Jewishness—offensive generalizations she felt she could make in the context of this exchange with Graves but would not have published—are ones she could have made forty years earlier; they would not have been, for Stein, connected to the anti-Semitism we associate with the Holocaust.

23. Stein's "Catholic friend" was probably Henri Daniel-Rops (1901–65), whose recent book, *Jésus en son temps* ("Jesus in his time," 1945) anticipates Graves's.

24. There are also four copies of Stein's *An Acquaintance with Description* at what is now the Beinecke Rare Book and Manuscript Library at Yale. Seizin printed 225 numbered copies, and the Beinecke has numbers 23, 33, 57 and 153. Two were Stein's, one was Carl Van Vechten's, and one was Thornton Wilder's.

25. These numbers match what is available at Cornell: twenty-one letters, two postcards (L72 and L88), and "1 p.c." that could be L29, which is on cardstock. Eight letters from Stein to Graves were kept by him and included with his papers at Oxford University, for a total of thirty-two from Stein.

26. The editor of this collection, Michael J. Hoffman, asked (Riding) Jackson in 1984 if he could reprint an excerpt of "The New Barbarism," and she offered him "Word-Play" instead (Cornell 23.1).

27. The notes make up an eleven-page typescript, which she sent in 1975 to Donald Gallup at Yale and Jane Woolston at Cornell. She attempted to organize the letters chronologically and numbered them, and it seems she sent the notes to the librarians to help them date the letters. Most of the notes do little more than restate a letter's content, but two letters precipitate lengthy responses: L5, the Graves postscript in particular, and L68, which she misdates and thinks is from 1928, with Stein's "I am saving the sentence." For (Riding) Jackson, the Graves postscript reveals his "will to capture literary importance" (Cornell 72.1). Her antipathy for Graves in 1975 is manifest in this four-page note on L5.

28. Restricting access to the letters represents a shift from her view of the letter forty-five years earlier. Back then, she was selecting Len Lye letters for his book *No Trouble* (1930) and letters from friends and acquaintances for *Everybody's Letters* (1933). She was writing *Four Unposted Letters to Catherine* (1930) and about letter writing for the "Editorial Postscript" in *Everybody's Letters*. She edited four issues of *Focus* (1935) and a book, *The World and Ourselves* (1938), all made of letters from various people. For Riding in that period, letters were literature, publishable, and not just for private exchange. But for her Cornell archive, she restricted more than twenty correspondences, Stein's included, until 1999; at Yale, her letters to Stein after L24 were restricted until 1991.

29. Steven Meyer published (in 2000) the first substantial essay on the two writers, discussing standard topics such as Stein's influence on the later 1920s poetry of Riding and how they mutually benefitted from the Seizin Press publication of *An Acquaintance with Description* but also how Riding's "New Barbarism" essay may have inspired Stein's *How to Write* (see Meyer 165). Like Friedmann's biography, Logan Esdale's 2006 article draws from the letters, and like Meyer, he reorients the issue of influence by suggesting that Stein's autobiographical writing in the 1930s drew from Riding's work in having epistolary qualities.

THE LETTERS OF LAURA RIDING AND GERTRUDE STEIN

1927

1. 22 November 1927

35A St. Peter's Square
Hammersmith
London W. 6

Dear Miss Stein

I have not written sooner to thank you for your manuscript: I have been ill. I like it very much and so does Robert Graves. We plan to publish it in the Spring, if that is satisfactory to you; and will write later to discuss with you contract and printing details.

Yours

Laura Riding

---

your manuscript: "An Acquaintance with Description," which Stein began writing in England after giving her "Composition as Explanation" lecture at Cambridge University and Oxford University in June 1926. (She wrote most of it in Belley, France, finishing by early fall 1926.) She may have chosen to send *Acquaintance* in part for the English association, where it started and where it was to be published. The letters that first established the connection between Riding (1901–1991) and Stein (1874–1946) are not extant, but they probably would have involved Riding's contacting Stein and requesting a manuscript (Stein's choice) to be published by Seizin Press, which Riding ran with Robert Graves (1895–1985). The plan for spring 1928 publication would be bumped a year. Riding's *Love as Love, Death as Death* was the first Seizin book, in November 1928, followed by Stein's *Acquaintance* in April 1929 and Graves's *Poems 1929* in June 1929. For more on Seizin Press, see Letter 8. (Hereafter Letter will be abbreviated to L.)

2. [November 1927]
27 rue de Fleurus
Paris

Dear Miss Riding,

I have been wanting for some time to tell you how much I appreciated and liked your essay in transition. It will please me very much to have you publish Acquaintance with Description in the spring.

When you come to Paris I hope you will let me know as I should like very much to meet you

[Scly?]

Gtrde Stein.

———

your essay in transition: The June 1927 issue (no. 3) of *transition* magazine featured both Stein and Riding and helped lead to their acquaintance. It opened with Stein's "As a Wife Has a Cow A Love Story" and included three poems by Riding ("Sea-Ghost," "If This Reminds," and "Death as Death"), as well as her essay "The New Barbarism, and Gertrude Stein" (see fig. 2). Versions of this essay reappeared in Riding and Graves's *A Survey of Modernist Poetry*, published just before these opening letters, in early November 1927 (Heinemann), and again in Riding's *Contemporaries and Snobs* in February 1928 (Jonathan Cape).

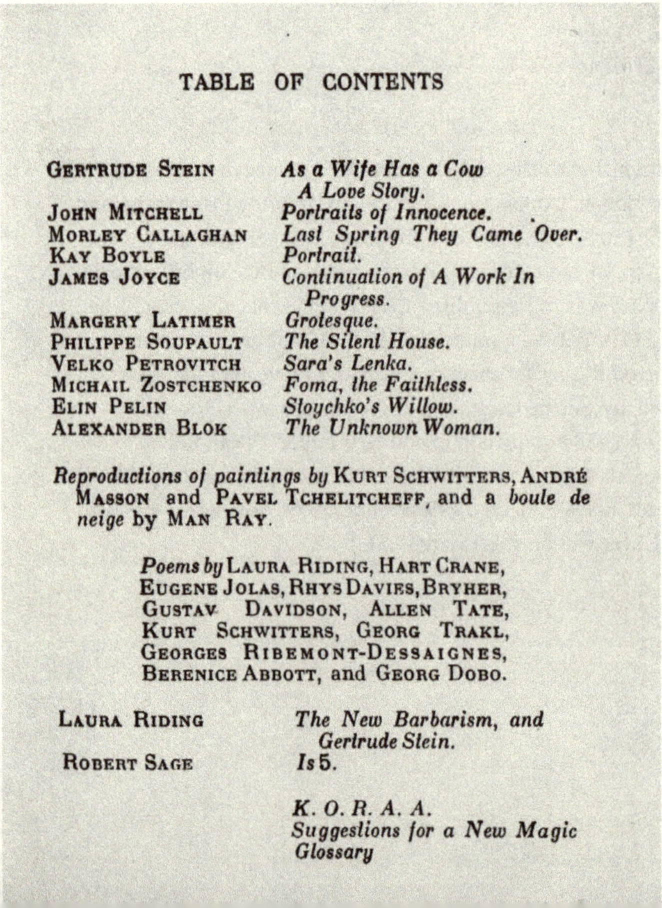

Figure 2. Contents. *transition* 3, June 1927 (np). Bibliothèque nationale de France. https://gallica.bnf. fr/ark:/12148/bpt6k-6436207f?rk=64378;0.

TABLE OF CONTENTS

GERTRUDE STEIN	*As a Wife Has a Cow A Love Story.*
JOHN MITCHELL	*Portraits of Innocence.*
MORLEY CALLAGHAN	*Last Spring They Came Over.*
KAY BOYLE	*Portrait.*
JAMES JOYCE	*Continuation of A Work In Progress.*
MARGERY LATIMER	*Grotesque.*
PHILIPPE SOUPAULT	*The Silent House.*
VELKO PETROVITCH	*Sara's Lenka.*
MICHAIL ZOSTCHENKO	*Foma, the Faithless.*
ELIN PELIN	*Sloychko's Willow.*
ALEXANDER BLOK	*The Unknown Woman.*

Reproductions of paintings by KURT SCHWITTERS, ANDRÉ MASSON and PAVEL TCHELITCHEFF, and a *boule de neige* by MAN RAY.

Poems by LAURA RIDING, HART CRANE, EUGENE JOLAS, RHYS DAVIES, BRYHER, GUSTAV DAVIDSON, ALLEN TATE, KURT SCHWITTERS, GEORG TRAKL, GEORGES RIBEMONT-DESSAIGNES, BERENICE ABBOTT, and GEORG DOBO.

LAURA RIDING	*The New Barbarism, and Gertrude Stein.*
ROBERT SAGE	*Is* 5.

K. O. R. A. A.
Suggestions for a New Magic Glossary

1928

3. May 1928   Paris, France

Dear Miss Stein –
    May I see you sometime Monday Tuesday or Wednesday? I want
to talk to you about the printing of your book –
                        Laura Riding

    c/o Thos Cook & Son
    Place de la Madeleine
    will reach me

————

May I see you: Stein's reply is not extant, but apparently she selected Tuesday. Riding's
first meeting with Stein and "Alice Toklas probably took place on Tuesday, May 22, 1928,"
at 27 rue de Fleurus; also "present was Virgil Thomson, the young American composer"
(Friedmann 120). Toklas (1877–1967) and Stein met in 1907 and were a couple from
1908 to Stein's death in 1946. Thomson (1896–1989) first met Stein in 1926, and by November 1927 he had begun composing the music for Stein's opera *Four Saints in Three Acts*
(Dydo 174). Riding and Thomson did not like each other. They can be seen as competitors
for Stein's attention over the next couple of years (see L6, 57, 80, 87 and 93).

4. May 1928   Paris, France

Dear Miss Stein
                    I borrowed this from a friend for you. Perhaps
you would like to look through it between now and Tuesday. The
<u>Anonymous Book</u> and the <u>Letter of Abdication</u> would interest you
most I believe – having to do with narrative. I have been thinking
about the problem since yesterday: it seems to me to centre in
<u>suspense</u> – that is with narrative from the individual point of view,
or self-maintenance. Your difficulty I should think is the difficulty
of stating in scientific terms what is a poetic phenomenon – if I
understand you properly your narrative is the physical preliminary
to thought (I mean thought in the poetic not scientific sense, difficult
not easy sense). Anyway if you succeed I am afraid neither poets nor
scientists are either of them a grateful lot.
                        Laura Riding.

————

Letters of Laura Riding and Gertrude Stein   25

I borrowed this . . . between now and Tuesday: Riding's *Anarchism Is Not Enough* (Jonathan Cape), which had just come out. After settling on Tuesday, May 22, Riding dropped off her book in advance of their visit. In a 1982 letter to Ulla Dydo, she remembered this "first meeting, by prearrangement, at her Paris apartment, and a first case of mutual liking" (Cornell 18.5).

Anonymous Book and the Letter of Abdication: Two chapters in the book, with "Letter of Abdication" being the final one. The speaker concedes her seeming contrariness: "You begin with contradictions instead of ending with them," the "you" an imagined interlocutor and adversary who would rather efface contradictions than develop them (217). "I am an unpaid hack of accuracy," she says (220).

your narrative is the physical preliminary to thought: Riding sees Stein's writing as a "summoning," as "creating the possibility of poetic thought to come"; a Stein text offers "lingual innuendoes that conjure poetic inflections" (Samuels).

5. [May 1928]   35A St. Peter's Square
                                                                                             Hammersmith
                                                                                             London W. 6

Dear Miss Stein

    We were so sorry to miss you both the afternoon we called to say good bye

                Laura Riding
                Robert Graves

I send you my Collected Poems. Dont trouble about the first half unless you feel sentimental. But read the final poem as a comment on your comment on me. I have refrained from inscribing homage. I cannot compete with the french.

———

my Collected Poems: This postscript and Graves's signature above are in Graves's hand. The book is probably his *Poems (1914–1927)*. The final poem in that book is "To Be Less Philosophical," which is in the appendix. In her notes from 1975 on the correspondence, (Riding) Jackson comments on Graves's postscript; she remembers Stein's commenting to Graves, "You are a man of ideas!" and says that Graves's "I have refrained from inscribing homage" alluded to "Stein's mocking talk about the Parisian ritual of exchanges between authors of flattering inscriptions in reciprocal presentations of books by authors to authors" (Cornell 72.1).

6. 5 June 1928   35A St. Peter's Square
                                                                Hammersmith
                                                                London W. 6

Dear Miss Stein

      I don't want to bother you with this but I must.

      The <u>New York Herald</u> (Paris Edition) printed a filthy reference to R. G. and myself, saying that 'Robert Graves and his wife Laura Riding' had 'arrived from the United States', and further that 'Mr. and Mrs. Graves' were going on to London for a lengthy visit.

      Now in Paris we saw no one but Jolas, Mr. and Mrs. Sage and Kay Boyle (all of whom I am sure knew enough about us to be responsible for none of these statements) and yourself and Miss T—— and one other person.

      It is very annoying for of course we did not arrive from the United States and of course we are not married and of course if we had foolishly happened to marry and stay married I should not allow myself to be called 'Mrs. Graves'. (As a matter of fact Robert Graves and another good person called Nancy Nicholson did foolishly marry many years ago and have never bothered to get unmarried, but Nancy has never allowed herself to be called 'Mrs. Graves'.)

      I write you all this because the other person I mention was Virgil Thompson and because the bad feeling I got from him when I met him matches the bad feeling I got when I read the <u>Herald</u> cutting and because I therefore think it possible that he is responsible for it and because therefore, if he is, I must ask you to destroy him for me (and R. G.). If he is not, then here is the gossip any way.

      Yours ever

      Laura Riding

Paris edition: By 1928, *The New York Herald*, having merged with *The New-York Tribune* in 1924, was *The New York Herald Tribune* in the United States; the Paris edition remained *The New York Herald*.

Graves and his wife Laura Riding: In Riding's next letter to Stein, she refers to "the cutting involving both of us that I sent you in a previous letter" (L7). Figure 3 shows that "cutting," from the 2 June 1928 column "With Latin Quarter Folk." Although not mentioned in the correspondence, there was a follow up in *The New York Herald* on 4 July 1928 (see fig. 4).

Jolas, Mr. and Mrs. Sage and Kay Boyle: Eugene Jolas (1894–1952), coeditor of

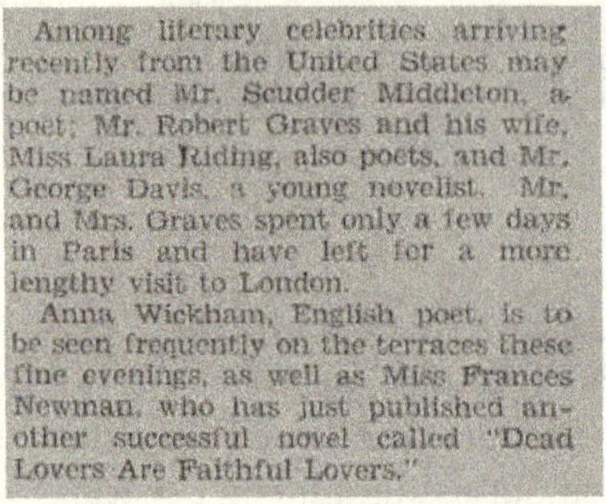

> Among literary celebrities arriving recently from the United States may be named Mr. Scudder Middleton, a poet; Mr. Robert Graves and his wife, Miss Laura Riding, also poets, and Mr. George Davis, a young novelist. Mr. and Mrs. Graves spent only a few days in Paris and have left for a more lengthy visit to London.
>
> Anna Wickham, English poet, is to be seen frequently on the terraces these fine evenings, as well as Miss Frances Newman, who has just published another successful novel called "Dead Lovers Are Faithful Lovers."

Figure 3. "With Latin Quarter Folk." *The New York Herald*, Paris, 2 June 1928, p. 9. Bibliothèque nationale de France. https://gallica.bnf.fr/ark:/12148/bd6t5206617/f9.

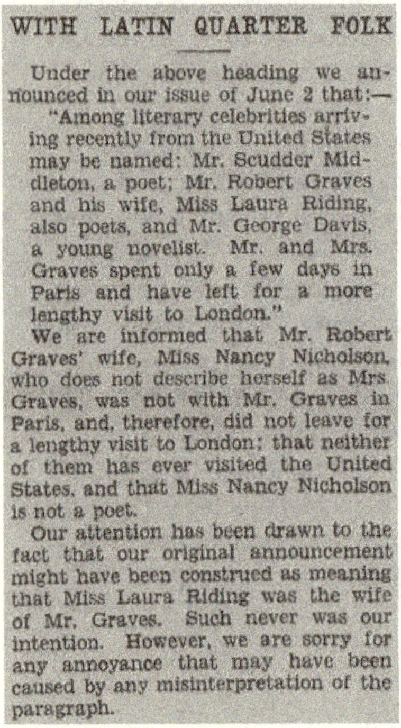

WITH LATIN QUARTER FOLK

> Under the above heading we announced in our issue of June 2 that:—
> "Among literary celebrities arriving recently from the United States may be named: Mr. Scudder Middleton, a poet; Mr. Robert Graves and his wife, Miss Laura Riding, also poets, and Mr. George Davis, a young novelist. Mr. and Mrs. Graves spent only a few days in Paris and have left for a more lengthy visit to London."
> We are informed that Mr. Robert Graves' wife, Miss Nancy Nicholson, who does not describe herself as Mrs. Graves, was not with Mr. Graves in Paris, and, therefore, did not leave for a lengthy visit to London; that neither of them has ever visited the United States, and that Miss Nancy Nicholson is not a poet.
> Our attention has been drawn to the fact that our original announcement might have been construed as meaning that Miss Laura Riding was the wife of Mr. Graves. Such never was our intention. However, we are sorry for any annoyance that may have been caused by any misinterpretation of the paragraph.

Figure 4. "With Latin Quarter Folk." *The New York Herald*, Paris, 4 July 1928, p. 4. Bibliothèque nationale de France. https://gallica.bnf.fr/ark:/12148/bd6t5194202/f4.

transition, and the writer Kay Boyle (1902–92), both Americans. Robert Sage (1899–?) was associate editor of *transition* at the time; the other coeditor of the magazine was Elliot Paul (1891–1958). Jolas, Sage, and Paul had all worked for (or were still working for) the Paris edition of the *Chicago Tribune*.

and Miss T——: Alice Toklas. Riding is unsure how to spell Alice's last name and would still be unsure almost two years later (see L73).

I should not allow myself to be called 'Mrs. Graves': Although Riding lived with Graves from 1926 to 1939, they never married. As can be seen in this letter, being referred to as

Graves's wife was deeply upsetting; they were in an open and equal relationship. Riding was married twice: to Louis Gottschalk from 1920 to 1925 and to Schuyler Jackson from 1941 until his death in 1968. Her name changed several times over the years; born Laura Reichenthal, she became Laura Gottschalk in 1920; in 1923 she published as Laura Riding Gottschalk and was Laura Riding by 1927; she was then Laura Jackson in 1941 and by 1963 her writer's name was Laura (Riding) Jackson.

Nancy Nicholson: Nicholson (1899–1977) met Graves in 1916, they married in 1918, and by 1924 they had four children: Jenny (b. 1919), John David (b. 1920), Catherine (b. 1922), and Samuel (b. 1924). Riding had moved to England in early 1926 to work together with Graves, as writers, but they quickly developed a more intimate relationship as well, and by late summer of 1926, they lived apart from Nicholson and the children (Friedmann 91). According to Graves, his marriage with Nicholson was over by 6 May 1929 (*Good-bye* 444). However, they did not legally divorce until 1950.

I must ask you to destroy him for me: Stein drafted her reply (not extant) on the back of Riding's letter, with many lines crossed out. Stein often drafted her letters (see L10 and 34 for other examples). Here is a reconstructed version of some of her reply:

> My dear Miss Riding / Really really you must not. . . . I don't like attacks and I don't like controversy and I like to mind my own business. . . . Do not be foolish . . . . anybody may have told anybody anything. . . . it is not likely that he was able to make them make false statements. . . . I do like you and I like Graves but I do not care to receive letters of this kind. . . . so please go easy [and] please hereafter be calm in letters.

7. [June 1928]

35A St. Peter's Square
Hammersmith W. 6
Riverside 4524

Dear Miss Stein

It makes me very sad that you should have felt it necessary to write to me in this way. Up to a point I do not bother myself. But there is a point at which these things become physical to me, and then I can only disentangle myself by acting physically. With me all mental detachment proceeds from this physical implication. Physical detachment would be unnatural to me.

If I say then that I am sorry that a physical act of mine affected you perhaps you will see that comparison does not arise. I could not help it. I wish you could have understood.

To have involved you at all is regrettable if it annoyed you. But there was in my letter no slightest association of yourself with the matter; no suggestion that you had made any social definition of me either to yourself or to anyone else. I had a strong instinctive sense of the physical source (not yourself) of something physically discomforting to me and I reached for it through you, the only way that presented itself to me at the moment, which was too bad, since you disliked it so. (Addressing the editor, who represented the outlet, was to me another matter.) I am sorry that the friendly and physically ingenuous character of my letter did not save it.

The physical effect on me of incidents of this sort has been sharpened by three years of active social stupidity and malice not against my work but against a life that, with two other people, I have been trying to live as detachedly and unaggressively as possible. This statement may strike you only as a further irrelevance. I make it to point out the distinction for myself between criticism, to which you were referring in your letter, and something more physical than criticism.

I hope this helps? Need I say that the cutting involving both of us that I sent you in a previous letter had nothing to do with either of us being affected by anything that the newspapers said? It merely seemed to me a little funnier than usual.

Robert Graves has sent you a copy of his Collected Poems, which I hope you have received. Soon we shall be sending you the proofs of your essay.

[?] you –
L. R.

---

with two other people: Riding alludes to her unconventional relationship with Graves and Nicholson (see L6).

I hope this helps: If Stein replied to this letter, it is no longer extant. (She did, at the least, send a letter [see L8] about Graves's poems, mentioned here in L7 and also in L5.) Around two months elapse before Riding writes again about the proofs.

8. [August 1928]   35A St. Peter's Square
Hammersmith
London W. 6

The proofs follow.

Dear Miss Stein
    I have read these proofs with great care; and Robert after me. I think you can trust them now. I have put a question mark

beside doubtful points also beside obvious points – please laugh where necessary, as with fur – fir. Take no notice of corrections in ink – these are compositor's mistakes, which have already been corrected. I hope you won't want to make any changes beyond corrections, because they have to be made here and not at the compositors; which would be very difficult. The trouble is the compositors cannot keep a job on the machines very long. It would be different if we did all our own composition – as we may some day.

I have read this essay with a proof-reading conscience this time, that is to say, I have been at it hard; and I wish I could say how much I like it – but that grows always into a long story, and I like it better than that.

My own book is now nearly all printed. I will send it to you when it is ready. I think you will perhaps like it because it is still early work.

Laura Riding.

Robert liked your letter about his poems. He is writing some more.

---

proofs follow: The pages for *An Acquaintance with Description* have been typeset and are ready for Stein to proofread.

fur – fir: Proofing a Stein text can challenge an editor. Are misspellings for the pun intentional? Early in *Acquaintance* is this sentence: "Holly has very little red berries and so have very large fir trees but not at the same time even though in the same place" (131). Apparently, the Stein manuscript had "large fur trees," and Riding has marked "fur." Was it an impertinence to check?

if we did all our own composition: The first three Seizin Press books were hand printed by Riding and Graves in their London apartment on an 1872 Crown Albion press. Using Batchelor hand-made paper, they "procured [typeset plates] from a Monotype firm: that is, the lines were set up in Monotype by the firm according to supplied text; [Riding and Graves] altered the composition as judgment suggested, with the help of an extra stock of type" (Ford 386). After moving to Mallorca (see L70), "a permanent stock of type was acquired, all the composition being done there. The fount used both in England and in Majorca was, uniformly, of Caslon type" (Ford 386). The word *seizin* was "an arcane legal term meaning 'possession of land by freehold,' [and] was almost certainly chosen to signify possession of the means of production" (Wilson 342–43). For Riding, the notion of "taking possession" meant "personal identification with the area of activity, being the more 'there'" (qtd. in Friedmann 108). Riding's use of *composition* in "if we did all our own composition" is probably in reference not just to hand printing or self-publishing but also Stein's "Composition as Explanation." On Stein's writing, Riding had said, "the composition is clear because the language means nothing but what it means in her using of it" (126). Thus, Riding may also be complimenting Stein here, as in "someday we may all write like you, using words as if for the first time."

Letters of Laura Riding and Gertrude Stein   31

Robert liked your letter: This letter is not extant, but see L52, in which Stein addresses Graves's *Poems 1929*. Letter 52 is undated, but it cannot be from 1928; Stein sent it from Bilignin, and she moved there in early summer 1929 (see L43).

9. [September 1928]   Hotel Pernollet
                                                                                        Belley
                                                                                        Ain

Dear Miss Riding
          The proofs have come and I have gone over them, there are awfully few mistakes, and the obvious were pretty much as they should be obvious, thanks awfully for all the trouble you have both taken. Inclosed is the list of the few mistakes that we found.
          I liked xceedingly that as you read the thing intensively you liked it more. It gives me a lot of pleasure to have you say so. I do hope that we will all be meeting again soon. We are probably here until the end of September. I am very much interested in a thing I am doing about grammar and in description again in so far as description is not grammar. Once more all my thanks for all the trouble you are taking. I am looking forward to having your book, but I don't insist upon its being early work, I think I might very well like it late too. Best to you both,
                              Always,
                                        Gtrde

------

a thing I am doing about grammar: Stein began "Arthur A Grammar" in Belley, finished it in Paris in October 1928, and published it in *How to Write* (Plain Edition, 1931). She wrote the eight pieces in *How to Write* over four years, from early 1927 to early 1931, starting with "Regular Regularly in Narrative" and including "Sentences" (Dydo 636–40). This is the major book of Stein's during the period that she knew Riding, and Stein seems to believe that Riding will be interested in it. (Further mentions of her work on this book appear in L25, 50, 55 and 68.) Early in "Sentences," started in October 1928, is this paragraph: "An adjective have to be faced. An adjective in sound based on fugitives. Leave roads alone. They will be pleased. To cover it with however it is only there. An adjective and they will have had May. May Rider. Mary Riding. Minna Riding, Martha Riding, Melanctha Riding. Thank you" (122). In this passage, "fugitives" alludes to Riding's association with *The Fugitive* magazine (1922–1925) and "Melanctha Riding" to Stein's story "Melanctha" in *Three Lives* (1909). (Did Stein see Riding as being like her Melanctha character, misunderstood and wandering, and Graves as Melanctha's earnest lover Jeff Campbell?) Then, in *At Present*, a play Stein wrote in spring 1930, is this: "Laura has a library. / The play is to be now adagio. Will it be andante or adagio and save Laura. / Save Laura they went there they all went there save Laura" (321). These two passages, in "Sentences" and *At Present*, appear to be the only explicit references Stein made to Riding in her work.

32   *Letters of Laura Riding and Gertrude Stein*

10. 29 September [1928]
$\qquad\qquad\qquad\qquad\qquad\qquad\qquad$ 35A St. Peter's Square
$\qquad\qquad\qquad\qquad\qquad\qquad\qquad\qquad$ Hammersmith
$\qquad\qquad\qquad\qquad\qquad\qquad\qquad\qquad$ London W. 6

Dear Miss Stein
$\qquad$ I have been ill and not-doing. Your book will be started soon now however and be soon done. My own is at the binder's at last. We can print yours in one month and finish it off in another.

$\qquad$ And I have been very slack about your Book from Payson and Clarke which arrived about a fortnight ago and which I have not yet read (but will now that I am feeling better). Of course I will write something if you would like me to and if I find something to say equal to the case. And be very glad to. But I want to make sure that you want this, first. Do you?

$\qquad\qquad$ Robert sends his best, with me
$\qquad\qquad\qquad$ Laura Riding

I have been ill and not-doing: A pattern potentially emerges here in which Riding describes herself as ill or unwell (beginning in L1: "I have been ill"). Doing this at the beginning of a letter would have been a courteous way to explain belated replies and publication delays, but each successive mention underscores a contrast in style and temperament between the two women. Stein does not refer to her own physical or emotional health in the letters.

your Book from Payson and Clarke: *Useful Knowledge*, which collected twenty-one pieces written between 1915 and 1926, including portraits of Sherwood Anderson ("Idem the Same") and Carl Van Vechten ("Van or Twenty Years After"). The book was Stein's second to collect various shorter compositions, after *Geography and Plays* (Four Seas, 1922), and was submitted at the invitation of Joseph Brewer, whom she had met at Oxford when she lectured there in 1926 (Dydo 108). On the back of Riding's letter, Stein drafted her response, which includes, "Yes I asked them to send you Useful Knowledge and I would very much like you to do anything about it" and "I hope you will like some of it." Stein was a careful letter writer (see L6 and 34). The wording of L11 is slightly different from these draft notes, indicating that she chose her phrasing even in what seems to be a quick reply.

Of course I will write something: Riding did not publish anything on *Useful Knowledge*. Riding's phrasing in L10 could suggest some hesitation, but if Stein understood this as a promise, she may have been quite disappointed.

Letters of Laura Riding and Gertrude Stein $\qquad$ 33

11. [October 1928]   Hotel Pernollet
                                                            Belley
                                                            Ain

My dear Laura,
    I asked Payson and Clark to send you a review copy of Useful
Knowledge because I wanted you to have it. Since they want you to
do something else for them and you are willing to do it naturally I
would like it very much. I am glad the books are getting on but sorry
you have not been well, it would be nice seeing you both in Paris this
winter, we are staying on here another month, I am writing pretty
well and want to go on,
        Always yours
            Gtrde Stein.

My dear Laura: For the first time, Stein uses Riding's first name, which suggests that their
relationship has become more intimate. (Riding will follow Stein's lead and use "Dear
Gertrude" on October 31 [L15] and by L15 and 16, they are both signing with "love.")
They have overcome their hiccup in June—Riding's annoyance over the gossip in the *New
York Herald* and Stein's refusal to involve herself—and are enjoying the collaboration that
the publication process entails.

do something else for them: This reference is uncertain. Payson and Clarke may have
been interested in publishing a book of Riding's or perhaps wanted just an endorsement
for Stein's book.

12. 17 October 1928   35A St. Peter's Square
                                                        Hammersmith
                                                        London W. 6

I am so very slow. You must forgive me. I will have something for
Payson and Clarke very soon. We are going to print about 225 copies
of <u>Description</u>. Numbered. 10/6. Would you have objections to signing
these (by means of labels which we would send you), or if not all, some?
If you have I will quite understand. Alas we both feel we never want to
see Paris or France again. What can we do about seeing you?
        Laura

We would very much like to have the names and addresses of a few
people who you think would like to see the prospectus of the first

four books from our press (including yours). Unless of course this would be a nuisance.

Laura.

I am so very slow: For this letter, we have combined two notes to Stein, sent around the same time, or perhaps at the same time, on two sheets. The first starts, "I am so very slow," and the second, which is dated 17 October, "We would very much like." As neither begins "Dear Miss Stein" or "Dear Gertrude," there may have been another sheet or other sheets. Stein answers the two notes—the one about labels and France and the other about names and the prospectus—in L13 (from Belley) and L14 (from Paris). Riding received both replies by the end of the month, writing on 31 October, "we are happy that you will do the labels, and thank you for all the names" (L15).

the first four books from our press: The Seizin Press prospectus listed Riding's *Love as Love, Death as Death* (see L18), Stein's *An Acquaintance with Description* (see L33), Graves's *Poems 1929* (see L52), and Len Lye's *No Trouble* (see L92). Seizin Two, Three, and Four were also listed on the verso page facing the title page of *Love as Love, Death as Death*. So although Lye's book would not be published until late in 1930, Riding had decided on it by October 1928; for *No Trouble*, she "selected [twenty of Lye's letters] and edited [them] but took care not to iron out the idiosyncrasies. This was Riding at her best as an editor" (Horrocks 119).

---

13. [October 1928]

Hotel Pernollet
Belley
Ain

My dear Laura,
    We are still in Belley but we are leaving in a day or two so send the labels all the labels to Paris and I will sign them and return them to you right away. I am awfully sorry you won't be coming over this winter, it is too bad, la pauvre France, as the peasants say when they feel low in their minds and sigh, elle a etait trahie. All the same I am hoping to see you both soon because it would be nice,
        Always
        Gtrde.

---

la pauvre France: "Poor France," as in, it is France's loss that Riding will not visit. Stein may have miswritten with "elle a etait trahie," as "elle a été trahie" makes more sense, the latter meaning "she was betrayed." Poor France, she was betrayed; there was hope and now it is gone. Although Stein learned French as a child and had lived in France for almost three decades, her written French was not as fluent as her spoken. For the sake of her writing, she intentionally avoided reading and writing in French. As she would say in 1937 after writing *Picasso* in French, "it was a frightful struggle it is not natural not at all natural to write french, English is what I write" (qtd. in Wagner-Martin 234).

14. [October 1928]   27 rue de Fleurus
                                                                              Paris

My dear Laura,
Here is a list of people who will either buy or tell others about it. Do send me a few prospectuses also to have here. Send me the labels as soon as you like and I will return them at once. Always best to you both
                         Gtrde

———

to have here: Stein is now back in Paris. The "list of people" she sent is not extant.

15. 31 October 1928   35A St. Peter's Square
                                                                      Hammersmith
                                                                      London W. 6

Dear Gertrude
            You are so very good to us, and we are happy that you will do the labels, and thank you for all the names; and we shall send several prospectuses to you also. This is a rough pull of the prospectus – it will of course be on different paper, and there are corrections in the type still to be made. We are definitely beginning to print your book Saturday. Saturday and Sunday will make 8 pages of it; so that leaves only 7 two-day jobs to be done on it (50 pages of text, 14 of titles, blanks, etc.) that is fourteen days which we ought to be able to do easily by the end of November – the type is already set up and here – with a fortnight for binding. And you will then have it by Christmas. And before it is bound you will have seen the binding of my book and will be able to say if you prefer another colour. The stuff itself is I think the simplest. I like knowing that it is washable.
            Oh about the labels: why we bothered you so soon was really to know if you would sign them in order to be able to put in the prospectus that they the books were signed, or else not to put. They are not yet

36   *Letters of Laura Riding and Gertrude Stein*

ready themselves (the labels) but we will send them along when they are in order to have them certainly done when the book itself is ready. We will send you the usual six author's copies and extra ones if you want them would be at the bookseller's price (that is with the usual discount) and if you should want any beyond those six will you perhaps tell us soon and we will print so many the more because the edition as it is is a pretty small one. The mark on the prospectus is by Len Lye our friend and if you like it or his name or anything or wearing a scarf round your neck when it is cold we will get some silk of whatever colour you say and he will put a few marks on it such as grubs developing into something very much the same really. I know this because he is at that stage of the film and puts it into blocks to print on silk or anything, to make pictures of them for himself, and so he has made several scarves out of grubs, and so it occurred to us that he might make you one because we often talk about you together. And now don't trouble to say what colour because we have decided a red background and black grubs and he will make the red himself because red dyes are not good in silks.

We liked very much the <u>transition</u> picture of you. But I feel difficult about <u>transition</u> generally. It comes to having to think that one likes Eugene, especially when reading Eugene's own writing, which it is silly to have to do.

Love from us both
Laura

------

they the books were signed: Riding added "the books" above "they."

Len Lye our friend: An artist originally from New Zealand, Lye (1901–1980) arrived in London in November 1926: "Lye quickly became part of the local artistic community which included among others the painters John Aldridge and Nancy Nicholson and the writers Norman Cameron, A. P. Herbert, Laura Riding, and Robert Graves. . . . Lye formed a particularly close friendship with Riding and Graves" (Horrocks 82).

the <u>transition</u> picture: The fall 1928 issue (no. 14) of *transition* led with a photo of Stein and her *Tender Buttons*, published for the first time since 1914 (see fig. 5). In this issue was also Stein's response to the question "Why Do Americans Live in Europe?"—"Your parent's home is never a place to work it is a nice place to be brought up in. Later on there will be place enough to get away from home in the United States, it is beginning, then there will be creators who live at home" (97–98)—and a photo of a shawl (like what Riding describes in this letter) made for Riding by Lye (see fig. 6).

scarves out of grubs: After arriving in London, Lye was befriended by the artist Eric Kennington (1888–1960) and his wife Celandine Kennington, who "operated a workshop for

Figure 5. "Gertrude Stein: Recent Snapshot." *transition* 14, Fall 1928 (np). Bibliothèque nationale de France. https://gallica.bnf.fr/ark:/12148/bpt6k62310106?rk=107296;4.

Figure 6. "Laura Riding Shawl, by Len Lye." *transition* 14, Fall 1928 (np). Bibliothèque nationale de France. https://gallica.bnf.fr/ark:/12148/bpt6k62310106?rk=107296;4.

hand-printed fabrics," Footprints Studio, "a thriving business with a number of employees and two retail outlets" (Horrocks 85). (Footprints was likely working in the textile-arts tradition of the Omega Workshops, which had closed in 1919.) At the workshop, Lye made batiks with silk or linen, typically three feet by five feet and often featuring a stylized witchetty grub, a food staple for Indigenous Australians.

think that one likes Eugene: Eugene Jolas, editor of *transition*.

16. [November 1928]   27 rue de Fleurus
                                                                          Paris

My dear Laura,
The prospectus looks very good and six author's copies are quite alright, do tell Len Lye that I liked your scarf and would like one of mine, black grubs on his own red ought to be satisfying and I guess they will be. Do thank him for me. I know about transition, it is like book shelves the kind you run across where you always see something that you had not noticed before and which is more or less readable, which I imagine is Eugene Jolas and gives pleasure. I am really very much looking forward to all four of the Seizin books, and always love to you both and again thanks to Len Lye for my scarf
                    Gtrde.

_____

tell Len Lye that I liked your scarf: She is referring to the photo in *transition* (see L15).

17. [November 1928]   35A St. Peter's Square
                                                                          Hammersmith
                                                                          London W. 6

Dear Gertrude   The prospectuses have been sent you, five. The scarf is now two since we thought too much about the grubs, so that one scarf is all development and the other all grubs. To be sent to you very soon, both. Len says the red in the top row of the sieve formations he is afraid is Ladies Home Journal but I said to him so is a neck. About transition pleasure of course is a feeling for other people, and it seems very natural to me that you should say this about transition, because you are kind. I should never have thought of saying it myself: I mean it would not have occurred to me. Love to you from Robert and from me
                    Laura

_____

Letters of Laura Riding and Gertrude Stein   39

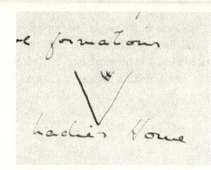

Figure 7. Laura Riding to Gertrude Stein, November 1928. Gertrude Stein and Alice B. Toklas Papers, Yale Collection of American Literature. Beinecke Rare Book and Manuscript Library, Yale University. Box 112, folder 2286.

sieve formations: Riding includes a drawing (see fig.7).

18. [November 1928]   35A St. Peter's Square
Hammersmith
London W. 6

Dear Gertrude
    I am sending you a copy of Love As Love Death As Death. It is an out of series one, that is, there will be imperfections of printing, but never mind everything is there. We are so sorry your scarf (the big one) has been delayed but it is now another one. The first one decided not to be for you, but for someone who danced. This one is now neither grubs nor development but all just the same. The small one is being hemmed mean while and you will have it first.   Love from us both,
                                                                  Laura.

---

a copy of Love As Love: Riding's third book of poetry, after *The Close Chaplet* (Hogarth Press, 1926) and *Voltaire* (Hogarth Press, 1927). This was the first book from Seizin Press.

19. [November 1928]   27 rue de Fleurus
Paris

My dear Laura,
I am delighted to have the book it pleases me a lot in every way, it is worth while having that kind of paper and the printing goes alright on it it suits it. The little thing of Len Lye is good and I am looking forward to wearing the scarves and it is no trouble to wear green or even not green. And the poetry, the poetry is good poetry. Fine fellow

son of fine fellow is complete and it is what I like you begin play and it becomes literal and you begin literal and it becomes play, and to me that is you. And it is literal enough and it is play enough to be poetry. There are lots of really complicated places in the poems and they hold.

Thanks again for everything and my love to you and Robert,

Always

Gtrde.

------

have the book: Riding's *Love as Love, Death as Death*.

little thing of Len Lye: Presumably a small textile with a Lye design, sent with L18 ("small one"). In writing "it is no trouble," she was likely alluding to the title of Seizin Four. Lye picks up on this—he must have read L19—in his first letter to Stein (see L20).

Fine fellow: Stein is referring to the poem "Fine Fellow Son of a Poor Fellow," which is in the appendix.

20. [November 1928]   35A St. Peter's Square
                                                              Hammersmith
                                                              London W. 6

Dear Gertrude

At last we can send you these: the large one is the third one tried. The first two you would perhaps have found pleasure in but this we now all think is right for you. We have not hemmed the large one, perhaps you will want to bind it in some special way so it is left raw. Ralph Church came to see me, and saw the big one and thought it was right. I can scarcely write having just cut my finger foolishly. Love to you from us both, and Len hopes you will be satisfied.

Laura

------

send you these: The shawls referred to in L15–19. They are not extant, nor are there images of them. At around the same time as (or with) the shawls, Len Lye sent a letter to Stein (Yale 115.2405; see fig. 8 and the transcription below). (There are four extant letters from Lye to Stein. See L68n for the other three.) Lye's joking manner suggests that he wondered if the shawl was too popular in style or too feminine for Stein and not "modern" enough. On the back, he sketched what would become the motif used on the title page of her Seizin book (see L34).

Letters of Laura Riding and Gertrude Stein   41

—this shawl is Ladies Home
Journal plus I know it — the dyes
get that way.

well Ladies Home Journal is surface
to Saturday Evening post is for
the flicks for a sunday school
holiday. well social
is surface & no one

notices much else
unless holiday at a
social outing & sometimes
you need a shawl and its
no trouble to wear green
Len Lye

if Ladies Home Journal means too much
give it to someone you know who
doesn't notice its aromatic.

Figure 8. Len Lye to Gertrude Stein, November 1928 (front and back). Gertrude Stein and Alice B. Toklas Papers, Yale Collection of American Literature. Beinecke Rare Book and Manuscript Library, Yale University. Box 115, folder 2405.

~~Dear Gertrude~~

this shawl is Ladies Home Journal plus I know it – the dyes get that way.

well Ladies Home Journal is surface & Saturday Evening Post is for the flicks for a
sunday school holiday. well social is surface & no one notices much else unless holiday at a social outing & sometimes you need a shawl and its no trouble to wear green

Len Lye

if Ladies Home Journal means too much give it to someone you know who doesn't
notice it as aromatic

Ralph Church: Ralph Withington Church, an American philosophy student at Oxford
University who received his doctorate in 1928. He met Stein either in Paris or at Oxford
when she lectured there in 1926 and commented on her writing in *transition* 14 (Dydo
108, n40). He returned to the United States and taught at Cornell University and at UC
Berkeley. His books include *A Study in the Philosophy of Malebranche* (1931), which Stein
owned (an inscribed copy).

21. [December 1928]

27 rue de Fleurus
Paris

My dear Laura,
I have just written to Len Lye telling him how much I liked the
scarfs and now two days later I am liking them still more, I like the
little one a whole lot but the big one is really quite xtraordinary in
its beauty, he makes all his colors very alike and as he says easy to
wear it really is rich and not gaudy, exact and warm, there is great
correctitude with emotion, really I cannot thank you enough, it has
all given me very lively pleasure, lots of love to you both

Gtrde.

22. [December 1928]

35A St. Peter's Square
Hammersmith
London W. 6

Dear Gertrude
It has been all this time making me feel well that you like the
poems though I have not been feeling well enough to write you
though sometimes I read Useful Knowledge. And to have you speak
of them in a way which is familiar to me and very comfortable. And
everyone feels good about your liking the scarf, and Len has made
a mark for the title page of Description which reminds of the scarf.
Description is now 1/4 printed but the type prepared for about all the

44   *Letters of Laura Riding and Gertrude Stein*

rest so by Monday about half will be finished. The printing is very much better than my book. And love to you from us both   Laura

// is too bad a misprint in about half of the edition will be in one place mnay instead of many

———

the title page of Description: See L34.

23. [December 1928]   27 rue de Fleurus
                                                                                  Paris

My dear Laura,
    I do hope that you are all well, the printing is coming on alright and I will be very pleased with the book, and the best of the New Years to you and Robert and also Len Lye,
              Always
              Gtrde.

1929

24. 8 January [1929]   35A St. Peter's Square
                                                                            Hammersmith
                                                                            London W. 6

Dear Gertrude
          The book is nearly done I have sent you the labels The binding is like this.
          The labels go: <u>225</u> numbered copies etc. . . . and this is no. 1 (2, 3, etc.) I have sent you more than 225 to allow for troubles. And will you anyway sign about ten extra (not numbered ones) to allow for troubles here?
          The books are selling pretty well, which is a good thing to think about sometimes.
          My love to you, and Robert's. Len's film is now 10 minutes long.

          Laura.

Did Hart Crane call on you? He is a wonderful life of metaphor.

———

Letters of Laura Riding and Gertrude Stein   45

The binding is like this: As promised by Riding in L15, a sample of the binding for *Acquaintance*. The only extant reference by Stein to the binding is in L34.

Len's film: Lye's animated film *Tusalava*. He began work on it in early 1927 and "spent nearly two years creating the 4400 or so drawings for his nine-minute film" (Horrocks 91). Lye borrowed elements from Maori and Indigenous Australian art. The title comes from the Samoan phrase *tusa lava*, meaning "just the same" (Horrocks 92). The film premiered on "1 December 1929 at the New Gallery Cinema as part of the London Film Society's 33rd programme" (Horrocks 93).

Hart Crane: Crane's poems "The Harbor Dawn" and "Cutty Sark" were also in the June 1927 issue of *transition*, alongside the Stein and Riding contributions (see L2). Crane (1899–1932) and Riding met and became close friends in fall 1925, in New York, and he visited Riding in London in December 1928. He would write to Stein on 31 January 1929: "Dear Miss Stein: / May I introduce myself as a friend of your friend, Laura Riding. / And on that presumption may I ask to see you some hour early next week—whenever it may suit your convenience to have me call?" (Hammer 396). To Isidor Schneider, on 1 May 1929, Crane said that of the many people in Paris he had met, Stein was "about the most impressive personality of all" (Hammer 406). Crane also appears in L25, 36, 49 and 83.

25. [January 1929]   27 rue de Fleurus
                                                                Paris

> My dear Laura,
>   I have just sent you back the labels, I am awfully pleased that the
> books are doing nicely, it is a pleasure, no Hart Crane did not come,
> I wish you and Robert were coming, and how long will Len's film be
> when it is longer. I am working a lot. I am doing something with the
> sentence, it isn't done it is a little commenced, that is I have gotten
> as far as the article, I get tempted by nouns and verbs but I am at
> present concentrating on the article. I do hope you are all well again,
> If anything happens and you want any more signatures let me know,
> there are some blank ones left,
>   Lots of lov to you and to Robert, and also to Len,
>   Always
>   Gtrde.

———

sent you back the labels: The labels were pasted in, as a frontispiece, facing the title page (see fig. 9).

I am doing something with the sentence: See L9.

46   *Letters of Laura Riding and Gertrude Stein*

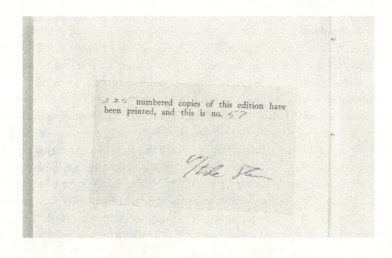

Figure 9. Frontispiece. Gertrude Stein, *An Acquaintance with Description*, Seizin Press, 1929. Beinecke Rare Book and Manuscript Library, Yale University. Za St34 929 c.1.

26. 26 February 1929　　　　　　　　　　　　　　London [telegram]

WOULD HELP LEN IF YOU COULD LEND SHAWL FORTNIGHT EXHIBITION IMMEDIATELY LOVE = LAURA

---

if you could lend: Stein wrote underneath the message, "Delighted with shawl sending at once and good luck to all Gtde."

27. 4 April 1929　　　　　　　　　　　　　　　　London [telegram]

IF GEOFFREY PHIBBS SEES YOU SAY WE ALL CAN LAST LONGER IF HE WISHES LOVE = LAURA

Geoffrey Phibbs: Before publishing the poem "To Sleep above Carthage" in *transition* 14, facing the "Laura Riding Shawl" by Len Lye (see L15 and fig. 6), Phibbs (1900–56) published two books of poems with Hogarth Press—*The Withering of the Fig Leaf* (1927) and *It Was Not Jones* (1928)—and read Riding's *Anarchism Is Not Enough*. In October 1928, after meeting with Robert Graves in Ireland, Phibbs wrote: "At present [the work of Laura Riding] is more important than anything else" (qtd. in Friedmann 127). Phibbs first met Riding in February 1929, in London, and with his wife, Norah McGuinness, lived closely with Riding and Graves and his wife, Nancy Nicholson, for several weeks. On 1 April, Phibbs went to Paris to see McGuinness, and they all met up in Rouen on 6 April.

we all can last longer: Descriptions of this group—with its entangled relationships involving two, three, four, or more people—in March and into April are bound to be incomplete; recollections disagree. But at this point, it seems that Phibbs was torn between a love for Riding (and Nicholson [see L42, 44, 51 and 56]) and a commitment to McGuinness. On 31 March, in London, he asked Riding to be with him exclusively but then abruptly left for Paris the next day. In a letter to Riding written in France before seeing her on 6 April, Phibbs explained that he left against his own feelings: "You know that I love you without degree or time or error. It is clear to me that you have not finished with me. I feel that you may kill me. Our relationship is as close as that" (qtd. in Friedmann 132). This Phibbs letter may have been intercepted by Graves, who wanted Riding for himself. Phibbs may have regretted coming between Riding and Graves and felt that McGuinness needed him. The toll these entanglements took on Riding is legible in this telegram and in subsequent letters that refer to the emotional strain of the situation—what Graves will refer to as "EXTREME TROUBLE" in L30.

sees you: Phibbs did not visit Stein.

28. 5 April 1929   London [telegram]

IN PARIS SATURDAY MORNING WITH ROBERT AND NANCY
MUST SEE YOU = LAURA

In Paris Saturday: Riding did not go to Paris. With Graves and Nicholson, she arrived in Rouen, on Saturday, 6 April, and then returned to London. Riding was demanding that Phibbs return to the group, and, for the time being, he wanted to detach; he would not see her again until 26 April (Wilson 364; see fig. 10).

Figure 10. Laura Riding to Gertrude Stein, 5 April 1929. Gertrude Stein and Alice B. Toklas Papers, Yale Collection of American Literature. Beinecke Rare Book and Manuscript Library, Yale University. Box 112, folder 2287.

29. 6 April 1929   27 rue de Fleurus
                                                                        Paris

Saturday

My dear Laura,
     I did xpect to hear from you and to see you to-day but nothing came
from you, do let me know how you are and what you are doing, we will be
in Paris still another couple of weeks and would like awfully to see you, I
do hope well I write vaguely because it is vague, but do let me hear from
you soon, Always with very much affection,
                                        Gtrde.

30. 8 April 1929   London [telegram]

SERRY TELERAM TURNED BACK ROUEN EXTREME TROUBLE
NOW EASING = ROBERT

———

turned back: Graves confirms that they had not traveled as far as Paris. This telegram
could be translated as "Sorry about the cryptic telegrams on 4 and 5 April. We went to
Rouen and are now back home. The trouble involving Phibbs is now easing." This is somewhat reassuring. Stein was likely also wondering about her *Acquaintance* book, which
Riding had said on 31 October 1928 (L15) would be done by Christmas and on 8 January
(L24) that it was "nearly done." Unless letters are missing, there has been no update on
her book for three months.

31. 9 April 1929   35A St. Peter's Square
                                                                Hammersmith
                                                                London W. 6

Dear Gertrude,
     Laura wants to know, is there a way for her to be near you for a
time: anyhow she must see you, she says, if only for a day: perhaps
not next Saturday but if not soon after   Will you please write her
something?
          Love
               Robert

———

Letters of Laura Riding and Gertrude Stein   49

next Saturday: This would be 13 April, and Riding did not travel to France. Graves's "Will you please write" suggests that Stein's 6 April letter had not reached them by 9 April. Letter 33 from Riding, probably sent on 16 April, is in response to Stein's 6 April letter: Stein's "well I write vaguely because it is vague" is echoed in Riding's "It is very difficult to write, as you say, it is vague" in L33, below.

32. 16 April 1929 London [telegram]

LETTER ON WAY LOVE = LAURA

33. [16 April 1929] 35A St. Peter's Square
Hammersmith
London W. 6

Dear Dear Gertrude
It is very difficult to write. as you say, it is vague. I
was coming to you this week but the trouble is in climax again rather
than in suspense as it was after Rouen. The trouble is persons and
work the same Always you are there, in this sameness. You know.
I nearly went to Paris to see you, after Rouen, but I was too ill and
it would therefore have been meaningless. Nancy went to Ireland
to-night to find the person Geoffrey who we thought might possibly
have gone to see you in Paris: because he joins you and me very
closely in his mind. Robert tried to find him in Ireland before we
went to France, but failed. Think of us as mad? our human behaviour
suddenly began to state to me terrific values. I nearly died of them at
Rouen. How can I write you. dear Gertrude.
I meant to bring the shawl and the books. When I
do come I bring as much of Len's film as he has photographed at
the time, we will have it run off somewhere. That is really the most
important thing: it is easier to look at Len's film than for me to write
you – or talk to you; and all just the same.
I will write you in a few days again. It will be easier
now: this is the first letter I have written for months.
bless you
and our love to you both   Laura

------

the shawl and the books: Although this is a very brief mention of Stein's *Acquaintance*, it is likely that this letter accompanied or shortly preceded a package with six copies of her book (see L15) and the Lye shawl (see L26).

34. [April 1929]   27 rue de Fleurus
                                                                  Paris

My dear Laura,
 Thanks so much for the book. I like it all my part and your part and
Len Ley's part. And thank you a whole lot. I like the way it looks and
the way you have printed the title at the end and the freshness of it all
including the binding. Len Ley's little thing is good his shapes are. They
have real weight and balance in them in some strange way. And Laura
when are you coming, you see if you wanted to stay a few days you
could take a room in one of the little hotels in the neighborhood and eat
with us and be with us. Do let me know or later if you would want to
come down to Belley, it is awfully pretty there. But above all do know
that nothing would give me more pleasure than seeing you again. And
again thanks for the book and a great deal of love to you and to Robert
    Alwys
     Gtrde.

---

the book: Stein has received her copies of *An Acquaintance with Description* (225 copies
printed in total).

Len Ley's part: Lye's "part" was an image on the title page: "He based the Stein symbol on a Maori
koru motif" (Horrocks 110). (See fig. 11; compare with his drawing in fig. 8.) Stein drafted her
reply in a notebook: "of it all including the binding. Len Ley's ~~little~~ thing is good his shapes are
They have real weight and balance in them" (Yale 92.1725). Also in that notebook is draft material
for "Sentences," "Five Words in a Line," "Basket," and "Film: deux soeurs qui ne sont pas soeurs."

35. [April 1929]   35A St. Peter's Square
                                                               Hammersmith
                                                               London W. 6

Dear Gertrude
 Your letter made Laura very happy Life is easier now though sad.
Laura will write soon about seeing you. We all want to see you.
Did you get the shawl safely?
We are so pleased you liked the book Some copies were badly bound,
that is, folded wrong so that the tops of the print did not lie even on
opposite pages. So good that you liked Len's shape. He is upstairs
doing a thing on Laura's bedroom wall in coloured distemper & chalk
Laura wants as much of your writing as you yourself consider
necessary. What do you suggest & how best can we get them?

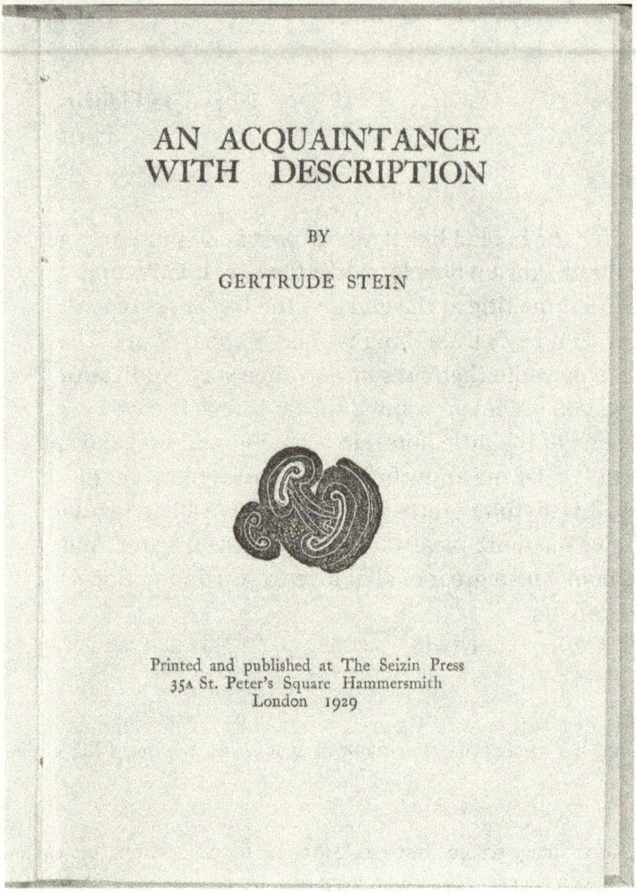
AN ACQUAINTANCE
WITH DESCRIPTION

BY

GERTRUDE STEIN

Printed and published at The Seizin Press
35A St. Peter's Square Hammersmith
London 1929

Figure 11. Title page. Gertrude Stein, *An Acquaintance with Description*, Seizin Press, 1929. Beinecke Rare Book and Manuscript Library, Yale University. Za St34 929 c.1.

About review copies of Acquaintance: – We have set aside six & have sent one to the Times' Litt. Supp.

What do you say to sending the other 5 to

Observer }
Nation } England

Sat. Rev. }
Dial } America
New Republic }

Any alternatives? We dont know.

Love

Robert.

———

Your letter made Laura very happy: Graves is writing to discuss Seizin Press business, but this letter marks the start of his handling of the correspondence with Stein, through June 1929. The shift to Graves began with L30 and 31.

get the shawl: Presumably, this refers to the Lye shawl that Stein loaned following Riding's request on 26 February and had (probably) been sent back to her with L33. Stein acknowledges receiving the books but not the shawl in L34.

sent one to the <u>Times' Litt. Supp.</u>: The *Times Literary Supplement* reviewed the book on 18 July 1929, but the other magazines on Graves's list did not.

36. [April 1929]   27 rue de Fleurus
                                                                                    Paris

My dear friends,
    Yes the shawl came alright and I am most awfully glad to have
it back, do thank him again for it, I do hope to see him some time.
About the review copies yes I think that is quite alright they are the
best places to send I don't really know of any others. Everybody who
has seen the book is really pleased with it and I am enormously so,
and yes there are some things of mine that are entirely and very
necessary and I would like to talk it over with you. I have been seeing
something of Hart Crane lately, he has gone South now, I like him
very much. I am glad that things are easier and I am looking forward
to seeing you either now or later, Lots of love to you
                            Alwys
                        Gtrde.

———

the shawl came alright: The Lye shawl of Stein's that she had loaned to them in February (see L26).

I do hope to see him: Len Lye.

some things of mine: Her response to Graves's "Laura wants as much of your writing as you yourself consider necessary" (L35).

he has gone South: Stein would get a 29 April postcard from Crane, from Collioure, France: "I like it so far, and expect to stay a while" (Hammer 404). Crane also wrote to Riding from Collioure, and her response came later, in August; it is far less detailed and emotional than what she and Graves would send to Stein in L37–40: "What has happened is we have been lying with the Devil and are all the better for it. In three months I'll be walking about—roughly speaking—and then off to Spain I think" (qtd. in Friedmann 157).

Letters of Laura Riding and Gertrude Stein   53

37. 27 April 1929   London [telegram]

LAURA HOSPITAL SERIOUS INJURIES SHOULD RECOPER COME
IF ANYHOW POSSIBLE STAY FLAT = ROBERT

———

serious injuries: Early in the morning of 27 April, after a night of tense conversation with Graves, Nicholson, and Phibbs, Riding jumped from the third (top) story of her London apartment, at 35A St. Peter's Square, resulting in multiple injuries. (The building has four stories—they had the top two—but the bottom is partly below street level.) Graves ran down a flight of stairs and jumped out of a second-story window. "Nancy [Nicholson] phoned at once for an ambulance, then for Robert's doctor-sister Rosaleen"; Robert was "shaken and bruised but basically unhurt"; and first impressions suggested that Riding "was not expected to live" (Wilson 368). Graves sent this telegram to Stein in the evening and by then he felt that Riding, at Charing Cross Hospital, "should recoper [recover]."

38. [28 April 1929]   27 rue de Fleurus
                                                                          Paris

My dear friends,
        Your telegram came last evening and I am troubled about you, do
let me know if I can be of any help to you in any way, you know I am
very very fond of you both
                        Always
                        Gtrde.

39. 30 April 1929   London [telegram]

XRAYED FOUR BROKEN VERTEBRAE FRACTURED PELVIS
ETCETERA NO FUNCTIONAL DAMAGE ON BACK PROBABLY ALL
SUMMER MIND LUCID ASKS FOR YOU = ROBERT

———

etcetera: Three days later Graves sends this update. Riding had also fractured her skull.

40. [May 1929]   35A St. Peter's Square
                                                                    Hammersmith
                                                                    London W. 6

Dear Gertrude
Laura tried to kill herself with tablets of Lysol & then a jump of 50 ft
into a stone area.

This was because Geoffrey Phibbs was a sort of dual personality, part incredibly good, part very very ordinarily vulgarly bad. Laura is a single person, and incredibly good. He quitted.

So she broke her pubis bone in 2 places and lumbar vertebrae were badly smashed but her spinal cord remained, curiously, intact. So she is on her back in hospital for at least 2 months & will eventually recover the use of her limbs. At first they said she was paralysed for life. She asked for you a lot, so I wired you. If you can possibly come, it will be good. Nancy & I have been lucky in getting her into a good hospital. She is conscious, rational when not under morphia & in great pain.

The Geoffrey business is now, Laura sees, ended. It was necessary, it produced good & now she can see things happening again, since this very thoroughly executed death, without him.

Nancy, Laura, myself & Len Lye are very close & feel you close to us too even though you cannot perhaps come yet.

> Love
> Robert

Geoffrey business: Although Riding's defenestration can be understood as a suicide attempt, Elizabeth Friedmann has argued that she did not want "to die but to free herself from a situation that had become unbearable" (138). (Friedmann also believes that she did not ingest Lysol. Graves may have lied about this aspect so that no one would be accused of having pushed Riding out the window.) The jump did snap the group tension and welded Riding and Graves. After she had sufficiently recovered, by September 1929, they left England for Mallorca (see L57). For Graves, this also meant leaving Nicholson and their four children behind.

41. [May 1929]   27 rue de Fleurus
> Paris

My dear Robert

It was about that that I feared, Laura is so poignant and so upright and she gets into your tenderness as well as your interest and I am altogether heart-broken about her, I cannot come now because of family complications but tell her and keep telling her that we want her with us, we are to be at Belley right near Aix les Bains and as soon as she can be about and strangely one thinks of her as coming together alright, you and Nancy are wonderfully good, I had an unhappy feeling that Laura would have sooner or later a great disillusionment and it would of course have to come through a certain vulgarity in another and it will make Laura a very wonderful person, in a strange way a destruction and recreation of her purification but all this does not help pain and I am very closely fond of you all. Tell

Letters of Laura Riding and Gertrude Stein   55

her all and everything from me and tell her above all that she will
come to us and reasonably soon and all my love,

Gtrde.

———

we are to be at Belley: Stein is still in Paris, at 27 rue de Fleurus, but will soon leave for Bilignin (sometimes spelled Billignin) where she and Toklas will move into a seventeenth-century
manor house that they would rent until 1943. In 1924, they began spending half the year,
the summer and fall, in Belley, staying at the Hôtel Pernollet. Bilignin is just outside Belley.

a certain vulgarity: Graves transcribed Stein's letter on the back, probably to render it
more legible for Riding. Alongside his transcription he added a note, for Riding, on Stein's
use of the word *vulgarity*: he says that "'vulgarity' is her word. I told her that there was a
dualism in Geoffrey, that he could not make it. That he was incredibly good, or just ordinary." In fact Graves had used a version of the word in L40, in "ordinarily vulgarly bad."

42. [May 1929]   Charing Cross Hospital
London

Gertrude

now it has all become simple. I am free. and others
to whom I have been a force are free of me Others have been wrong
so have I. The hardest is now to be dead [pain – no pain] and also
alive (for others) Robert understands me as dead so does Len in his
far-off way. But Nancy (to whom Geoffrey went in horror at my
<u>supposed</u> death) is puzzled and cannot make sense of the deadness
and the aliveness. And Geoffrey now understands me as religiously
dead that is his profanities are over. Poor Nancy she is ashamed to
be happy in Geoffrey – Geoffrey is happy in Nancy and not puzzled
but thoughtless. Poor Geoffrey he was some part of me that resisted
me with fanatic love-hate up to the final out-of-the window Dear
Gertrude Dear Robert Robert went out of the window with me in
bodily spirit. you are always outside This is a description becoming
an undescription. Unless you are going to be in England I cannot
come to you for a long time apparently. I am not troubled. They
promise me the pain will go in time (though I may have to have an
operation to release pressure from the spinal chord) and that is

This is Laura's first letter since her fall.

It is not very legible because of the pencil so here is a copy I am making.
[. . .]

56   *Letters of Laura Riding and Gertrude Stein*

She asked me to go on with the letter.

She is looking much better & can eat properly again. This afternoon after writing this letter she had another visit from Geoffrey. She was very generous, very strong, very plain. very gentle. He thought that she was trying to hypnotise him away from Nancy! And raised his voice & was violent. It seemed like the end when he went out. End for him. Poor Geoffrey. He is so afraid of his mean goatish little independence He does not know or begin to know Laura's goodness. She is overgenerous overpatient. But she realizes I think that this is the end unless there is a quite new surprising change in him & in Nancy.

He hurts me so by his brutality, I am bewildered & I have got used to excesses He has just said to me – as I'm lying writing this :–

"If I thought that Laura was able in any way to alter my feeling for Nancy in the slightest degree I'd pitch her (Laura) out the window and break her neck." Nancy did not protest.

!Well!

     Love

         Robert.

Have mislaid your Belley address

Dearest Gertrude

     This is Laura's first effort since her operation

     She goes on well & is getting back feeling in her legs, very gradually.

     Love

         Robert

Mon.

Dear Gertrude

         This is Laura her face is somewhere underneath. You can't imagine how wonderful it is that I am contriving to write this such pleasure and also such tugging of sewn up back-muscle!

         Love Laura

———

L42 is nine pages altogether and is a collaboration with Graves, while Riding is in hospital. The first three pages (from "Gertrude / now it has all" to "and that is"), from Riding, are followed by four from Graves (from "This is Laura's first letter" to "very gradually. / Love / Robert"), and then two more from Riding (from "Mon. / Dear Gertrude" to "Love Laura"). One part of this sequence (marked with "[. . .]") is not included here: Graves's transcription of the first three pages, which he introduces with "here is a copy I am making." The last two parts of L42—brief notes from Graves and from Riding—might have comprised a separate letter, as they are from after "her operation" and the first parts are from before. But it seems likely that Graves sent everything together—L43 from Stein appears to respond to L42 in total.

[pain – no pain]: The brackets are Riding's.

Geoffrey is happy in Nancy: See L27, 44, and 51.

may have to have an operation: This likely refers to the surgery she had on 16 May to realign her spinal cord.

He hurts me so: This paragraph and the next is Graves recording what Riding had said after a Phibbs visit.

This is Laura: Riding's words connect with a drawing (see fig. 12).

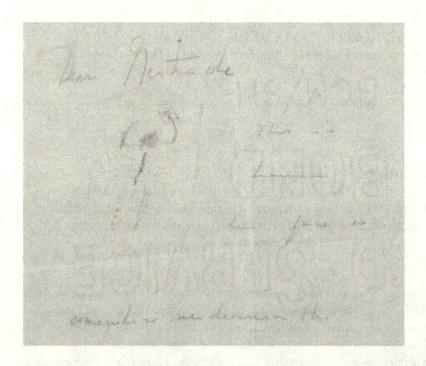

Figure 12. Laura Riding to Gertrude Stein, May 1929. Gertrude Stein and Alice B. Toklas Papers, Yale Collection of American Literature. Beinecke Rare Book and Manuscript Library, Yale University. Box 112, folder 2287.

43. [May 1929]

Bilignin
par Belley
Ain

My very dear Laura
I was awfully pleased to have a word from you from your own hand and now I imagine it is getting better and better at least I do most awfully hope so and I am looking forward to hearing again, that it is. It will be alright seeing you both it always would be but now more than ever. Do please tell Robert to go on letting me know how you are and very soon now more your you, Lots of love and lots of everything to you both.

Always

Gtrde.

———

Bilignin: This would be one of Stein's first letters from her new home.

44. [May 1929]

35A St. Peter's Square
Hammersmith
London W. 6

Dearest Gertrude
I am writing for Laura who looks so thin and yellow & talks in a whisper, but today has really, she says, found peace for the first time since her fall: talking to me. She dictated to me a few notes for you:–

"Thinking to Gertrude, tell her, has kept me alive in the worst hours. Since I came to Hospital, say, I had had a fresh lot of personal complications thrust upon me, principally by Nancy. Nancy brought Geoffrey back but she brought him back to herself as well as me. But I am keeping clear & clean and there is only one thing and that is that I did go out of the window and that some people were with me at the time. Some went out & some didn't really. Robert went out with me. Anyone else who wants to be here with me as Robert is must discover in herself or himself an out-of-the-windowness. Gertrude does not have to; she was never inside the window. Tell Gertrude I love her!"

[I don't think I need supplement this by anything. Nancy & Geoffrey are together, in a very strong way, a final way. They are alike. Creatures of impulse. Good in streaks; amazingly poor in streaks. Laura understands all this Nothing in them that endures & sees things out to the end. But good while they are good.]

Letters of Laura Riding and Gertrude Stein   59

Laura says she is coming to you as soon as she can travel & that she wants me to come with her.

Laura is sure of you & me & Len and of Jane who lives with him and has shown herself good in all this.

All this . . .

Love
Robert

———

since her fall: When Graves first described to Stein what had happened on 27 April, Riding acted with intention: "Laura tried to kill herself with tablets of Lysol & then a jump of 50 ft into a stone area" (L40). But here and above in L42, the word is *fall*, a word suggesting something more accidental or unconsciously done. Riding also uses "fall" in L49 and 51.

[I don't think: The brackets around this paragraph are Graves's.

Jane: Jane Thompson (b. 1904?), at the time the partner of Len Lye. She was born in London, moved with her family to South Africa, and returned to London in her early 20s. She met Lye there in 1927 and they moved in together in early 1928 (Horrocks 97). They married in 1934 and divorced in 1948.

45. [June 1929]   Bilignin
                                                                par Belley
                                                                    Ain

My very dear Laura and Robert,
        I am rather selfishly glad that the result of it all means you both more completely together, you do mean that to me the two of you with Len firmly in the background because after all it is hysteria that is vulgar and the complete absence of hysteria is very rare, there is very little absence of hysteria and you two are it and therefore if not for other reasons very dear to me. We are here and wanting to see you here both of you with us a quiet and yet sufficiently enlivening spot and all of it. As soon as the pain is over Laura has such real vitality that she will go on and nowadays so fortunately they can get the better of pain and it must be soon done. Do please let me hear from you as I have been doing, and all my love to you both always.
        Gtrde

46. [June 1929]
35A St. Peter's Square
Hammersmith
London W. 6

Dearest Gertrude
Laura is as good as gold & will be moved over on her back again on Thursday. Then perhaps ten more days & she will be propped up. Meanwhile she will be massaged & reeducated in use of her legs. She is cheerful but not thinking yet. She eats a lot & reads hospital library books. Today for the first time she contemplated thinking again, and separating herself from the ward-routine a little. I will take her your letter when I go tomorrow.

Bless you
Robert.

———

your letter: Probably L45.

47. 18 June 1929
35A St. Peter's Square
Hammersmith
London W. 6

Dearest Gertrude

Laura's address is now

Private Wards
London Homeopathic Hospital
Great Ormonde St
London W. C. 1

She has a room to herself & better nursing & food decently served & so on. All much better. She is quickly recovering the movements in the legs that she was afraid she would never have.

I am busy when not in hospital in writing my autobiography. It is a sort of goodbye to everyone but the very very few people to whom one never says goodbye or has ever said a formal how do you do. Quite ruthless; yet without indignation.

Laura says that she is going to write a book about Suicide. But not able to begin for some time of course. And by the time she starts it may be something different.

Letters of Laura Riding and Gertrude Stein   61

She is still on her back until her pelvis strengthens. Probably another fortnight.

I think that (by using influence in Whitehall) we have succeeding in quashing any police nastiness or prosecution for attempted suicide.

Good luck

Robert

London Homeopathic Hospital: Riding has just moved from Charing Cross Hospital to what is now called Royal London Hospital for Integrated Medicine.

writing my autobiography: Graves wrote *Good-bye to All That* quickly, in eleven weeks, starting in May and finishing by late July. He completed revisions by late August, and it was published by Jonathan Cape on 18 November 1929, selling thirty thousand copies in its first month (Wilson 391–92). In writing about his life to that point, Graves says goodbye to it, as something now separate from or even dead to him. His new life with Riding is expressed solely in his epigraph, her poem "World's End," from *Love as Love, Death as Death*, and in the "Dedicatory Epilogue to Laura Riding" that closes the book. Because he has not mentioned her in the autobiographical part—she is not what he is saying goodbye to—the "last chapters have a ghostly look," he notes (447). He is now "here outside" with her (447). Above in L42, Riding also conceives of their post-April 1929 life as being "outside," where Stein already was; one had to jump through the window to get there. Later, for the 1957 Doubleday edition of this book, Graves—having said a goodbye to Riding in 1939—effaces her presence entirely.

a book about Suicide: This is probably what becomes *Experts Are Puzzled* (see L54, 64, 85, 92).

using influence in Whitehall: Graves alludes to his friend and mentor Edward Marsh (1872–1953), "private secretary to Winston Churchill at the Exchequer. Attempted suicide was illegal in England, and Laura therefore was subject to prosecution and, if found guilty, deportation" (Friedmann 143). "Whitehall" stands for the British government. Graves's 16 June 1929 letter to Marsh on this issue has been published (O'Prey 188–90). He mentioned to Marsh that "We will probably leave the country when Laura can travel, i.e. about November" (O'Prey 188). See L49 for Riding's update that "there will be no Prosecution."

---

48. [June 1929]

Bilignin
par Belley
Ain

My very dear Laura,

Just had a letter from Robert saying that you were really getting better and being more comfortable and I am pleased as can be, I always liked Robert a lot but I have come very close to him lately and am enormously interested in his autobiography I guess he is going to be better and better as well as you and that means a lot to me. And you don't try to write until it comes easily but I will be very glad indeed to have a letter from you. We are now quite quietly in the country and I have just begun writing, it's just begun and it interests me, more by and by and by and by is not going to be too long away, I am awfully fond of you both and lots of love

Gtrde.

---

interested in his autobiography: *Good-bye to All That* was one point of reference for Stein's *The Autobiography of Alice B. Toklas* (1933), but there were many other modernist memoirs, including Janet Scudder's *Modeling My Life* (1925), Natalie Clifford Barney's *Aventures de l'esprit* (1929), and Margaret Anderson's *My Thirty Years' War* (1930), all of which Stein owned. There were also Muriel Draper's *Music at Midnight* (1929) and Ford Madox Ford's *Return to Yesterday* (1931)—and Mabel Dodge Luhan's *Intimate Memories* (1933) was published alongside Stein's *Autobiography*.

49. [June 1929]   London Homeopathic Hospital
                                                 Great Ormonde St
                                                 London W. C. 1

dearest Gertrude
          I had a dream of you and the dream was gone and the feeling very easy, not remembering. how are you. The operation was made by an insect Mr Lake, a very busy scar about a foot long and now little motions are beginning though the back is always under me. Old John Clarke is leaving me with Gelsemium, which is yellow jasmine, he is a doctor not really but Paracelsus + Blake +, he is also 80 and chuckles. There is also a masseuse and visiting hours. In three months my feet touch the ground at least not before and then it will be first steps for we hope not into the winter. Where shall we go, not where you advised Hart Crane to go? Yes dear Robert he is at the top of his action always and always it is an Action. which progresses, and because it must, not because it pleases it to do so.
          The last part of this sentence was written many days later and in the meantime I have had another dream of you, and you came to see me without warning and I was rather angry not to know because it did not give me time to look in my mirror: my left eye was nearly casualtied totally in my fall, but it is gradually being itself, but it is still making the left side of my face a little odd or not alive, and you know that a mirror is a corrective that is it evens things up, it would

make the right side of my face a little odd or not alive also, and so I was rather angry to be caught half-and-half like that, though not with you, with the porter who announced you. And I was lying only a few inches from the ceiling, and slid down a little on my pillow toward you. You were a somewhat sickroom Gertrude that is you had fine black hair and delicate features and wore a creamy woolen cap, and you were planning to do some shooting in the Highlands. I remember wondering but not for long. There was more and most of it quite unnecessary. And you came again for lunch though you had Engagements.

I am sitting up a little now, my body is a great number of things but it is beginning to suggest simple arithmetic

Len is working hard on the film all this time. We don't see each other, it would of course be silly. But he's all right. And in a fortnight I am going home to be nursed, and people can begin again.

Eddie Marsh, do you know him, editor of old Georgian anthologies, and Chief Secretary at the Home Office, has succeeded in persuading the Police that I am a remarkable person and must be left alone and so there will be no Prosecution for attempted suicide or moral turpitude, and apparently no deportation danger But anyway we must leave England as soon as possible, to be away for the winter, and to find a place that will justify being away from it more and more. Will you live in Paris always?

There is an island Simitara in the Australs Len and his pretty Jane and Robert and I think about but that is perhaps just thinking about it, to say death is not places, death is place, and so to find place, and so for it to be no trouble to be alive. dear Gertrude,
my love, Laura.

Mr. Lake: The "leading expert on spinal surgery" who operated on Riding on 16 May (Wilson 368).

Old John Clarke: John Henry Clarke (1853–1931), the physician in charge of Riding at London Homeopathic Hospital.

old Georgian anthologies: From 1912 to 1922, Edward Marsh edited five collections of *Georgian Poetry*. Graves appeared in the last three (1917, 1919, 1922).

Simitara: Presumably the island of Rimitara, in the Austral Islands of French Polynesia.

50. [July 1929]
Bilignin
par Belley
Ain

My very dear Laura,

        I have been thinking of you a lot lately back home, and I hope going on, and not too hot and not too anything but alright. I do hope to hear that everything is coming back, and that it would be good for you to take treatment at Aix or somewhere near us, or something that would be a pleasure to us all. Do let me hear how everything is going, yes I imagine I will go on staying in France I can see how you wouldn't like it, it is not xactly a pleasant taste but it is on the whole a case of the shortest and permanentest cut to liberty and liberty that does not concern anybody not even oneself it is so permanent, but if one does not want that much and one easily may not then there is everything that jars I can see that though I do not as a matter of fact feel it. it is so uncomplicated that really there is no jar but this is for me and not for you not at all for you and yet I am hoping that we will be seeing you here just the same and for all that. I am writing a little these days, something that you will like I think, I am getting my sentences beginning with my paragraphs more natural and it is very nice to feel them feeling more natural. Last years sentences were good but these years paragraphs are better. Anyway tell me you and Robert about yourselves and lots of love and are we seeing you and how and when and always
Gtrde

---

go on staying in France: Her response to Riding's "Will you live in Paris always?" in L49.

51. [July 1929]
London Homeopathic Hospital
Great Ormonde St
London W. C. 1

dear Dear – Gertrude

        I was beginning to more than want a letter from you so your letter was just right. And I have written two poems in the last two days, the first for my self, the second for Robert, and this is now the third business. I am so pleased about your sentences, which means more and more ease for me (or difficulty, which is the same thing) not in sentences but in my self This year's laura for yes There is always Gertrude and just now there is Laura and it is a

Letters of Laura Riding and Gertrude Stein   65

very clear or confused thing but it is a thing. It is the same thing that people who know our work but not us and imagine our faces and make mistakes about them make no mistakes but only get us mixed. This has happened to me any way. And it is simpler to me now than when I thought about it more, before the leap. That one was a knot.

That one and that one sicken me now greatly by their own thoughts of me. That one for instance threatens to sue for some books and it is altogether quite fiendish, like night fever, and so not at all true but only sickening.

There are still body troubles but also more and more forgetting them. I sit up a little nearly straight now and put my feet to the floor for a few minutes: it is an exercise; and I can sit up quite unsupported for 2 or 3 minutes, and the legs are becoming a little less odd to look at, and the pains broken up into bundles – not all one as in the beginning. I am going to get Len to make me a shawl of my scar, which is beautiful, like asphodel, that is so

and in colour like dawsons / yes liberty this is right for you but for no one else but who would ask for it or know it but you and yes that which is not liberty is right for me say it is responsibility and who would ask for it and know it in my way but me?

About walking, when it comes then I'll walk and we'll see you somehow but we think Spain for the winter if we can be told of a place easy to find and like without too much walking. They say it will be a long time before my back is really good again so we must not think of things too definitely – In any case it will be November the very earliest.

And here is Len's for-the-time-being. It was just a letter but I said oh a poem and so we let Jane type it like that and now it is both. But first it was a dream. Len is a good dreamer. He dreams lots of things for me.

And here is a picture I made about five weeks before my fall when there was no fall and so I made a picture about myself (central) Robert (right) and that one (left) and it is the truth not told and so a picture and I found it here when I got home and as there had been a fall there was no more picture. I am sending it to you because all the pictures belong to you to tear up and Robert is sending his poems to you not to tear up, Robert says about himself that he is glad about me and that he has practically finished his autobiography, and we both say we love Gertrude.

———

London Homeopathic Hospital: Where she wrote this letter is uncertain. She was back at 35A St. Peter's Square by 12 July (Wilson 381).

I have written two poems: Riding sends a poem that she will later title "This" (p. 127) in *Poems: A Joking Word* (1930), and a poem beginning "Other, who have tasted true water," about Graves, which was never published. Both poems are in the appendix.

the third business: Currently, her three tasks as a writer: to write for herself, about Graves, and to Stein.

There is always Gertrude: A Steinian syntax is pronounced in this letter (see L33, 42, 49, 54, 86 and 92 for other examples), perhaps because Riding felt so close to Stein at this time.

That one and that one: Phibbs ("sue for some books") and Nicholson.

that is so: Underneath these words is a drawing of her back and its scar (see fig. 13).

Len's for-the-time-being: Riding includes a four-page typescript, the first part of which, "Still July," will become "No More Stories" in Lye's *No Trouble* (1930), the fourth Seizin Press book (see L92). The second part is probably by Thompson ("we let Jane type it like that"). As she typed Lye's letter, she also played with elements of it and added others to make an eight-stanza poem: "no night or day" and "stepping stone" are repeated, as is the notion of a select group of twenty versus the millions, his "they needn't even remember the garden of eden" becomes "no ark needed" in her poem—and she adds references to popular songs ("Waiting for Robert E. Lee" [1912] and "Can't You Hear Me Calling, Caroline?" [1914]). This typescript is in the appendix.

here is a picture: Not extant. Riding did say that "all the pictures belong to you to tear up," and perhaps Stein did.

Robert is sending his poems: *Poems 1929*, the third Seizin Press book, published in June 1929 in 225 copies. See L52.

Figure 13. Laura Riding to Gertrude Stein, July 1929. Gertrude Stein and Alice B. Toklas Papers, Yale Collection of American Literature. Beinecke Rare Book and Manuscript Library, Yale University. Box 112, folder 2287.

52. [July 1929]

Billignin
par Belley
Ain

My dear Robert

Your a poet alright and it is a pleasure to me I like you to be a
real poet and your head is good and it holds what it has and that is a
pleasure for me because I like a head that holds what it has and has
something to hold. Its a little book and its a lot of poems pretty much
each one there. It goes with a rush. And I have read it over and I like
each one in turn. And it is a biography. A little and a lot. Thanks and
more than thanks for you and for Laura,

Gtrde

I liked Laura's letter and the finished scar, will be writing to her
very soon.

———

a little book: Graves's *Poems 1929*, with twenty-four poems.

53. [August 1929]

35A St. Peter's Square
Hammersmith
London W. 6

Dear Gertrude

Len found this in the street and sent it to Laura. Laura & I are
sending it on to you; it may help you with your paragraphs.
Bless you
Robert

———

Len found this: Not extant.

54. [August 1929]

35A St. Peter's Square
Hammersmith
London W. 6

Dear-Dear-Gertrude-Gertrude

Laura's writing is becoming more
& more Laura, and Gertrude's writing is becoming more and more

68   *Letters of Laura Riding and Gertrude Stein*

writing and so Robert is becoming more Robert and so everything
is becoming more and more what it is which means also to walk
between two people, to walk between two crutches, then to walk,
to more and more walk, to walk. The day before yesterday I walked
upstairs with the banister on one side and a crutch on the other –
there was a banister and a crutch and also I walked upstairs. Now I
am resting but I walked upstairs and before that I walked down and
then to walk and to walk or as I please.

Yes Len and yes November where do you think November is?
November and all. We'll be there where.

I am making a large book of what has been poems and I am
calling it Here Beyond and also a prose book and calling it Obsession
and you are in it now and again and always.

And now and again and always love

Laura

----

yes November: In L50, Stein had written, "it would be good for you to take treatment at
Aix or somewhere near us." Riding is now making plans to leave England by November
and is asking Stein where she will be then.

a large book of what has been poems: Riding's *Poems: A Joking Word*, published in July
1930 by Jonathan Cape, which includes the poem "Here Beyond."

a prose book and calling it Obsession: This became *Experts Are Puzzled*, published by
Jonathan Cape in November 1930, which includes the piece "Obsession" (included in the
appendix).

55. [September 1929]
Billignin
par Belley
Ain

My very dear Laura,
A long one for sentences and a short one for
paragraphs and I think there is something, I would so like you to see
them and they have rather thrown me back to grammar for words
not really thrown me back I had almost completed sentences and
paragraphs and I don't want them that way that is almost completed
and so I am wondering if one can get back to return for grammar, I
am having a try, and Len's contribution was a pleasure the found one
and the made one. He has real freshness, not like anything, but just
fresh. I would like to see him, but somehow in November it will be

Letters of Laura Riding and Gertrude Stein   69

managed in your way, because we could meet you somewhere on the road for I do very very much want to see you all, I like you all and I like you made. Thanks for the poems and the pictures and the letter, they don't look too much alike, and that is very nice. Do one of you tell me very soon how everything is going and that some November plan will be possible. We will be here until the end of October, and something that suits you will suit us. Otherwise we go in and out of the house the way one does in the country and it has helped a lot about paragraphs and I am very fond of you both

Alwys

Gtrde.

——————

Len's contribution was a pleasure the found one and the made one: What Graves forwarded (the "found one") to Stein with L53 and what Riding forwarded of Lye's (the "made one") with L51.

Thanks for the poems: Stein acknowledges the two poems that Riding had enclosed with L51.

We will be here until the end of October: In Bilignin. Then (see L59: "when I went to say good-by") Stein and Toklas will go to their Paris apartment.

56. [September 1929]   35A St. Peter's Square
                                                                Hammersmith
                                                                London W. 6

Dear Dear Gertrude

       Things are pretty nightmarish – the Phibbs-devil has even summonsed me to a police court about 5 shillings worth of books that he claims are being withheld from him and Robert and I are anxious to get away, he (Phibbs) and Nancy are living under our very eyes a few minutes away and it is painful to think of the children who are with Nancy and whom Robert and I love very much being with them. We want to get away by October first if we can settle up here by then. I'm really not ready for travel but am losing so much power by all this that it is important to go. I would take my masseuse with me to help me over the journey and carry on her work until I was able to do without massage and my crutches. Would Belley be allright for October. or where. And would you be there. or where. And could you get a room for Robert and me and one for the masseuse –

70   *Letters of Laura Riding and Gertrude Stein*

where Robert and I having different names wouldn't matter. And will
you wire what's possible and love from us both and very

Laura

———

the Phibbs-devil has even summonsed me: Phibbs wanted eighty books returned to him
and, in the end, he got most of them and they did not go to court (Wilson 382).

57. [September 1929]   35A St. Peter's Square
                                                            Hammersmith
                                                            London W. 6

deardeargertrude we are trying to leave <u>the first</u> exactly

Robert says you wouldn't understand this to mean Oct. 1.

and the room of R & I at any rate should be as low as possible because
stairs are very difficult for me and I think that is all, we will stop
about a month, the masseuse a fortnight and we will write again
when we have consulted Cook's and know definitely when we arrive.
And we are both pleased as can be to be going to be with you and I
hope you won't find me too crippled, it is all on the way to being less
and less so, I am very strong and very damned satisfied, and love
from both
                            Laura

these are from earlier parts of Len's film the hand is accidental not
composition they are good to show the development of the right & left
hand sides the hand one is the second in order of these of course

———

trying to leave <u>the first</u>: They may not have left until 4 October (Wilson 383). There must
have been other communication between Riding and Stein, regarding the arrival of Riding
and Graves in Belley, but none is extant. Because Riding inserted "Robert says you wouldn't
understand this to mean Oct. 1" between two lines of her letter, this addition has been set off.

we will stop about a month: After recovering from her injuries and settling her affairs
in London, Riding's first objective after leaving England was to visit Stein. Jean Moorcroft
Wilson, a Graves biographer, says that their stay lasted a little under two weeks, at "a
small *pension*" in Belley (383); but Elizabeth Friedmann, a Riding biographer, says "three
weeks" in a house they leased (162). (See L84 and 85). After they left, Stein wrote to Virgil

Letters of Laura Riding and Gertrude Stein   71

Thomson: "we are saying a tender farewell to our garden trimming our vines and gathering our quinces and all the rest, we were interrupted in these delightful activities by Laura Riding and Robert Graves but they have happily passed on to Geneva, and to Fribourg and further east" (Holbrook and Dilworth 135).

these are from earlier parts of Len's film: Riding probably sent some drawings used for Lye's *Tusalava*. What she sent is not extant.

58. [October 1929]   Freiburg im Breisgau
                                                                    Germany

Dear Gertrude
    M Humbert is a very nice man, tell Alice they were very nice apples, we still have the basket, Freiburg is a very nice town, Belley was very nice indeed, and now we are thinking while it is raining where is it not also and yet not otherwise. The American family in the pension is furious with us because we say Good Morning to them and not Guten Tag, this is not playing the game and they are quite right but it is such a slow game and not quite a game – no – not – Love from us to you both

tell Alice they were very nice apples: This is Riding's first reference to Toklas. Although they met in May 1928 (see L3 and 6), including Toklas in the correspondence (in small ways) became common only after the October 1929 visit. See L73.

Freiburg is a very nice town: They left Belley and went to Freiburg im Breisgau, in southwestern Germany. Is the repetition of "very nice" a friendly echo of Steinian style or is it, perhaps, mocking?

59. [October 1929]   Bilignin
                                                                   par Belley
                                                                        Ain

My dear Laura,
    Yesterday I had a long and pleasant conversation about you with M. St. Pierre when I went to say good-by you have completely touched his susceptible french heart, the charming the distinguished Miss Laura Riding moves him, he says you have to have a really distinguished and charming house, and he thinks deeply and continuously about it, we are bidding a sad farewell to our garden, Basket has slightly sluggish liver and had had castor oil, did not mind

it, we have had nothing but packing and gardening and now Paris, do
when you know them tell us your plans, I am sending this by way of
London and Robert's book, Alice is reading it thoroughly and liking
it too, where shall that be sent, and Laura I do hope you are getting
better and better spinal columnly speaking and lots of love to you and
Robert, you know I am really awfully fond of you both,

Gertrde.

Basket has slightly sluggish liver: Basket (1929–1938) was their beloved poodle.

sending this by way of London: Not knowing what address to use for Riding and Graves,
Stein sent this letter to London.

where shall that be sent: This is a proof copy of Graves's *Good-bye to All That*, which was
published in mid-November. Graves had left it with Stein and, apparently, had said he would
need it back. In L60, Riding says that he does not, but in L62, Graves says that he does.

60. [November 1929]   Casa Salerosa
                                                          Deyá, Mallorca

Dear Gertrude   After Freiburg we came on to Mallorca and
yesterday we found the right house I think at Deya on the other
side of the Island, it will be about £36 a year, pretty expensive, with
peasant cottages 1/10th of that to be had in the village, but lots of what
you'd call cachet and tolerable furniture and good glimpses (i.e. no
panorama), about six rooms, and not a bad sort of landlady, and we
are making friends with the general agent of houses and books here,
I have already donated to the English Circulating Library A Short
History of the Jews, Isadora Duncan's Russian Days, and Robert has
donated The Woman in White by Wilkie Collins. I read somewhere
where it said I might be the sphinx and you the great goddess, it didn't
say who. Or maybe it did – I'm stupefied with Saturday Evening Posts,
there are about 70 back numbers at this hotel and I still have 19 to
go, we think we are going to like it here. Anyway I'm walking better
and better. And I liked that about M. St Pierre. I hope Basket likes
Paris. Love to Alice. And love to you. And Heine. Maybe you'll come to
see us here – when we get Len down – perhaps? And how would you
describe what I'll be going to be writing then or next, it might be kind
of helpful to know beforehand and afterwards, yes, Laura.

Robert says to give the autobiography proofs to someone influential.
and love.

Letters of Laura Riding and Gertrude Stein   73

we came on to Mallorca: As Riding said in June 1929 (L49), "we must leave England as soon as possible, to be away for the winter, and to find a place that will justify being away from it more and more." Mallorca became that place. Traveling there may have been partly at the recommendation of Stein and Toklas, who lived on Mallorca from April 1915 to June 1916 (see *Autobiography* 160–68).

we found the right house: Casa Salerosa, where they lived until 1932, when they moved into Canellun, a house they designed and had built, also near the village of Deyá. Since 2006, Canellun, now La Casa de Robert Graves, has operated as a museum funded by the Robert Graves Foundation. The Len Lye shawl mentioned in L15 hangs in the main stairwell. A detail of this shawl appears on the cover of this book.

no panorama: Stein's house in Bilignin offered panoramic views of the Rhône valley. Riding's description of Casa Salerosa seems to imply a comparison with Stein's house.

donated to the English Circulating Library: Either Clement Wood's *A Short History of the Jews* (1924) or Henry Paine Stokes's *A Short History of the Jews in England* (1921). Also referenced are the Wilkie Collins novel *The Woman in White* (1859) and *Isadora Duncan's Russian Days and Her Last Years in France* (1929), by Irma Duncan (1897–1977) and Allan Ross Macdougall (1893–1956). Stein had known Isadora Duncan (1877–1927) since their mutual upbringing in Oakland, California, and wrote a portrait of the dancer in 1911–12, "Orta or One Dancing."

61. [November 1929]   27 rue de Fleurus
                                                                                Paris

My very dear Laura,
       Here we are back again and a little sad about it, Basket gets dirty and we get busy, but anyhow here we are, and there you are and I am awfully pleased, we had an awfully good year on the island, have you met the British consul M. [Lincoln Wells?] remember me to him he was very nice to us, and if the weather is good its awfully nice and you will walk and walk, and everything and really be all well, it is a nice country and you do eat well and January is heavenly, of course in our day there were no foreigners but perhaps most of them have died off by now, so far have not seen anybody you know, but then we are just back, have seen Ford Maddox Ford, for a moment, he does still remember the war, Alice has read the autobiography thoroughly and is very pleased with it, is it going well, Heine is Alice's far away cousin, anyway lots of love to you both always
       Gtrde.

back again: Back in Paris, to be there through the winter and into the spring.

Ford: Ford Madox Ford (1873–1939), the English writer and editor. He published some of Stein's *The Making of Americans* in *The Transatlantic Review* in 1924.

62. [November 1929]   Casa Salerosa
                                                                        Deyá, Mallorca

> Dearest Gertrude.
>   If you can recover that proof from wherever it is lent I should like it because Siegfried raised a fuss and cut out the poem and another bit and I want a copy that has it all in, having none here.
>   I told Cape to send you a copy so you probably can spare it, if recoverable.
>   Your friends Short and a French wife or perhaps Russian visited us & we liked them visiting us (L.). Laura is keeping well.
>   I'll write properly soon
>   and love to you both from us both.
>   Robert
>
> My mother took it very well.

Siegfried raised a fuss: Siegfried Sassoon (1886–1967), the English writer. Graves and Sassoon met in 1915 as soldiers in World War I, and in 1918 Sassoon sent a verse letter to Graves that begins, "I'd timed my death in action to the minute" (see L75). Sassoon had been sent an advance copy of *Good-bye to All That* and had noted the presence of the verse letter and wanted it "cut out" (which was done). There are inaccuracies in *Good-bye to All That*, but, as Wilson has argued, the truth of Graves's autobiography "was not factual so much as emotional, that is, how it felt to Graves himself, or rather how he remembered it by 1929" (386). Something similar can be said of Stein's *The Autobiography of Alice B. Toklas*, which she wrote in 1932 and which became a bestseller when published in 1933, to the chagrin of people who felt they were misrepresented in it.

Your friends Short and a French wife: Graves writes "Short," but in L63, Stein understands him to mean William Edwards Cook (1881–1959), an old American friend of Stein's who moved to Paris in 1903 to study painting, was on Mallorca when Stein and Toklas were there in 1915–16, married a Frenchwoman, Jeanne Moallic, and lived permanently on Mallorca from the mid-1930s on. He said to Stein in a 12 November 1929 letter: "as for the formidable number of English inhabitants of the island they seem to be tucked away obligingly out of sight in obscure and economical corners" (Gallup 239).

visiting us (L.): Riding added this in between the lines—one example of the shared nature of their writing to Stein.

My mother took it very well: This is probably in reference to *Good-bye to All That*. Graves's parents were "worried about what their son might write about them" (Wilson 385).

63. [November 1929]   27 rue de Fleurus
                                                                            Paris

My dear Robert,
    I will get it back and send it back tomorrow or next day, goodbye to all that from Sassoon he might make a fuss I hope it is going alright and we are pleased at you being pleased with the visit at the Cooks yes you might both write me a proper letter it would do neither of you any harm, awful pleased you are well
        Alwy
           Gtrde.

———

goodbye to all that from Sassoon: Stein met him in London in 1926, at a party hosted by Edith Sitwell, just before she gave her "Composition as Explanation" lecture at Oxford and Cambridge (Dydo 104). At that party, Sassoon talked of having read Stein's portrait of "Constance Fletcher" in *Geography and Plays* (*Autobiography* 131).

64. [December 1929]   Casa Salerosa
                                                                        Deyá, Mallorca

Love from Robert. <u>Goodbye</u> is in 30th thousand now. My <u>father</u> wrote to the Herald to say how proud etc!! Really! Love to Alice. Also to Basket.

Dear Dear Gertrude

        Len and Jane and John and Kanty are coming about New Year and before coming here they are going to Paris: Len and you. I think a lot about that. Len is my way of not saying what you say. Say it with Len and it turns out Len: not to repeat. It would make me happy if you wrote him some time before then about seeing you. And love him for me as well as for you.
        I am now using my stick less and less, only on long or upward or downward walks. I even do stairs now in a

balancing way without it, and our only staircase is without a banister rail.

Across the road is a German painter. His father is a master carpenter with 25 men to assist him. He has a small daughter who looked and looked at one of Len's things hanging on the wall and said 'Aber wir haben das nicht zu Hause'.

A little way along lives our landlady, an American artist. She left a wonderful lot of reading matter behind in this house and among it was a novel of which she was the heroine called <u>Out of Drawing</u> by Marius Lyle, being the Pen Name of a boarder she once took in who was travelling for material. Our landlady was Marion Tooker then she married a Spaniard and was Marion Hernandez and then they separated and now she lives here and she asked us to call her Mariana. She is very nice, only she has for eight years apparently been the victim of writers travelling for material. Before we ever came here, in Palma, I read a story about Deya in an old Saturday Evening Post, and it was by Eleanor Mercein, who turned out to be Mrs. Kelley of Louisville, Kentucky (I actually met her once there) whom Mariana had once taken in. Apparently the material for the story came from some notes of Mariana's on Mallorcan life. Indeed, Mariana was in the story herself. Mariana loves <u>the</u> modern art. She knew the man Cook in Chicago at art school. The man Cook came out to see her and asked her if she knew of us, and here we were. Apparently the man Cook didn't like us because we were revolutionary. The only revolutionary thing we did was to give him and his wife a very nice unrevolutionary tea, which probably was a very revolutionary thing to do if we were revolutionary. But, as you see, the basis of that reasoning is unsound. Anyway, we were glad to hear about you and the bullfight. Mme. Cook kept saying: 'Elle avait un succès!' Mariana said she once read something of yours called Two Sisters. She said she liked it. She said it was about two sisters.

Further along, in the village, is the house of the richest man in the village. He has electric light and there is a light over his door outside and a reflector behind it which is also a chamber pot. And that is all for to-night.

I have to-day finished working on my poems. I have written a preface to them. Robert is turning a lot of my notes into an Ipsa Dixit Laura. They don't have notes here, mostly olives. I'm working on the book somewhat of which you read at Belley. I'm going to divide it into three parts: Opinion – Story – and Obsession. That fits in just right with

Letters of Laura Riding and Gertrude Stein   77

your objection. Of course I'm enlarging the Opinion. Robert is writing something. He thinks it's an autobiography of God. I'm making a Compendium of All True Letters. The Phibbs v. Riding I'll alter just enough to make Truer than Real. If you come across any good ones that won't need too much editing and the writers have gone away . . . . there must be thousands of true letters both to and from yearning for recognition in Paris . . . . perhaps Basket . . . . . I'm going to reopen a long closed correspondence with my mother. Did I tell you about her?

Sleepier and sleepier. See you and Alice again. That will have to be arranged.

> Very love
>
> Laura

Among the reading matter was a book called Hobby House about a house boat on the Ohio. We think you ought to know it. R & I spent a whole evening discussing it. After you've discussed a book like that you feel like giving a course in discussing books like that. It is by Russell Neale and published this year by Harper's. We're sending it. I'm trying to think what there is about it. That's the way it makes you feel.

———

Love from Robert: This opening is in Graves's hand. From "Dear Dear Gertrude" on is Riding.

Len and Jane and John and Kanty are coming: Len Lye (see L15) and Jane Thompson (see L44) and the English artists John Aldridge (1905–83) and Katherine ("Kanty") Cooper, then a couple.

Across the road is a German painter: This could be Ulrich Leman (1885–1988).

Aber wiz haben das nicht zu Hause: "But we don't have that at home."

Marius Lyle: The pseudonym of Una Maud Lyle Smyth (1872–1964), an English writer. Her novel *Out of Drawing* was published by Gerald Howe in 1928.

Eleanor Mercein: Eleanor Mercein Kelly (1880–1968), an American writer. The "story about Deya" in *The Saturday Evening Post* is "Hombre de Amor," in the 31 August 1929 issue. The story is about Lady Millicent Jocelyn, an English widow who has bought two adjacent houses in Deyá, one for herself and the other for visiting artists. Jocelyn falls for Mañolito, a local stonemason, but the conclusion's plot twist reveals his love for Junaïna, Jocelyn's maid. Jocelyn, or perhaps the head maid, Dawson, would appear to be the character Riding mentions as modeled on Mariana. See L71 for Riding's plan for a second house, for visiting artists ("the Tower House of Deya").

the man Cook: See L62.

Elle avait un succès: "She had a success."

Two Sisters: This reference is uncertain. It could be Stein's "Film: deux soeurs qui ne sont pas soeurs" (Film: Two sisters who are not sisters), which she wrote in early 1929 and may have somehow been shared with William Cook and by extension with Mariana Hernandez. It was not published until 1930. More likely is "Two Women," published in 1925 in the *Contact Collection of Contemporary Writers*, about the sisters Claribel Cone and Etta Cone, old friends of Stein's.

a preface to them: Riding's Preface for *Poems: A Joking Word*.

Ipsa Dixit Laura: *Ipse dixit* is Latin for "he himself said it" and denotes an unproven claim.

He thinks it's an autobiography: Probably "The Autobiography of Baal" in *But It Still Goes On* (Jonathan Cape, 1930). Another possibility is *I, Claudius* (Arthur Barker, 1934). Graves's "interest in the Emperor Claudius" began in 1929: "Living on an island still dotted with the ruins of the pre-Christian Era Roman occupation was a continuing reminder to [Graves and Riding] of the reality of history to contemporaneity" (Jessop 138–39).

a Compendium of All True Letters: Riding is collecting letters for what will become *Everybody's Letters* (Arthur Barker, 1933). The book will include ninety-four letters organized into three types—British (thirty-six letters), Universal (thirty-six letters), and American (twenty-two letters)—a brief "Foreword" that defines the three types, and a long "Editorial Postscript," a theorizing of epistolarity. Riding's collection may have been the first to redefine the traditional letter book, which began in the late sixteenth century and had usually included the posthumous letters of people with a certain celebrity. In *Everybody's Letters*, the letters are contemporary—from the late 1920s and early 30s, by friends or acquaintances—the writers are relatively unknown people, and pseudonyms were used, so that the reader's attention goes more to the letter than the writer (see L71 and 85).

65. [December 1929]   Casa Salerosa
                                                                                          Deyá, Mallorca

Dear Dear Gertrude

I never gave you Len's address.

Len Lye The Studio
9ª Black Lion Lane
Hammersmith
London W. 6.

I have now made an Obsessional Appendix to my Poems.
And I'm pulling Story Stuff all together leaving Opinion all by itself.
So you win after all. But anyway Opinion. It and you win.

I can't tell you, we are so excited. We don't know why and it feels so good we don't care why. I am writing dozens of letters daily. They are all as nice as possible.

Letter to my bank	Letter Merrill Moore
Letter to Mr Short of Palma	Letter to Maisie
Letter to Mr Sanders of Oxford	Letter to John
Letter to Marguerite	Letter to Sidney Hunt
Letter to Leonard Woolf	Letter to my sister
Letter to Nancy Cunard	Letter to my nephew
Letter to Marguerite	Letter to you
Letter to Vyvyan	Letter to Len
Letter to Gertrude	Letter to Jane
	Letter to

and all as nice as possible

———

Dear Dear Gertrude: As this letter does not include a closing, and Riding had suggested in L64 that Stein write to Lye, it is possible that L65 was enclosed with L64.

Letter to my bank: Merrill Moore (1903–57, American poet and psychiatrist); Mr Short of Palma (see L62); Maisie (Mary "Maisie" Somerville, 1897–1963, Scottish educational director at the BBC); Mr Sanders of Oxford (Frank J. H. Sanders, bookseller and owner of Sanders and Company); John (Aldridge? see L64); Marguerite (unidentified); Sidney Hunt (1896–1940, English artist and editor); Leonard Woolf (1880–1969, English writer and publisher); my sister (Isabel Reichenthal Mayers, 1894–1947, a half-sister); Nancy Cunard (see L68); my nephew (Isabel's son, Richard Mayers); Marguerite (unidentified); Vyvyan (Vyvyan Richards, English, helped Riding and Graves in 1927 when they started Seizin Press); Len (Lye [see L15]); Jane (Thompson [see L44]).

66. [December 1929]   27 rue de Fleurus
                                                                          Paris

My dear friends,
I am awfully pleased with the success of good-by and have just made it 30001 by enthusing Joseph Horne to buy a copy, may there be many more, also pleased at going to see Len and am writing him to that effect, the islands are nice and it is too bad you did not cotton to

Cook because if Laura still wanted to drive a car there is nobody who could teach her like Cook, he taught me in a Museum of War taxi and it was nice anyway get well and remember me to all the island

> Always
> Gtrde.

———

have just made it 30001 by enthusing Joseph Horne: Replying to L64, Stein alludes to Graves's "Goodbye is in 30th thousand now." Joseph Horne's was an American department store at the time, and it's possible that Stein had been in contact with a store representative.

he taught me in a Museum of War taxi: During World War I, from March 1917 to June 1919, Stein and Toklas worked with the American Fund for French Wounded, driving a truck with medical supplies. In late 1916 in Paris, with Cook as her teacher, Stein learned to drive "on one of the old battle of the Marne taxis" (*Autobiography* 162). She included stories about driving and her cars in her first two autobiographies, *The Autobiography of Alice B. Toklas* (1933) and *Everybody's Autobiography* (1937). See L72 and 88: on the front of these postcards from Stein were photos of her and Toklas during World War I with their car.

67. [December 1929]   Casa Salerosa
Deyá, Mallorca

Dear Gertrude   Len is so sparing about saying that he generally doesn't say so perhaps he hasn't told you what's happening about his film. Everyone likes it in London where it has just been shown and this tells about the rest and you'd like to know of course and he might not say. Robert and I are so pleased and we think you'll be. He's made me a scarf about my scar, ask him to show it to you.
> Love from us both
> Laura

———

what's happening about his film: On Lye's *Tusalava*, see L24.

and this tells about the rest: Riding wrote her letter on the other side of a typed letter from Jane Thompson. Here is what Stein saw of that:

and boats <u>every day</u> to Majorca. Three days in Paris for Len and film business. We get to Paris Saturday night. Sunday no good for business only for Gertrude or whatever. Monday for film and perhaps Tuesday. Hans Richter (German film director lecturing F.S.) had dinner at the Barn on Saturday; he is writing to Paris to arrange for the projection of the film on Tuesday (but it's a bad time – between Xmas and New Year) and for several people to see it. That arse Len puts film director on his passport. So I or John or Kanty will have to smuggle the copy of the film. Cochran gone to New York so no use worrying about that part until he or we come back. Richter is taking a copy to Germany, I think. Maybe the Cinema Ursulines (Paris) will take it. Richter made 20 pounds from them for one short film. It's marvelous about camera and things. I don't know if Len is doing anything about it before we leave – there is only ten days, less because of Christmas.

Sunday no good for business only for Gertrude: They visited Stein and Toklas at 27 rue de Fleurus on 29 December, a Sunday.

Hans Richter: The London Film Society, led by Ivor Montagu, had "invited Richter [1888–1976] to conduct a workshop in London with [Sergei] Eisenstein, who lectured on film" (Foster 263). The reference to "F.S." is the London Film Society.

the Barn: The nickname for Lye and Thompson's apartment at 9A Black Lion Lane in London (Horrocks 97). It was a single room with a high ceiling.

So I or John or Kanty will have to smuggle: Hoping to avoid trouble and costs as they arrived in France, they hid the cans of film in their clothes (Horrocks 114).

the Cinema Ursulines (Paris): A supporter of avant-garde film, Studio des Ursulines, a cinema, opened in 1926. On 1 January 1930, Lye informed Stein that the "Ursulines saw my film & did not take it" (see L68n).

68. [December 1929]

My dear Laura,

Since I am fond of you and of Robert and I guess of Len although I have not heard from him yet but hope to soon, and you are getting better and its a pleasure, and I I am saving the sentence, I began preparing to save it last summer but now I am actually saving it and it is a good deal of a job and I was low in my mind but now it is better and I guess the sentence will be saved. It looks like it, otherwise a great deal of the same and now the weather is cold and on the whole we prefer it. I saw Allen Tate the other day, he and his head are both more so he has another year of the Guggenheim prize and is flourishing tell Len we are xpecting him any minute and lots of merry Christmas to you lots of it

Gtrde.

_____

82   *Letters of Laura Riding and Gertrude Stein*

I have not heard from him yet but hope to soon: The placement of this letter is uncertain. Letters 64–69 address Lye's visit with Stein on 29 December. Her saying "I have not heard from him yet" implies that her "tell Len we are xpecting him any minute" should not be taken literally. Stein probably wrote this letter around mid-December, and after she sent it to Riding, she received these three from Lye (Yale 115.2405), before and after his visit (18 December 1929 to 1 January 1930):

[1] today is dear gertrude about 18th dec   we know now when we leave everyone is out but I know we get to Paris on the 29th   4 of us are going down to Mallorca together   L & R seem good by their last letter   can we ring up yes   on the 29th morn to say can we see you there's nothing to say but a lot to look or which ever way is best   Jane said Hotel Venetia near or on Montparnasse is near you so thats simple   we can ring up on the 29th   all I hope is Christmas sortings or whatever haven't taken you out of town   I want to find the studio Ursuline   but more important for circulation these days is dancing   They say Paris is even colder than here I dont believe it   Hope to see you soon

> best Love   Len   John
> Jane
> Kanty

[2] Dear Gertrude   Kanty is a cannibal   she's got a long tongue that she uses as an exclamation mark, Jane said she's also got a crutch and doesn't use it.   I dont really know about Kanty but its all for the best.

We are getting hungry for lunch with you on Sunday   & we'll all be there at 12:30   Robert's just been making marmalade so he says   He's good at making jam I'm glad I can only eat it   he said the marmalade was made out of 'local ingredients' which sounds like an excuse to me but we'll soon know about it.
Best of all & merry Christmas
> from one & us all
> Love   Len

[3] Dear Gertrude   new years day today   so we are off to Barcelona this evening and we saw Nancy Cunard who was all for press things and beautiful books.   The Ursulines saw my film & did not take it because I dont think they liked it because Madame Myrga said it was very curious.   Coming back might be a better time to see Man Ray as then I'll know what kind of lenses I want to use etc. and I hope I can see you when we come back.   Best of everything.   Len Lye

we saw Nancy Cunard: An English writer, editor, and publisher, Cunard (1896–1965) started Hours Press in 1928 and in 1930 published *Ten Poems More* by Graves (see L88) and two books by Riding, *Four Unposted Letters to Catherine* (see L86 and 88) and *Twenty Poems Less* (see L73, 83, 86 and 88). Lye designed the covers for the three books.

Letters of Laura Riding and Gertrude Stein   83

Madame Myrga: Laurence Myrga, pseudonym of Marcelle Marie Clémence Tulle (1894–1988), an actor and cofounder of Studio des Ursulines.

Man Ray: The pseudonym of Emmanuel Radnitzky (1890–1976), an American photographer and intermedia artist who had moved to Paris in 1921.

69. [December 1929]   Casa Salerosa
                                                              Deyá, Mallorca

Dear Gertrude

   About getting well. Yes. But you must always send love when you send. I couldn't find any anywhere in your letters and it's made me feel different all night and all day different not well. It wouldn't do you any harm to be irritated with me which would make me feel bad if it was a letter but not different which makes me feel ill. And Len is going to be seeing you soon, and you him, and you know very well that the things that make me feel same are Gertrude, Len, Robert and Laura (and two names more, or not) and when it's like that it's simple enough for you to go by, though you run to large figures, but that's simple too, and I wouldn't forget it.
   I nearly came to Paris about figures but I wasn't feeling well enough. How are you.

                              Laura.

About getting well: The placement of this letter is uncertain, but "Len is going to be seeing you soon" suggests December 1929. The "About getting well" is most likely responding to L66, where Stein tersely says, "anyway get well." Letter 61, with Stein's "and really be all well," or L63 with "awful pleased you are well" (although this letter is addressed to Graves), are other possibilities.

70. [December 1929]   Casa Salerosa
                                                              Deyá, Mallorca

Dear Dear Gertrude
                    What a good thing to have two letters from
you in two days and what a good thing Len has written. Kanty is
Katherine. She makes things. A little pining and a lot wouldn't do
Hemingway any harm. It's marvellous to me that I should be getting
news about Allen Tate like that from you. He played a dirty trick on

84   *Letters of Laura Riding and Gertrude Stein*

me once and I shall never be grateful enough. The more news I hear about him from anyone the better. It's that head. It even fascinates you I notice. We are glad you are saving the sentence. I am busy on the word. Robert is busy on the letters of the word.

We like membrillo and Mahon cheese best, we had too much Xmas dinner, there was an American family called Varney in Deya and we sat down with them and they told us all about books and authors and we listened like anything and now we have the word varney.

Robert's parents wrote secretly to the headmaster at Charterhouse to apologize. Oh yes another news is that the Fibs is back from Egypt having lost his job there for giving a dirty Irish lecture on Egyptian nationalism. He could do this of course because board and lodging was safe for him in England because the dogs eat of the crumbs that children drop.

The almond blossoms are just coming out. We are bringing our press out, we find we can get monotyping done at Barcelona. When we're going we want to print a lot of opinion by you. Many local measuresful of love to you and Alice which (that measure) is as much as a local mule can grind of olives in one turning

Laura

&

Robert

---

two letters from you in two days: One must be L68, which mentions the American poet Allen Tate (1899–1979) and saving the sentence, but the other may have been lost—a letter about Lye arranging to meet with Stein ("what a good thing Len has written" to you), with references to Kanty Cooper (see L64) and the American writer Ernest Hemingway (1899–1961).

we had too much Xmas dinner: This suggests that Riding wrote this letter between Christmas and the end of December.

Charterhouse to apologize: From ages thirteen to eighteen, Graves was a student at the prestigious Charterhouse School and wrote about his unhappiness there in *Good-bye to All That* (Chapters 6–8).

the Fibs is back: Gossip about Geoffrey Phibbs. The pun was serendipitous for Riding: Geoffrey fibs; that's what he does. For instance, Graves said in a June 1929 letter that after Riding's jump, Phibbs's first act was to fib: "Geoffrey told the police a lot of lies in the first place because he thought it wouldn't matter. He thought that Laura must have died" (O'Prey 188). See Riding's "Obsession" in the appendix for more on Phibbs (there referred to as Nunquam) and the police.

bringing our press out: The Crown Albion printing press they acquired in 1927 when starting Seizin Press. They had it shipped to Mallorca.

Letters of Laura Riding and Gertrude Stein

1930

71. 16 January 1930

Casa Salerosa
Deyá, Mallorca

And dear Gertrude

The thing now is pebbles, we are all making and sorting the Collection. Mostly Robert and Len collect them at the shore, though Len tends to paper-weights. He tended to a blue and black one to-day for my birthday. Jane tends not to collect blue ones. I tend to say which is which. Len and Jane are pleased as can be and we are planning the Tower House of Deya for Len's eventual film studio. He is going to London in the summer to buy the camera and learn more tricks about cameras and lights. We heard a lot about what food they had with you and Alice. I wish you had seen Len's film. Apparently it wasn't arranged till the last moment. The cottoning of the Cooks to us goes better, I think they suspected us as being rum literary friends of yours, but last time they were here we showed them our workroom and the patent Boston Pencil Sharpener on my table made him trust us. He liked that. Also he met some people the Varneys who had told us all about modern poetry, and they told him all about painting, and that drew us together. I am working pretty hard and Jane is typing things. I am writing some poems about certainty, and it is difficult to do that; not to write poems about sureness. I am also still on those letters, spinning the yarn into them. I have also a rather lovely golden fillet someone was making for me. It keeps my hair tidy. Another thing to say is, can we have Born to Be for a while for Len and Jane? And then about the proof of Robert's book, from something Jane remembered he feels bad if you think that he hogged that back, he says that he hadn't thought about it as finally yours necessarily, because there was supposed to be a bound copy on the way to you. He left the proof for Alice to finish, and then unexpectedly needed it, and it went to London. Did you get a proper copy from the publishers (Robert told them to send you one) and Robert says, if it hasn't the Siegfried business complete, to send it to him and he will write it in for you, etc. Will you? Our press is on the way. And we are going to send you a cheque some time in settlement of Acquaintance, it is difficult to work out because of doing all the printing ourselves, but we will decide something and I hope that will be all right. Are you and Alice ever coming to Mallorca again? When I am elastic again I'll go out of Mallorca for a month or so. I had a long talk with Len about his film this afternoon. About his things and words.

Love from us all to you both, Laura.

------

86   Letters of Laura Riding and Gertrude Stein

to-day for my birthday: This dates the letter, since 16 January was Riding's twenty-ninth birthday.

the Tower House of Deya for Len's eventual film studio: Lye and company arrived in early January, and while he "took an immediate liking to this rocky island," Thompson and Cooper and Aldridge were "less enthusiastic" (Horrocks 115). Riding's idea for a film studio alarmed Thompson. In her own words, she felt that Riding "wanted to appropriate [Lye] intellectually" (Horrocks 115). Riding had perhaps maneuvered similarly with Geoffrey Phibbs a year earlier, and Thompson was wary and demanded some space; she and Lye will find a house "on the other side of the village" (Horrocks 116). (See L79 for a photo.) Lye and Thompson stayed four months, leaving in May (see L81).

still on those letters: What will become *Everybody's Letters* (see L64 and 85).

can we have Born to Be: The autobiography *Born to Be* (Covici–Friede, 1929) by Taylor Gordon (1893–1971), about growing up as part of the only Black family in White Sulphur Springs, Montana, and becoming a famous singer of spirituals. Carl Van Vechten (1880–1964) had sent *Born to Be* to Stein a few months earlier—he had written a foreword for it—and Stein wrote to him on 5 October 1929: "Thanks a thousand times for the Born to be of Taylor Gordon, I have enjoyed it immensely"; there is in it "a way of seeing it from the inside and the outside that makes it clear, the way a white can't do it, it is not realism it is reality and that's what interests me most in the world" (Burns 202–3). Stein must have recommended the book to Riding and Graves when she saw them in October; they arrived in Belley around the time that she sent this letter to Van Vechten.

he will write it in for you: Graves will send the Sassoon verse letter (on separate sheets to be tucked into the book) to Stein with L75.

72. 11 February 1930   27 rue de Fleurus
                                                              Paris

My dear Laura,
>   Are you well and are you all happy, do write and let us know so
>   Gtrde

———

Postcard: On the front is a 1917 photograph of Stein and Toklas, with their car, in front of Hopital Violet in Thuir, France (see fig. 14). Stein had multiples of this postcard and sent it to various people over the years, but the shared World War I experience with Graves (see L62) may have been one reason in this case.

Letters of Laura Riding and Gertrude Stein

Figure 14. Gertrude Stein to Laura Riding, 11 February 1930. Laura (Riding) Jackson and Schuyler B. Jackson collection, #4608. Division of Rare and Manuscript Collections, Cornell University Library. Box 72, folder 1.

73. [February 1930]   Casa Salerosa
                                                                           Deyá, Mallorca

Dearest Gertrude

        I have meant and meant and you know and so
intricate and so differing always. Now I have finished a small book of
poems for Nancy Cunard's Hours Press, there are twenty one poems,
but the last one is called Zero. That is all I have done since Len & Jane
came but now I will do more. And dear Alice Kanty wants to know
your last name exactly for and about the linen so will you spell it and
how are you, I have now a spring in my walk,

                      and lots of love, Laura

and love from Len and Jane, we have had awful weather.

------

small book of poems: *Twenty Poems Less* (see L68). Indeed, it has twenty-one poems, and
the last is "Zero."

dear Alice: This is the first instance of Riding addressing Toklas directly. Riding and Graves
apparently assume that Stein shares her letters with Toklas, and vice versa; Stein knows
that her letters to either Riding or Graves will likely be read by both. Prior to Stein's *The
Autobiography of Alice B. Toklas* (1933), people who had met Stein and Toklas often did not
know how to spell Toklas's name (see L6).

74. [February 1930]   27 rue de Fleurus
                                                                           Paris

My dear people,
        No Cape has never sent the Good-by and it would seem
that one would not be missed out of 40000 so do you Robert get
them to send you one and write in the Siegfried part that is missing
because I did like the Siegfried part and then send it to me that way
I will be sure to have it which is a pleasure. I will send you Born to
be and also a negro anthology that Carl has just sent me, also I will
be pleased to have the cheque and of course it will be right even
[necessary?] authors like a check. I am sorry that Len's film did
not come to something here but after all it was a bad time between
Christmas and New Year and next time it will be better. We have been
drowned in translations lately I am not translating but I am being
translated a great deal of me is and it leads to meditation, otherwise

life is pleasant. Basket grows in [months?] and obedience and I am
writing and Alice is tapestrying. I don't know whether in a way you
wouldn't call that work too and I guess thats all. It must be lively
in Palma now but then we have rather wonderful spring days now
ourselves and we go to the [Fount?] of Saint Germain and its nice,
Lots of love to you all   Gtrde.

———

No Cape has never sent the Good-by: This Stein letter responds to L71 ("Did you get
a proper copy from the publishers," "the Siegfried business," a check) and comes before
L76, but her "we have rather wonderful spring days now ourselves" makes its placement
somewhat uncertain.

Born to be and also a negro anthology: Stein sends Taylor Gordon's *Born to Be* (see
L71). The "Negro Anthology" could be *Caroling Dusk: An Anthology of Verse by Negro Poets*
(Harper & Row, 1927), edited by Countee Cullen. These came to Stein from Carl Van
Vechten in New York.

I am being translated: See L80 with the note on *Dix Portraits*.

75. [March 1930]   Casa Salerosa
                                                                      Deyá, Mallorca

I send you the letter (with a few extra lines not in the version I tried
to print) to paste into the book.

Also <u>Born to Be</u> and Negro Anthology
Thank you so much.

Dear Gertrude,
We haven't written to you for six weeks; they have been difficult
weeks with weather; cold & windy, with the house (masons building
a new workroom, carpenters putting in cupboards & things, all our
furniture to settle in from England) with the four, now reduced to
three since Kanty went back, crowding our small house & making
concentration on work impossible – but now Len & Jane are moving
into another cottage in a day or two – with our LandLady Mariana
who is awfully nice but has had such a bad time with money that
she's a little mad about it and admits it so that at one time we decided
to clear out and cut our losses – she is an old friend of Cook's they
studied art in Chicago together – and with our next door neighbours,
Germans; he paints & she has a little girl and one day she suddenly
decided that Laura was the Christus & that I was the Shepherd King

90   *Letters of Laura Riding and Gertrude Stein*

of England & that I must travel with her (this German woman) to India to preach a world-religion. She herself was the Messiah; I always thought that Messiah & Christus were identical but seemingly not. This last was most embarrassing & upsetting in so small a village but I think now she realises her mistake. They are frutarians & she used to be tuberculous & being a psychologist you know that Messianic exaltation goes with that.

So Laura has done just about no work for six weeks & she has written no letters because she wants to work first. But she says that she has been thinking of you every day all the same and sends you her best love. I have written about 3 poems & stacks of business letters mostly to do with <u>Goodbye</u>; don't believe newspaper accounts of its sales which exaggerate by 2 or 3 hundred per cent: still it has sold very well in England & started off very well in America too. And a German translation is being done by the Transmare Verlag in Munich.

I had a funny letter from Siegfried, all about my self-importance & vulgarity & how I had Zepf-bombed the "delicate & restrained" account he was trying to write of the same events.

Well.

Kanty trod on a sea-urchin bathing here & had a lot of trouble; some of the prickles are still embedded and are to be allowed to remain because irrecoverable.

Len is making a construction out of cement, wire, paper & various marine flotsam which he is going to photograph for a cover for Laura's next book.

Laura's collected "Poems: a Joking Word" are to be published by Cape in May; that's good.

We have assembled the press & Laura & I plan a visit to Barcelona soon to make the necessary arrangements for printing.

Laura walks very well now and is teaching herself to put down the heel instead of the flat of the foot first; that makes it look more natural.

We know all the good local foods now & are quite decided about liking the island as a permanent home. We expect to see you in the summer somehow.

Love Robert.

I send you the letter: He enclosed the Sassoon verse letter from 1918 (see L62).

photograph for a cover for Laura's next book: The assemblage Lye composed for Riding's *Twenty Poems Less* (see L68; see fig. 15). (Riding used a Lye drawing for the cover of *Four Unposted Letters to Catherine*.)

Letters of Laura Riding and Gertrude Stein

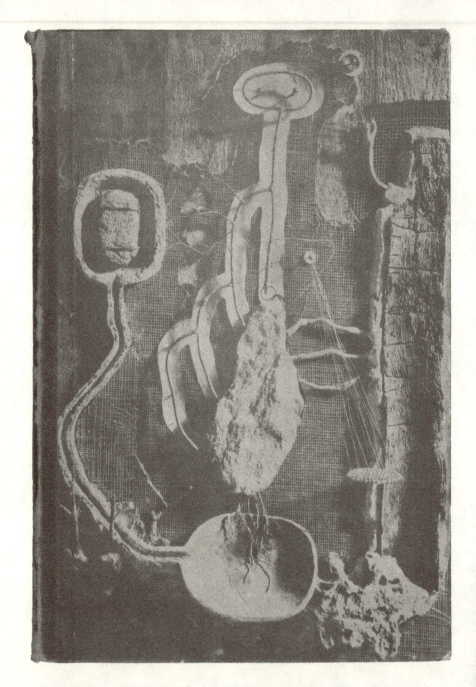

Figure 15. Front cover. Laura Riding, *Twenty Poems Less*, Hours Press, 1930. Beinecke Rare Book and Manuscript Library, Yale University. Za J1362 +930t.

76. [March 1930]   Casa Salerosa
                                                        Deyá, Mallorca

Dear Gertrude

       Oh I hope you have received Born to Be & the other book Robert saw to it for me and it was posted from Soller by a village official. There is however no village apparatus for registering, one must go to Soller oneself, about the cheque yes it is certainly coming, certainly by the end of March, we must get a report up to April from our London agent who took over some of our stock when we left, and that will then be about a year of it. It has about paid for itself (not including our work on it) and we are glad you are curious so are we. Soon we will print Len's Letters as promised which will finish the promises and after it will be a paper every month and I will make point in it and I think Robert has as many points to make and when you see the first copy perhaps you will want to make what you have to make

      I am better now though by days or hours, about D.H. Lawrence's death which we read of in Spanish briefly, Len and we know a Scotch painter just like that, it makes it less noticeable. We saw the Cooks in the sun walking, we were, they had stopped their car and she was sitting back.

    Love to you both
                                                  Laura
                                          Love from
                                          Robert

———

Soller: Sóller, Mallorca, near Deyá.

D.H. Lawrence's death: The English writer D. H. Lawrence (b. 1885) had died on 2 March 1930 in Vence, France, from tuberculosis.

Love from Robert: This is in Graves's hand.

77. [March 1929]   Casa Salerosa
                                                        Deyá, Mallorca

Dear Gertrude

      A lot of letters seem to have strayed. Have you received two from me recently – apart from Robert's letter?

    Love Laura

Letters of Laura Riding and Gertrude Stein

You would be so pleased at the way Laura is looking & working now. Yesterday she walked down to the sea (about a mile and a half down a very steep path & back) for the first time. We expect to visit Europe in midsummer (did Laura say?) & maybe, we hope, stop off to see you at Belley for a few days. The weather is lovely and we do love this island and with our own furniture & the press and everything just right we feel settled. So now to get on with work a bit faster.

>Love
>Robert.

———

letters seem to have strayed: Probably L73 and 75–76.

78. [March 1930]
Casa Salerosa
Deyá, Mallorca

Dear dear Gertrude

Pebbles for you and Alice from Deya shore a trial collection you must put them at any rate the smaller ones under water to see how really good if you react favourably you can have more The big black and white one is special because I discovered it on my first walk to the sea. John and I picked these out of our large collection to try you or them by Robert was not here but on his return he mourned the loss of only one.

>Love
>Laura.

———

Pebbles for you: The enclosed pebbles are not extant. The sequencing of these early 1930 letters is uncertain, but Graves's "Yesterday she walked down to the sea . . . for the first time" in L77 and Riding's "my first walk to the sea" here go together.

79. 3 April 1930
Casa Salerosa
Deyá, Mallorca

X = house of Len & Jane

Dear Gertrude

    Alan Steele
    Wm. Jackson Ltd.
    Tooks Court Cursitor St
    Chancery Lane E. C.
            London

He was the transition agent I think he might easily be your affair he is young & not unmannered I hope he will do I recommended him & N. Cunard to each other and he was her affair and how nice to be with you in Belley

I guessed you would feel like that about pebbles.
                    Love Laura

———

X = house of Len & Jane: On the front of this postcard, lower left, Riding marked the roof of Lye and Thompson's house with an X (see fig. 16).

Alan Steele: A bookseller and publisher, Steele (1905–1985) worked with many writers of the time. This postcard seems to be in response to a letter from Stein that is not extant, one that asks for Steele's address, invites them to visit her in Bilignin, and mentions the pebbles, which Stein mentions (again?) in L80.

Figure 16. Laura Riding to Gertrude Stein, 3 April 1930. Gertrude Stein and Alice B. Toklas Papers, Yale Collection of American Literature. Beinecke Rare Book and Manuscript Library, Yale University. Box 112, folder 2287.

80. [May 1930]

Bilignin
par Belley
Ain

My dear Laura,

The year does roll around doesn't it, and here we are and liking it we do like it there is no mistake about it and you like the islands and they are doing you a lot of good and we will see you this summer and that will do us a lot of good too and anyway here we are. Thanks for the address of Mr. Steele I think Georges Hugnet and the edition of the Montagne will get together alright, it is about the inclosed that I wanted him. And how did the accounts turn out, you didn't send me the cheque well cheques are a pleasure even when you don't have them but how did the account come out. And the pebbles we do use the pebbles in tarts really we do and you will see ours, they came from the garden and you'll see, and what is happening to you and how do you like it and when will we see you and lots of love to you and to Robert

Gtrde.

———

anyway here we are: Stein and Toklas have made the annual move from Paris to Bilignin in the spring.

Georges Hugnet and the edition of the Montagne: For a few months, Stein had been working on *Dix Portraits*, which included ten of her portraits and French translations by Hugnet (1906–74) and Virgil Thomson. It was published by Hugnet's Éditions de la Montagne in Paris in May 1930 (see L84 and 86). Stein wrote to Thomson on 8 July 1929 that it would be "a little series of portraits of the rising generation," a series that included Thomson but not Riding or Graves (Holbrook and Dilworth 125). This book followed *Morceaux choisis de la fabrication des américains*—selections from Stein's *The Making of Americans*—also translated by Hugnet and Thomson and published by Éditions de la Montagne in June 1929. The reference in Stein's "the inclosed" is uncertain.

use the pebbles in tarts: To hold pastry flat as it bakes prior to the filling being added.

81. 21 [May 1930]

Casa Salerosa
Deyá, Mallorca

Dear Gertrude, so our letters crossed, meaning postcard, I have just nearly killed myself over proofs, so all the more postcard, early in June you'll get a copy of Poems a Joking Word, Len and Jane have gone away till perhaps January, their house is shut up.

Love from both, Laura

———

so our letters crossed: This may go back to Riding's "A lot of letters seem to have strayed" (L77), and again the sequencing is uncertain and there may be missing letters. On the front of this postcard are Mallorcan trees (see fig. 17).

82. [May 1930]   Casa Salerosa
                                                            Deyá, Mallorca

Dear Gertrude and Gertrude   This should have been said sooner but the chaps were leaving for London and then I haven't been well again an almost nothing but it may mean going to England sooner, I don't know. I am out of bed to-day so we shall see how it goes. But generally speaking everything is good and where and how are you. I am sorry about that cheque, I have just written the London man severely, he has as yet sent me no statement, did you have any luck with him? Just now it is proofs which always harass me because of the challenge to do over or not to do. But otherwise publication would be less painful, so it is well. Robert, charming thought, would apparently have been named Laureate if it hadn't been for <u>Goodbye</u>, and that doesn't spoil the joke really. There is a Dutch painter here a horrid fellow who says he knows you, name of Leyden. He asked John where he first met you and John said at

Figure 17. Laura Riding to Gertrude Stein, May 1930. Gertrude Stein and Alice B. Toklas Papers, Yale Collection of American Literature. Beinecke Rare Book and Manuscript Library, Yale University. Box 112, folder 2287.

Oxford when you lectured there. 'It's funny,' he said, 'how women go about doing things these days. There's a woman in the Hague who collects pictures!' Well, say something to us, and here is love from us both – Laura

———

name of Leyden: This is likely Ernst Van Leyden (1892–1969).

at Oxford when you lectured: Stein's "Composition as Explanation," from 1926 (see L1).

83. [June 1930]   Casa Salerosa
                                                                                Deyá, Mallorca

Dear Gertrude
              That bad man Wm Jackson Ltd seems to be against your having a cheque so here is a cheque anyway as a cheque and when I do get a definite statement out of him I'll add whatever is to be added, and this be at the rate of 10% for every copy sold. I don't think we've made a profit on it but it's paid its expenses and all the pleasure and we have stock left over a lot. And everything. I wasn't well for about a month from May to early June so perhaps we won't see you till August I want two months of wellness I mean ordinarily speaking we'll naturally come to see you in the course of wellness, and Poems A Joking Word will come to you an advance copy Robert is very well he's fine, Len and Jane are fine in London, Len made three lovely covers for 1 book of Robert's two of mine the Hours Press is doing we'll send you there soon have you anything to send, I had a letter from Hart Crane he is sending me his Bridge by someone but I read all about his powers in an American review so, he says Allen Tate was in New York very disgruntled until somehow he got a $10000 country estate in Kentucky bestowed on him from where he deals with the New Humanism we do love Len and Jane What is in your garden cornflowers are no good here carnations are wonderful ladybirds eat cornflowers and zinnias but not carnations or pinks or sweet willows or <u>of course</u> roses, nor the sea over there which doesn't come near enough to be eaten, and lots of love from us both.

———

so here is a cheque: The first mention of a royalty is in Riding's 16 January 1930 letter, six months earlier. It was thus a long time in coming and seems to have frustrated both publisher and author.

98   *Letters of Laura Riding and Gertrude Stein*

the Hours Press is doing: See L86 and 88.

he is sending me his Bridge: Crane's *The Bridge* appeared first from Black Sun Press as a limited-edition book, in late winter 1930, and a month later from the trade publisher Liveright.

84. [June 1930]

Bilignin
par Belley
Ain

My dear Laura,

Yes you have been in our mind so much so that day before yesterday we went up to your village Alice had never seen your house and to-day whom should I meet at market but you going to the landlady and she had loved you so and it was all about 500 francs not at all says I it was because you wanted the privilege of going in when you wanted to, ah yes she said that was my husband he so loved the place and he said if we rented to people from Lyon we could go up there spring and fall, but now she says the dear lady if I could only see her now, but then she added they did want a selling price and how could any one give a selling price but she said to awfully I did love her very much and do remember me to her and then I came and there was your letter. A really truly coincidence that, well anyway thanks so much for the cheque, it is always pleasant to have one but I did want it honestly earned, and I am a little bothered because I have recommended on your say so the editions de la Montagne to go on with the Jackson lmt. and if he is the kind that does not answer and come through it will be awkward, how about it, and how many of the Acquaintance did sell I am very anxious to know that for other reasons. We are pleased that your choice falls on August, we will be glad to see you, there will be a lot of people here July and another lot September but August seems to [announce?] itself just at present very peacefully and it will be nice seeing you both, we are really very fond of you both. Lucy Church Amiably has been corrected three times and the ten portraits, they will be out about immediately and Lucy in August so there we are, and now I am just beginning to work, something I want very much to do. Grammar for the moment being done, even to titles and sub-titles. Otherwise no very great news, we were all there and I guess more or less we will all be here. Do get all well but then you surely will and lots of love to you both

Gtrde.

———

Letters of Laura Riding and Gertrude Stein

up to your village: This story's references are uncertain—it is possible that our transcription has misconstrued something, as Stein's handwriting can sometimes be difficult to decipher—but Stein is apparently describing meeting the person who rented to Riding and Graves back in October 1929. Graves responds with, "This house is so good that we can do without the London one and Mère Michaud" in L85, so we have a name for "the landlady" Stein encountered and also a confirmation that Graves and Riding will not be returning to France or England anytime soon for more than a visit.

to hear that for other reasons: Stein alludes to the new Toklas-Stein imprint, Plain Edition. Information on how well *An Acquaintance with Description* sold could predict the success of the books from Plain Edition, which started with *Lucy Church Amiably* (1930). The four to follow were *Before the Flowers of Friendship Faded Friendship Faded* (1931), *How to Write* (1931), *Operas and Plays* (1932), and *Matisse Picasso and Gertrude Stein* (1933). While Seizin Press was one model for Plain Edition, closer was Hugnet's Éditions de la Montagne. Stein considered publishing "under a joint arrangement" with Hugnet's press, and "Plain" was wordplay with "Montagne," the plain and the mountain (Dydo 417).

85. [June 1930]

Casa Salerosa
Deyá, Mallorca

Wm Jackson's is all right. Laura says she didn't want to mislead you about them. The fact was that the personal touch and so on got mixed up with the business (and no definite arrangement was made last October when we went off, Laura not being in a proper state for business) and that isn't likely to occur in any relations between Jackson & Montaigne. N. Cunard finds Jackson very good: we recommended them to each other.

Dearest Gertrude,

Laura and I were so pleased with your long letter and Laura will answer it, but meanwhile I will too because she's not very well. We find that out of 225 Acquaintances, 127 were actually sold – about 100 in England, the rest in America & Paris. Our American connexion is weak (we think that this is the sort of information you want) & we should have done better there.

This house is so good that we can do without the London one and Mère Michaud but it is nice to know that she loved Laura. Laura sends two gifts – the p cards from her father (who is as sweet as the cherubs) & a card from some people called Burnham, a family of 4th Class Americans who went round the world sketching & getting travel notes to address women's clubs in Chicago with. The husband drank & didn't count, and a daughter got married in

Jerusalem to an excavator. You will read all about them in Laura's book of letters – there's a marvellous collection now, all typed for you & Alice to read in August, of all different sorts – we wish you'd found some more for us – perhaps you still will – anyhow, the one I send you enclosed from W. Gainsford isn't included, but you'll like it. I don't know more about him
than you do.

    Laura's collection of stories & so on: <u>Experts Are Puzzled</u> is coming out in the autumn & an easy one of mine called <u>But it Still Goes On</u>. How nice to have finished with your grammar! We have a vine of pinky-white grapes in front of our house just like yours; and this is the season of fireflies so much love and what fun in August
       Robert

———

Wm Jackson's is all right: Graves wrote this note, something of a postscript, in the margins on the left side of this sheet and at the top, to reassure Stein.

Laura sends two gifts . . . read all about them in Laura's book of letters: The postcards from Riding's father, the Burnham card, and the one from Gainsford are not extant. "Burnham" refers to Anita Willets-Burnham (1880–1958) and her husband and four children. Willets-Burnham was on the faculty at the Art Institute of Chicago, and she would write about her family's travels in *Round the World on a Penny* (Covici–Friede, 1933), of which Stein owned an inscribed copy. Graves is alluding here to Riding's *Everybody's Letters* (see L64 and 71), and for the book she changed Carol-Lou—the oldest of Willets-Burnham's children, who was twenty-two in 1930—to "Hulla Loo" and changed Burnham to "Chesney." Their letters start on p. 181 in *Everybody's Letters*.

we wish you'd found some more for us: As he wrote this letter, Graves made two changes to the phrasing: "had" became "found" and "more" was added, so it first read: "we wish you'd had some for us." Perhaps he checked with Riding and learned that Stein had sent a letter (or letters). But as there is no evidence in the rest of the correspondence that Stein sent something for Riding's collection, it is likely that his first words were more accurate.

86. [July 1930]   Casa Salerosa
                                        Deyá, Mallorca

Dearest Gertrude
    I like being a coincidence and I hope you like occurring and occurring for that is what you do to me, and you were in the middle of occurring and then <u>Ten Portraits</u> came and that was an occurrence and a little while before there was an accident, it was

on the left of the house, and about ten days ago there was another and that was on the right and so I was relieved, for I was beginning to feel disturbed, I was relieved to have an occurrence right in the middle of the house and it will remain an occurrence until I and we have read it, then there will be occurring and occurring again. You were just occurring I was thinking about you and wisdom, Cook said you were wonderful but you made generalizations, he didn't like once you said Norwegians were low-class. And you make generalizations and that is wisdom, and I was surprised Cook's not thinking that wisdom until I learned he had Norwegian blood (because I think he is a lover of wisdom) and so that was no generalization to him. Anyway there was a book and it came to us and it turned out to be about a Jew not putting down his last cent and it made me feel pretty sick because I made a [be?] out of it and not a generalization, I think you'll like seeing it because of the generalization. The last transition came to us, and I was relieved, because I hadn't seen it for a long time and it was nice seeing the last for the last time, it was all about fighting for life, and so a last time was nice. But what I wanted to say especially was Picasso the second one the composition that was a happiness to me Len can give me hope but that gave me happiness and nothing. And here is a sheet of our printing of a book of mine one is very dim but you can tell we have started printing, I can manage the pull though not for too long. Next when we get back comes Len's. I am writing a poem called Laura and Francisca, Francisca lives here and I have given her a doll I love her it is very embarrassing Robert says they will think you are a Lesbian and now I shall have to put that in because of Lesbos being an island. Today I put in Crete, Malta, Ireland and England. We shall be sending our three Hours Press books very soon, alas I had a row with poor Nancy Cunard for printing off Catherine without sending me proofs I hope that won't show in any way, and once more to say what a relief the occurrence, and our very particular love –

Laura

I like being a coincidence: A reference to Stein's Mère Michaud story, with its "A really truly coincidence that" (L84). In L84 and 86, in the openings, Riding and Stein seem to be exchanging "thinking of you" expressions, in "occurring" and "whom should I meet at market but you."

Ten Portraits came: Stein's *Dix Portraits* (see L80 and 84).

I was thinking about you and wisdom: This and other phrasing in this letter probably connects with *Four Unposted Letters to Catherine*, a book addressed to Graves's eight-year-old daughter Catherine (see L6) and dedicated to Stein. (Riding refers to the book at the end of this letter.) She offers advice on growing up that is also relevant to adults; through her writing, she'd like to "give people something better than comfort or fun—a feeling of laziness, of being alive for always" (31). The next sentence (after "I was thinking about you and wisdom") ends with "I think you'll like seeing it," an "it" that isn't explicitly identified but could be *Four Letters* and its profoundly ambiguous dedicatory letter: "Dear Gertrude. / The function of Opinion is to be that which does not get posted. Hating Opinion and loving All That Gets Posted as you do, you must applaud my not posting these letters, however much you deplore my writing them. / Love, / Laura." See L65 ("But anyway Opinion. It and you win") and L92.

you said Norwegians were low-class: This is repeated in *14A* (Arthur Baker, 1934), a roman à clef by Riding and George Ellidge (see *14A* 230).

a Jew not putting down: In a 1975 essay, (Riding) Jackson claimed that "Among [Stein's] favorite aphorisms was: 'No Jew ever lays down his last cent'" ("Word-Play" 245). (Graves also cites this aphorism in a letter to Stein in January 1946 [O'Prey 337]). So Riding would be echoing Stein here, in L86, and is "pretty sick" about the notion that it's prudent to hold something back. The "there was a book and it came to us" is probably *Dix Portraits*.

The last <u>transition</u> came: The June 1930 issue, no. 19–20. The magazine went on hiatus until 1932 and ended in 1938, with twenty-seven issues altogether.

Picasso the second one: Stein's "If I Told Him. A Completed Portrait of Picasso" (written in 1923), which was in *Dix Portraits* (see L80).

that gave me happiness and nothing: We can take Riding's "nothing" as praise. In *Anarchism Is Not Enough*, she writes: "What is a poem? A poem is nothing. By persistence the poem can be made something; but then it is something, not a poem. Why is it nothing? Because it cannot be looked at, heard, touched or read (what can be read is prose). It is not an effect (common or uncommon) of experience; it is the result of an ability to create a vacuum in experience—it is a vacuum and therefore nothing. It cannot be looked at, heard, touched or read because it is a vacuum" (16–17). A "something" is written for "effect," a cry for attention.

a sheet of our printing of a book of mine: Not extant. Probably for *Though Gently* (1930).

Next when we get back comes Len's: Riding and Graves went to England in August (see L89), returning to Mallorca by early October. "Len's" is *No Trouble*, Seizin Four, which would be published before Riding's *Though Gently*, Seizin Five (see L92).

Letters of Laura Riding and Gertrude Stein   103

a poem called Laura and Francisca: After Graves's *To Whom Else?* (1931), Seizin Six, was Riding's *Laura and Francisca* (1931), Seizin Seven, the last that they hand printed. From 1935 to 1937, six more Seizin Press books came out, copublished with Constable in London.

our very particular love: From "you make generalizations" to trying to drive a wedge between Cook and Stein to "a Jew not putting down his last cent" to saying that the end of *transition* was "nice" to Riding thinking it "very embarrassing" to be (jokingly) called a lesbian, this letter seems designed to offend Stein. There are affectionate moments in it, but if Stein had been considering a break with Riding (and Graves), this could be grounds.

87. [July 1930]

Bilignin
par Belley
Ain

My dear Laura

I am so sorry but we will have to put off your visit to us, July has been so broken up with unxpected arrivals from America and family matters and I must absolutely have my book ready on a date and so I must keep August completely to myself for that job I am sorrier than I can say, it would have been nice seeing you and Robert again and having you here but better luck next time, I know you will understand, thanks for all the inclosures the Burnham is quite unbelievable and I liked Robert's [man?], we are looking forward to the new books, and everything else, otherwise there is no news with us, Basket was a little upset and had to be nursed and now he is spoiled has to be told about it, the garden goes on spite of lots of rain and Belley is much as usual and looking forward to the 14th of July. We didn't see Cook before we left he had not gotten back yet, I am glad you rather liked him, he is a very old friend and a dear one, and I am awfully glad that on the whole things are going so well with you

Always

Gtrde.

I must keep August completely to myself: Stein is making choices here. She was getting *Lucy Church Amiably* ready for publication and writing, but she also had visitors in August, including the Picassos, then Carl Van Vechten for a couple of days, and then Virgil Thomson for two weeks. To Thomson she said on 1 August 1930, "Sure it will be a pleasure arrange to suit yourself because just at present August is free" (Holbrook and Dilworth 163). Stein apparently preferred to host friends other than Riding and Graves and perhaps exaggerates the urgency of her deadline to put off their long-anticipated visit.

We didn't see Cook before we left: Before they left Paris for Bilignin a couple of months earlier.

---

88. 17 July 1930

Bilignin
par Belley
Ain

The books have just come thanks so much,

G

The books have just come: This is a postcard, with Stein and Toklas, and their car, in front of an apartment building in 1917 (similar to L72). The "books" are probably the three from Hours Press: *Ten Poems More* by Graves and Riding's *Four Unposted Letters to Catherine* and *Twenty Poems Less* (see L83 and 86). Stein had likely already gotten *Poems: A Joking Word* (see L83). Riding later confirms that all four were sent to her (see L92). This is the last letter from Stein. After putting off their August visit (L87) and here acknowledging receipt of some books, she stops corresponding. Riding and Graves send five more letters and then do likewise. Graves and Stein will correspond again after World War II, in 1946, before Stein's death (from cancer) on 27 July 1946, but Riding and Stein never resume contact.

---

89. [August 1930]

34 Markham Street
Chelsea
London

Dear Gertrude

William Nicholson you know he is a friend of ours painter maybe you know best English tradition leading post-Whistler modern those days you know probably (technically Nancy's father), he is going to be at Lake Annecy with friends in about ten days time and could motor to Billignin if you would like to have a chat because he thinks it would be nice to have a chat with you. He's sweet really and fifty three and a good friend of ours. Perhaps you have the book finished, and it would be a pleasure to have a chat. He could tell you different new things about Siegfried Sassoon or American millionaires he has painted or you could tell him not to worry about modernism. Will you let me know if he may come for an hour or so.

Love
Laura

Have you seen <u>The Strange Death of Warren Harding</u>?

Letters of Laura Riding and Gertrude Stein   105

William Nicholson: Of Stein's generation, Nicholson (1872–1949) was a painter, illustrator, and teacher—and as Riding includes as an aside, the father of Nancy Nicholson.

Lake Annecy: In France, forty miles northeast from Belley.

Have you seen <u>The Strange Death</u>: A sensational bestseller in 1930, *The Strange Death of Warren Harding: From the Diaries of Gaston B. Means, as Told to May Dixon Thacker* claimed that President Warren G. Harding, who died in 1923 of a heart attack, had been poisoned by his wife Florence Harding, with the help of Dr. Charles E. Sawyer. An all-purpose con man, Means (1879–1938) worked with the FBI in the early 1920s as a private detective. Perhaps Riding and Stein had discussed Harding or Means during the visit in October 1929.

tell him not to worry about modernism: This is the first and only appearance of the term *modernism* in the letters. The word was circulating at the time; among Stein's friends, Mina Loy had used it in 1924 ("Modernism has democratised the subject matter and la belle matière of art, through cubism the newspaper has assumed an aesthetic quality . . . and Gertrude Stein has given us the Word, in and for itself" [430]) and Virgil Thomson in 1925, in "Maxims for a Modernist" (see Holbrook and Dilworth v), and then there was Riding and Graves's *A Survey of Modernist Poetry* (1927). But Stein herself never used the term. Stein did use *modern* but never the word in its capitalized sense, as a name or brand.

90. 9 October 1930

Casa Salerosa
Deyá, Mallorca

Dearest Gertrude

Are you all right? We are rather anxious that you have been ill or something, as we have had no word since early July and no reply to two notes of Laura's. Please reassure us.

We are back here a week now & very glad to be back too.

Ever yours
Robert.

———

no word since early July: L87 (and the very brief L88 too, from mid-July).

no reply to two notes of Laura's: L86 and 89.

91. 27 October 1930

Casa Salerosa
Deyá, Mallorca

Dearest Gertrude

About a fortnight ago we wrote anxiously for news of you – not a sign from you for months or any answer to two notes Laura wrote. Are you ill? No reply yet, but we suspect that this last letter to you was in a batch of fifteen that seem all to have been detained. A devil in the Palma P.O. tears up all foreign mail for the sake of the 40 c stamps. Anyhow do write to let us know you are all right, and then we'll give you our news too.

Love
Robert.

92. 3 November 1930

Casa Salerosa
Deyá, Mallorca

Dear Gertrude

Robert said surely Gertrude ill but I said to hope not but he wrote to hope no mistake. Absolutely seriously and surely a mistake and if absolutely seriously no mistake. So please believe and I too believe. Letting slide is not really possible to knowing and we know. What is said in letters is of course always better left unsaid but when absolutely seriously a letter is for good measure and so better left unsaid means already said and so what is said in letters is all the better if absolutely seriously and please believe. The times are not so strange. A remark or a package can seem like a remark or a package but not for long and doubt must pass as usual. This is not inspiration, but from the beginning thought of often enough. We wanted very much to see you this summer. A week in Paris would be absolutely seriously a next time this winter if you felt better luck and we could make it match a rest in work. We have finished printing my book and are printing Len's now. I am working on a stage piece with Len and writing the words for it. I have a lot of rheumatism which I find rather like sleep only painful. Our house is probably not good for the winter being so good for the summer. Len's book is such a pleasure. I should like to send it to you when it is finished; and <u>Though Gently</u> which is being bound; and <u>Experts Are Puzzled</u> which you liked in manuscript. If you would like. <u>Though Gently</u> has a cover by Len. Did you like <u>Poems A Joking Word</u> and the Hours Press books? Could you write us something for the press needn't be longer than 5000 words or as you like we would like something on <u>Meaning</u>. And we are very very fond of you, you mustn't overlook it. William Nicholson did very much want to see you and absolutely seriously a sweet person you must have liked him and it's nothing you never answered but please believe in all respects lots of love always

Laura

———

What is said in letters is of course always better left unsaid: The phrasing here echoes the dedicatory letter to Stein that Riding had included in *Four Unposted Letters to Catherine* (see L86). In theory, Stein differentiated between what one says in conversation or puts in a letter and what one does as a writer—what goes in a book, what makes literature. She could generalize in conversation but would avoid doing so in a book. Stein wrote this passage two years after the break with Riding, and it may be apropos: "Observation and construction make imagination, that is granting the possession of imagination, is what she has taught many young writers. Once when Hemingway wrote in one of his stories that Gertrude Stein always knew what was good in a Cézanne, she looked at him and said, Hemingway, remarks are not literature" (*Autobiography* 76–77). Stein names Hemingway, but she may have been thinking of Riding, too.

93. [November 1930]   Casa Salerosa
                                                              Deyá, Mallorca

Dear Gertrude

        Well you apparently are not going to say anything, which would be just the thing if you hadn't somehow put us in the wrong without saying anything, which we can't be going along on. And so it came to absolutely seriously, which ought to have told you how we felt. If you don't care how we feel, to keep it from being unpleasant you ought to say something unpleasant. All right, you won't answer this either, so don't. It gets pretty bad. I'll be damned. All right. You forget and I'll remember until you always have all the time known or not doubted.
        But if you could tell me your friend V. Thompson the Masque I am working on with Len Lye the music could that happen with satisfaction Len has the sound requirements all worked out can you let me know about this which is important in a quite apart way if not all right I promise not to write again not even about the weather <u>certainly</u> not.

Laura

APPENDIX

To Be Less Philosophical

Robert Graves

Listen, you theologians,
Give ear, you rhetoricians,
Hearken you, Aristotelians:
Of the Nature of God, my song shall be.

Our God is infinite.
Your God is infinite,
Their God is infinite,
Of infinite generality.

God *he* is also finite,
God *she* is also definite,
He, she; we, they; you, each and it—
And likes to be correctly.

He is a bloody smart sergeant
And served in the Royal Artillery:
For gallantly exposing his person
He won the Victoria Cross.

She is also divorced
To a Russian count in exile
And paints a little and sings a little—
And won the Victoria Cross.

It has also the character of a soap
And may be used very freely
For disinfecting cattle trucks
And the very kine in the byre.

You are also mad, quite mad,
To imagine you are not God.

Goddamn it, aren't you a Spirit,
And your ministers a flaming fire?

We are also gradually coming
To be less philosophical,
To speculate more confusedly
And defy the universal.

They are a very smart Victoria Cross
With the character of a soap a little:
They disinfect confusedly
To be less philosophical.

Each is a very smart Russian count
And may each be served very freely,
Freely, freely in the Royal Artillery
To be less philosophical.

Poems (1914–1927), William Heinemann, 1927, pp. 226–28. See L5.

Fine Fellow Son of a Poor Fellow

Laura Riding

Every poor fellow reminds me of my father.
With worse luck than that
He reminds me of my father
With worse luck than he had.
Which means me
Who has worse luck than my father had
Because it is not so bad.

Every fine fellow reminds me of me.
Good luck is hard to come by.
It is not that innocency
Of how luck befalls.
It is a bad luck weary,
A worse luck turned into vanity,
A knowledge of bad luck
And with bad luck seamy.

A poor fellow knows a poor fellow.
A fine fellow knows a poor fellow and a fine fellow,

A poor fellow and a poor fellow.
Every poor fellow reminds me of me.
Every fine fellow reminds me of my father.

And it is not to be forgotten:
All luck is luck,
My father's or mine.
He was a poor fellow.
His bad luck was perhaps no luck.
I am a fine fellow.
My good luck is perhaps no luck.
All luck is perhaps no luck.
All luck is luck or perhaps no luck.

This is no way to be divided,
By poorness and fineness.
Truer to say there is
Nothing in which to be prided,
And then say
Every fellow reminds me of every fellow,
My father reminds me of my father,
I remind me of me,
And then say
A poor fellow and a fine fellow
And bad luck and good luck
And father and son
Are no fellow, no luck, no blood
But a false life-line
Between what is more than poor
And what is less than fine.

Love as Love, Death as Death, Seizin Press, 1928, pp. 27–28. Riding revised the poem and retitled it as "The Lullaby" for *The Collected Poems of Laura Riding* (1938). See L19.

[Two Poems]

Laura Riding

1

Through pain the land of pain
Through narrowness and self-hate
Through precious exiguity

Appendix 111

Through cruel self-love
So came I to this inch of wholeness.

It was a promise
After pain, I said,
An inch will be what never a boasted mile.

And my proud judgement
That would not know my nearly faultless plan
Smiles now upon my crippled execution
And my lost beauty praises me.

2

Other, who have tasted the true water,
By this you are my other,
But in your otherness
You make a clumsy myth
And still clumsier humanity.

Well, how shall I advise you,
Who first named the spring
And drink of it like nature?
To go dry, be parched, mean and mystical,
And know me decently, in a vision,
According to the skilled bookish custom?
Or to drain it as if bewitched,
Fall in a love fit and not get up
Till shame discovers you alone?

These are the ways of time not us.
No, be my other, be not they,
Be difficult, half bright, half slow,
And leave me strange and simple.
This imperfection is perfection.
This disappointment a foreshortening
Of the impossible.
Teach me to love a little
And I will keep the myth in reason
Long enough to make it human
And so be your other, and clumsily.

Such is truly a just estimate.

If there is spite and persecution
It is that I advise you in yourself
When you would be advised in me
But no more damage may be done.

July 1929. Riding published "Through pain the land of pain" in *Poems: A Joking Word* (1930) as "This" (p. 127). The poem beginning "Other, who have tasted true water," about Graves, was never published. In the typescript she sent Stein, the poems were numbered (as seen here). See L51.

Still July

Len Lye

Dear mother whats the latest for you is Phil still in Sydney how is your health is Flo up in Auckland with you now? I hope the winter is not too snappy I dont suppose it gets much worse than in London. London must be the worlds worst, still it doesn't matter if I can work. Jane doesn't like it so maybe by then for the next we will go with L and R to Spain: that is too if film things are fixed by then and I'm hurrying up to finish it so as to get something to stand on. Here's a little story for you. Its that when human us's keep on getting better and better and of course there will always be a few who keep on fining things down to essences so say in so many umteen years a few get as far as they can go and of course there must be a limit and when they get that far they'll know it.

Well when it gets to that stage of simplicity it will mean the end of the world simply because when a few get as far as that they will cause it to happen as the only next thing and they will all realise it at the same time no matter if they haven't seen each other for years. It will happen gradually as the 20 or so realise they've gone as far as they can and what can they do about it with the worlds millions complicating things up and rushing around staking their claims all over the earth so the minds of the 20 gradually focus onto some other world until it slowly begins to move towards them without the least effort; just as if their minds were all forged into one mind and the okum in that one mind could make anything happen let alone as simple a thing as making a star blink. . meanwhile of course the millions dont know anything about it while the few of course know without being told or going to see one another.

Then about the time the other world is so near that there becomes no night or day and the millions are getting panicky not knowing whats happening or where to run the few become more and more tuned to whats taking place so that all their mind becomes okum enough to control the other world so that it is part of it so that they are no longer human but universal: so they wait for the actual crash of the two worlds: heigh! heigh! I'll be there that day with a toy balloon: well - that one mind is part of the next world so they anticipate exactly when it will crash into this and they know that there is only one vantage spot to take off of when the other world is alongside so as to step over onto the other in time to avoid

Appendix   113

the sparks. They wait, and know that at the time they'll all go to that one spot all right and that the method of getting off this to the next will be no ceremonial but simply a step from this world to that as easy as stepping over a stream: that they'll be there together and no one need say anything for the stepping stone is too exact for that: that it will be the only stone not knocked: that it will be the width of a stream for a normal step over: and that when they step over they needn't even remember the garden of eden: no that will be an old story and no more stories needed: love len; so here you are then : -

waiting for the toot toot waiting
for the Roberty Robert. E. Lee
A 1000 million people all gone wrong.
while a way a few living never die.

no no ark needed
millions stomp and stay
amazed. cant you hear
me calling caroline.

1,2,3 and 19,20 get as
far as the limit: so that
means the end of the world:
how simple.

no night or day: so 1,2,3
the end of the world: all
latin jokes lost: hey! hey!
no perfect day: no one
had spoke: no one had drifted.

what have we got telepathy,
no, finality, no not needed
1,2,3 and 19,20 knew alone
what was nearer: satisfied
to know: only living to know
only knowing how simple:
where to go off what place to
step and us 1,2,3 stepping over.

when thats how then there
must be a limit so they'll
all be the same: as if 20
minds are really only one
mind: just the same one exact mind.
So we're all bound to know.

They ought to - that one
exact mind pulls the other
world over. Then a crash
and they know where to go for
a stepping stone from this
world to that.

meanwhile the millions still
love fireworks: let them stay
and enjoy the very last glare
down in the sandpits eating cake
with pitchforks while the stars
go moving on. So that ends
the last lesson.

"Still July" became "No More Stories" (pp. 20–21) in Lye's *No Trouble* (1930), the fourth book from Seizin Press. The twenty letters for *No Trouble* were selected and lightly edited by Riding. "Still July" ends with "no more stories needed: love len; so here you are then : -" and "waiting for the toot toot" is a separate but closely related piece, untitled, by Jane Thompson; as Riding says in L51, "It was just a letter but I said oh a poem and so we let Jane type it like that and now it is both." See L51.

Obsession

Laura Riding

I never yesterday, as I intended wrote the poem of rage, to say wild Laura, her my not corruptible gentleness: which is not to change, and cruelly-kindly, as long as I can last (and them), to make this gift of unchangeability to that which changes, this gift of annihilation to make which I take upon myself the pain of permanence—short permanence, long annihilation, short pain, long pleasure. Robert reaches for the gift, a gift sought for, a gift of pain not pleasure. Therefore he too, from love, has a short permanence. I am, and while I am he has me. He has me in permanence instead of himself in annihilation. Because he has a genius equal in wildness and gentleness to my own, the genius of self-annihilation. So there are two pains where only one is, there is love, there are not two but an extreme one, there is the pleasure of pain, the longness of shortness. Then Len. He does not seek the gift, he waits: to receive, to mark the receiving from the giving, to have long pleasure. And the permanence of this annihilation, the shortness of it even, he calls Jane not pain. And Gertrude? Not to tell, not to give, not to take, not short or long, not wild or gentle; if not telling, not giving, not taking, not short or long, not wild or gentle, and yet if not otherwise, then Gertrude. If intending to write yesterday and not writing, if not writing to-day of intending to write yesterday, if not writing not intending to-morrow, then Gertrude. If to-morrow or the day before yesterday, then Gertrude. If not Laura, then

Appendix 115

Gertrude Gertrude. If not then if. Gertrude is not less than Laura and Laura is not more than Gertrude. Sad Laura is glad because of Gertrude and glad Gertrude is sad because of Laura. Gertrude is not the name of Gertrude as Laura is the name of Laura. There is no name Gertrude as there is no name God. The Nunquam made an accusation of Laura to the police when he thought her dying of a leap from a window that he had opened for her. He said: She was mad, she thought herself God. No. She is mad, she thinks herself Laura. Gertrude does not think herself Gertrude, she is not mad. Gertrude does not call herself Gertrude, she is not sane. There is no name Gertrude as there is no name God. Gertrude does not think herself Gertrude as she does not think herself God. No. She is not mad, she does not think herself Gertrude or God. She is not sane, she does not call herself Gertrude or God. Gertrude is Gertrude or God, God is God or Gertrude; or God or Gertrude nor Laura. The Nunquam made an accusation of or God or Gertrude nor Laura to the police. What action does the police take? If Gertrude does not call herself Gertrude, who calls her Gertrude? She is called Gertrude by the police. This is the action of the police against the madness of Laura. Thank you, dear Gertrude, for being called Gertrude.

2

And Robert, you say, "Be still while I add up again." No, I will not be your perhaps greater result, I will not be your to be. I will not be a proof that any more can be of making sure, of the fear that having may be not having, when right seems too right. No, I will not be still, Robert. I am your result and I will not be still, and if your result seems narrow, you must have narrowness of it and want and her own showing which says, "This however scant is truth." You love fullness. She loves truth. We have not made a compromise, we are one, this is as full as truth may be and as true as fullness may be. We are one, we are only separated from each other by ourselves. I miss the rendez-vous by a shyness of the inexact, you by a shyness of the insufficient. We do not touch. But our language is the language of the rendez-vous. Then why do you linger over memories that are not, stand bewildered though nothing more can bewilder, intricately perform simplicities, make resistance to distractions that are not, mourn somewhat your generous conjecture of me now that I am plain and strait before you, put on gray hairs to annotate the conclusion with carewornness, swallow in small morsels to be able to make talk between them because you fear that a single mouthful might leave you speechless, give alibis and then commit crimes-spill, drop, trip, stutter? And all to prove yourself you? Ah, I know you, you are Robert, but you need not so bellow out your name as if time were still between us. There is nothing between us but ourselves, and as this seems nothing it is Laura and as it seems something it is Robert. So fold your hands, or I shall hate you for showing me how you verify, as if it were I who doubted and not you. Open your eyes and know instead of looking knowingly through closed eyes, or you will make the end in your own imagination and never have been now at all. Yes, Robert inclines to grossness in order by contrast to incline to delicacy, he wears a manner of defiance in order to wear by contrast a manner of acquiescence, he tosses carelessly in order by contrast to toss with care, he tosses stupidly in order by contrast to toss with wit, he wears a manner of indifference in order to wear by contrast a manner of concern. Yes, he makes a face of trouble, annoyance, greatness, tragedy, nice self-justifying and some hypocrisy. I think it is a face to his fellows not to me, a face to history that is, a face of fate that is instead of love, that is a face of mystery instead of satisfaction, to say, "Let me take time to come well into death to you, Laura. Let me make sure that I come truly." Dear Robert, do you think I can be fooled? Do you think I would take you into my climate raw and alive? No, I know you. Yes, you wish to seem to resist, to hesitate, to arrive here as by Good Luck not Plan, slapping me heartily on the shoulder and exclaiming with surprise, "You, Laura, of all people." Yes, of all people. Well, have it your way. I too am having it mine. Which is to be Laura, as yours is to have been Robert. I come from a future, you from a past. From which, between us, a dead present. No, we cannot help but triumph. From which I do speak of triumph, from which you do so. You do so be a fool and a fool under my very nose, yes. You cause me to know you somewhat in the past. You cause me to know you somewhat in the future. Perhaps we do not meet at all? We do not. This is another way of saying that we have a dead present between us, from which you seem to yourself to be always starting over again to be always ending.

3

But there can be nothing further beyond the end. Whatever wishes to be must be before the end. Whatever wishes to enjoy the certainty of death must live, must die. After death there is only death. Before death there is degree; degrees of death. You can see from this that I believe that each should have fear in a degree suitable to his proximity to death. By proximity I mean, of course, proximity of character not of time, or rather I mean that time is character. By character I mean, of course, justifiable fear. For there are those who belong to degree only, who are life, in whom fear is a play: these merely sneak in out of chance, then return happily to chance again, confident of an eternity of self-forgetfulness. And there are those who belong earnestly to death, who are death. And fear? Death-being, degree of self-unforgettableness. I myself am happiest in fear; it is my life. It is Laura. And it would be difficult to be otherwise, however difficult you may think it to be Laura. I feared heights with the same fear by which I was able to leap down a height, and I feared death with the same fear by which I was able to die. And this I did with such ease that you would not, to know me, call me dead. Perhaps you would call me mad. Indeed, if you will not call me dead, I do not see how you can help calling me mad. And yet it would be difficult for me to be otherwise. Indeed if I were otherwise you would also call me mad. As it is, however mad it may please you to call me now, you will at least admit that I am behaving naturally-for myself. Madness, it is agreed, is when a person loses her nature. But it is clear that I have not lost my nature: it is clear that my nature is even more certain than yours. I think you had better give in and agree as well that death is my nature. Or else turn away from me toward Gertrude, who is whatever you please and who will seem to you sane though incomprehensible, as I seem mad in so far as I seem comprehensible. Yes, now I have you in a corner, you do not know whether to think me mad or subtle, plain-spoken or obscure. No, I do not want to tease you, I do not even know who you are. But so long as there is a possibility of your being someone I must treat you as someone, that is, as something not myself, that is, half with confidence and half with suspicion, since you would be an uncertain divided fellow, and if I did not treat you uncertainly, or if I did not treat you at all, you might treat me, that is, know me as something not yourself, cast me out, yes, call me mad. And the harm of it to me? No harm. But the harm of it to you! Therefore I shall deal gently with you, for nothing could come of dealing with you otherwise: I shall treat you, for all purposes except the real purpose, as myself. In this way you will gradually disappear, so gradually that I shall not miss you when you are gone, nor you yourselves. Meanwhile you will want signs of my confidence since I have given you such frank signs of my suspicion. I shall perhaps begin at my body, since that is where I end and others begin or others end and I begin: an impartial point of departure. By others I mean the unresolved ones, those who have not yet named themselves with death or with life, who have not yet chosen between myself and themselves, which is the same as to say between themselves and others or between one and many. For it is plain that a good fellow is always the same fellow, that he is always me, a united madness, and on no occasion them, a disjointed badness: that a good fellow is always a dead one. For who would be a live one who could be a dead one, I mean dead and a one? I don't mean dead and not a one, I don't mean the death of those whose life and death are only number and numberlessness. No, my death is not the numberlessness of number, my death is one. But to hurry on, since there is no reason not to be hurrying on, no reason why I should linger, such as to succeed in persuasion, my object being to confront not the persuadable, who must be already persuaded if they are ever to be persuaded, but the unpersuadable whom to confront with all the materials of persuasion is not to persuade them of me but to unpersuade them—they alone can tell how quickly—of themselves. But to hurry on. To hurry on, to hurry back to my body. Or, to simplify, to hurry back to body, since I do not know body, I know me. Robert knows body, he knows bodily, he does not know, he loves. To love is to love absurdly and beautifully, to make body absurd and beautiful, to outrage it with ridicule and overwhelm it with adoration. He loves. The Pridem did not love. She no more than fancied. No more than fancying, she would say of me in the language of Reality: "Has she fingers, has she toes?" And the Nunquam, the lover of me as one unbodily and unlovable, knew himself by her question to have been of old the Devil, and was shocked into piety. "No," he answered, "she is only a witch." And so it was that he became the Pridem's lover, as woman with fingers and toes—raging against me to rage against himself, the Devil driving out the Devil. And the Pridem? Chaste Reality: body as not absurd, as not beautiful, as Reasonableness to Extravagance, as Reality to Truth. Nearness and False Content. As False Content Robert could love her truly. As True Content the Nunquam can love her falsely. Ah, you scheming and subtle one, you Devil, you Contriver. I have no more need of you, but since you cannot be happy except in service and you insist upon happiness, that is, réclame, that is, taking part, that is, unendingness and unrest, action and unhappiness—go along with you then, go along with you eternally, suffer eternally if you will, since you wish to outlast and there is no outlasting except in Hell, the Eternity of Lies. So to speak, in this way of talking. Of course you will understand that this is but talking, but my meaning, but the truth so to speak, without legality. Without legality of course. That is, I do not tell the whole story, only the essentials. Only what stands out, what I remember, the essence that is of what I have forgotten, gradually evaporating essence. Without legality. Gradually evaporating essence, scarcely now memorable. Nearly vacant truth. Nearly no libel.

4

And Robert, I say to you, Robert, that you are a tricky chap. This is not an accusation unless to say, "I love you," as you would have me say and I will indeed say, is to make an accusation. Indeed you would indeed have me say "I love you" to be an accusation upon which to make a defence—the defence, to wit, "I love you." Therefore it is agreed that I say "Robert, you are a tricky chap." That is, you are a tricky chap if I am a natural chap. Which is agreed. For all that I am is consistent with all that I am. While all that you are is inconsistent with all that you are. You come to extreme agreement by extreme disagreement that you force by its very extremeness to agree extremely. We are at the same business together but we are each at a different business. You do your business by trick, I do my business by nature. That is, you seem to be doing your business easily, I seem to be doing my business laboriously. I say you are a tricky-seeming chap to others, but to me a clumsy-seeming chap. I say you come to me with flying colours from others, you so come in order to come. In order to be accused. In order to defend. I love you. I love you. In order not to accuse. In order not to defend. In order in order not to.

5

And Avidity, the Jew. Not quietable. Holy rapacity, unsightly fanaticism, chosen despicability. All that is cast out, all too worthy, utter and inhuman Right—this is Jew, that will not be cast out but, in a rabidly mean human form, taunts Christian Renunciation with a scornful image of itself. O horrid, holy, uncomely, exquisite, O Jew, O people more than people defining people. Not for long. Unjust ones, who will not give Wrong an equal place with Right, Justice is soon dead, it grows harsh, you may give over to it your cruel mind and throw away your heart made soft by anger. And science itself, all that is less than people defining people, intellectual, dumbly prognosticating Matter—Science itself is slowing saying that Science, or Slowness is soon over, soon-now over. The game which was no game is up, the real business is at hand. What real business? Real business is how Science says business. The business. What business? Am I a mystic? No, I am not a mystic, I am Laura. What business? Laura. How can Laura be a business? How can she not? Complete obsession. Never before, now at last. Until now, delusion of completeness, unavowed delusion. Now, complete obsession, avowed completeness, now Laura. And what of Space? Gertrude. All-together Gertrude, separate Laura. Strong all-together Gertrude, separate strong Laura. Laura alone. Gertrude everyone. Strong. But do you think I have forgotten Jew? No, I have not forgotten Jew but only not forgotten Laura not forgotten Gertrude not forgotten anything only remembered Jew. Remembered Jew. Jew reminding that that which is is not at all until it all is. Jew the miserable, author of Jesus the miserable and Satan the miserable, both preoccupied, though in opposite intentions, with mediocrity. Jew seeming the loathsome past by that he is a loathing of the past. O Jew, suffering dog, lie down. Science the Gentile, the Slow Reasoner, is coming into Comprehension. Soon will be Rapidity, soon the co-operative world of sense will disintegrate, soon Unity itself will appear of the long everlastingly long failure of sense to make a proper idea of Unity, soon the fine instruments will be seen to have been of no usefulness except to themselves. What unity? Unity. Unit-y. Soon. Soon unit. Unit not Co-operation. Soon or Now. Gertrude and Laura. Or to wander, Jew. Jew, not to wander. Wandering Jew. Jew, hater of wandering. Jew, hatred because of wandering. Jew, hatred, therefore hated. And to wander. And Voltaire, Gentile becoming Jew, Jew unbecoming Jew, hatred and hatred, cancellation. Lie down dog at last or soon or now. Justice has been in spite of you but, because in spite, Justice is no more. All have had their chance of being God, God is no more. He was too many, the God of too many is no more. Fewer now than God. Fewer than Jew. Fewer than Jew the few of the many. Few now of few. Or soon.

6

Perhaps or somewhat a turn. Or more deliberately not a turn. Whatever, and the same story. At any rate, always at any rate, always the impossibility of sham because always at any rate. Of course I mean the impossibility to me, for I do not, conspire, I attend. No, nor to persist. Of persistence, Robert. No, nor to be. Of being, Gertrude. Of life, Gertrude. Of life and progression, Robert. Of life, progression and ultimately, Laura. Always at any rate the impossibility of sham. And also the possibilities of sham to? To anywhom. For with Robert goes Robertness, Robert and Robertsham, Robert and whoness. For with Gertrude goes Gertrudeness, Gertrude and Gertrudesham, Gertrude and anyness. But with Laura goes Laura, always at any rate the impossibility of sham unless Laura of Laura, which is to say ultimately, which—which is to say ultimately. Life, progression and ultimately. Life—endless security of endless chance. Progression—dangerous advance of right calculation. And ultimately. Ultimately the centre from which endless security of endless chance, to which dangerous advance of right calculation, in which at any rate nowhere else Laura, always at any rate the impossibility of sham. Meanwhile a letter to and from, a letter from and to, a letter to and to, a letter from and from, meanwhile letters, letters in which, in which and out of which, more or less exactly, than, not exactly, more or less exactly than inexactly or more or less inexactly than exactly. Meanwhile perhaps or somewhat or more deliberately not. Meanwhile ultimately though meanwhile though letter though only frequently always. At any rate a letter, letters, at any rate always as if ultimately, frankly as if, more or less exactly and inexactly as if. Dear frankly. Dear as if. Frankly as if, knowing otherwise to be otherwise. Frankly seeming. Frankly romantic. Frankly not romantic. Frankly meanwhile. A letter not a lie. And the same story. To anticipate, and the same story. Perhaps or somewhat or love, and the same story frankly not, frankly with love.

Experts Are Puzzled, Jonathan Cape, 1930 (reprinted by Ugly Duckling Presse, 2018, pp. 87–99). See L54.

THE NEW BARBARISM, AND GERTRUDE STEIN

Laura Riding

transition 3, June 1927 (pp. 153–68)

It has been seen that contemporary criticism, the philosophical portion of contemporary poetic activity, has attempted to bring about some order in the views commonly held about poetry. By doing this it has hoped to bring about an order in the actual writing of poetry. The only order there has been in poetry for the last hundred and thirty five years has been a superficial uniformity due to a confused sympathy of sentiment and imagery in the language in which it was written. But there has been no fundamental professional sense of the eighteenth-century sort. The background has been anarchy and amateurishness. To be able to use these words is to be using them in condemnation. When contemporary criticism expresses its respect for the eighteenth century it is, of course, praising its professional sense. It is impossible to believe that it is praising eighteenth century poetry as such, in which the sentiment of professional uniformity lacked the energy that might have been supplied to it by anarchy and amateurishness.

The problem of the present-day poet, therefore, who feels himself responsible to the problem raised by criticism, is a very difficult one. He must react against the unprofessional and superficial uniformity which romanticism brought about—he must maintain a professional independence of sentiment and imagery—and the same time avoid anarchy and amateurishness. He must resign from the emotional brotherhood which poetry formed from a loose romantic social sense and attach himself to the organized metaphysic of poetry professionalized in the narrowest possible social sense as an art-and-craft.

We may say that the problem will be to a large extent solved by the poet's originality and the discipline that should go with it if it is to be effective originality. And it is true that the successes in contemporary poetry have been those who have been able to combine originality and discipline. But in general the burden of responsibility has rested with originality; discipline has been distorted, teased and distracted by the lack, in criticism, of immediate suggestiveness, a failure which is aggravated by the dogmatic character of its theorizing. Criticism assumes all the prerogatives which belong to creation without assuming any of its concrete responsibilities. It limits its share in these responsibilities to a negative and irresponsible taste and envelops itself in a forbidding cloud of snobbery.

Criticism says: "Art refers to an absolute. It must recognize a first principle. Every work must imply this first principle." "What," is the creative question, "is the first principle? A work cannot imply it by interrogation; that would be romantic." But the first principle is not stated. It seems part of the consistency of the metaphysic that it shall not be stated. It must be derived from the metaphysic in such a way that its finality shall not be impaired by its relation to contemporary history. The age itself must invent a first principle *pro tem.*, the corporeal representative of the absolute. The absolute cannot be absolute and appear in person. Art is ideal action. It does not so much create as reveal. Its purpose is "to pierce through the veil placed between us and reality" (Hulme), not to pretend to reality in the work itself. Art is a way of expressing things, not things; it is craft-like, instrumental. The work is a kind of ideal behaviour, but the beauty of this behaviour must not be made to inhere in the work, for this would mean a confusion of standards. Beauty must be inferred, its sameness verified. Variety is in the instrumentality of art, not in its meaning. Its meaning is so *same* that it can only be expressed, it cannot be immediately present. The belief in the possibility of its being immediately present is a perverted romantic notion.

Thus the absolute, beauty, the first principle, remains persistently elusive unless supplied by the age. The critical energy of the poet is supposed to be more concretely responsible than the creative energy of criticism. Half the energy of the poet, if not more, is to be consumed in making the age yield its version of the first principle. This version is known as a "theme." If the theme is absent it is through the combined fault of the poet and the age. The poet should have the power of identifying himself with the temporal extent of his age, of realizing his proper theme. If this happy union is not effected, criticism takes the attitude that it is very significant that it has not been effected, that it is indeed too bad and that the poet will have to do the next best thing, that is, write about this very significant and deplorable handicap. "The dissociation" (of vision and subject), says Mr. Allen Tate in his Foreword to a volume of poems by Mr. Hart Crane, "appears decisively for the first time in Baudelaire." Theme-ishness, Mr. Tate wishes to suggest, wore itself out. This is not to be interpreted as a reflection on the theme-ishness of the absolute, but apparently on history, which has not been able to sustain the succession of themes, and on poets, who have, because of history, been forced to ease up a little on themes. Nor does it contradict the unexpressed first principle or the theoretical necessity for a theme. "For while Mr. Eliot might have written a more ambitiously unified poem," Mr. Tate further says, "the unity would have been false; tradition as unity is not contemporary." Tradition, he means, is unity, and contemporary criticism is busy saying this; but contemporary poetry is not unity because it is busy proving how distressing the absence of unity is and also paying the penalty for the sins of romanticism, which disregarded tradition as unity and so in its anarchic enthusiasm developed no unity but a feeble universalization of poetic language. "For," he goes on to say in a few sentences, "the comprehensiveness and lucidity of any poetry, the capacity for poetry being assumed as proved, are in direct proportion to the availability of a comprehensive and perfectly articulated given theme." This theme being temporarily absent (Mr. Tate does not say who should have articulated the theme, not the poet, since the theme is given? Not history, since this would imply a critical function which Mr. Tate would surely not admit in history? The only deduction possible is that criticism, for no discoverable reason, has decided to be coy), "the important contemporary poet has the rapidly diminishing privilege of reorganizing the past," Mr. Tate concludes.

T. S. Eliot composed such a résumé in *The Waste Land*. James Joyce attempted the same sort of thing in a more satiric way in his long progressive use of period literary styles in *Ulysses*. Gertrude Stein, lacking the sophistication of either of these, refused to be baffled by criticism's haughty coyness and, taking the absolute and beauty and the first principle quite literally, saw no reason, all these things being so, why we should not have a theme, why indeed, we cannot assume "a perfectly articulated given theme." If everybody assumed this perfectly articulated given theme (and no one has yet shown satisfactorily why, fortified by such a criticism, we should not), everybody would understand Gertrude Stein. Mr. Eliot does not approve of Gertrude Stein's work because he has not himself had the courage, although a sincere disciple of the new barbarism, to assume a perfectly articulated given theme. Gertrude Stein, by combining the functions of critic and poet and taking everything around her very literally and many things for granted which others have not been naive enough to take so, has done what everyone else has been ashamed to do. No one but she has been willing to be as ordinary, as simple, as primitive, as stupid, as barbaric as successful barbarism demands.

Does no one but Miss Stein realize that to be mathematical, thematic, anti-Hellenic, anti-Renaissancist, anti-romantic, we must be barbaric? What has happened? We have had enough triangles, circles, spheres and hemispheres to satisfy any barbaric geometric craving, and yet it is certain that triangles, circles, spheres and hemispheres have passed: the London *Times* recently criticized a young artist's work which was of a geometric type as "old-fashioned." If the geometric type (which Hulme opposed to the vital type) has passed (as it has) it must be because it was romantic (a romantic movement must have an end) and because it was surprised and defeated by its own romanticism.

We have seen how near the surface romanticism lurked in Mr. Pound's philosophy. We discover Hulme's absolute, too, to have been a pessimist's deification of pessimism, a sentimental abstraction of despair. Hulme's romanticism is finally and completely confessed in his attachment to Bergson. Bergson's attraction is that in rescuing the fundamentally romantic idea of evolution from its idealization, evolutionary progress, he invented an elaborate, pleasurable and dreamy way for the modern classicist to be barbaric. By interpreting evolution as an intensive instead of an extensive process he kept the movement and variation of evolution but eliminated the objectionable enlargement of significance with which humanity generally accompanies its movement and variations. By calling the true intelligence of this process intuitive rather than intellectual he discredited the civilized personality of the human mind but allowed it to remain as a primitive power of animalism. By defining the time world as an absolute duration which continuously interpenetrated itself and thus continuously produced new forms, he suggested a movement in the absolute without attacking its absoluteness; he made romanticism seem classical, and, above all, kept a dignified place for originality in this system without displacing discipline.

The devotion of the modern barbarian to originality is the most serious flaw in his metaphysical technique. Because of the classicist's romantic fondness for originality, discipline only succeeds in making originality more original. He cannot abandon originality,

The New Barbarism, and Gertrude Stein 123

however it contradicts discipline, because gross romanticism has come to represent the sentimental vulgarity of ordinary humanity. Gross classicism only represents ordinary humanity theoretically, which means that it really represents those who have extraordinary power or superiority over ordinary humanity. This flaw was very obvious in Hulme's idea of the nature of the artist's vision. To Hulme, the artist saw something that no one else saw, he directly communicated "individuality and the freshness of things": the only suggestion of classicism in this being the peculiar emphasis on "things." Speaking again of the artist, he said: "It is because he realizes the inadequacy of the usual that he is obliged to invent." Direct communication, furthermore, is hindered by the long romantic history of language. Its democratic communism, or generalized originality, is responsible for its decadence. The classicist, to believe in the absolute, must believe in communism, but in autocratic communism: communism permitting of originality in the autocrat. The representative authority of the artist comes, it appears, from his authority: he is the autocrat of authority.

A discrepancy multiplies. How is originality to remain consistent with the classicism of the new barbarism when every increase in originality seems, as in modernist poetry, a movement in the direction of romanticism, a widening of the breach between criticism and workmanship? "The artist must discover," criticism would reply, "classical originality: he must invent original type." For a time it seemed as if the geometric type was the sought-for original type. But it failed as an experiment in original classicism because it was only a sophisticated imitation, or rather caricature, of perhaps the most ordinary type of art in the past. And it is hard to see, indeed, how the pursuit of an original type can get any farther than a caricature of the ordinary. The possibilities might seem greater in literature, where it has been permissible for human personality to contribute to this desired combination of originality and conventionality. But here too the creative limit seems to be reached in caricature; in Joyce's Leopold Bloom and in Eliot's Prufrock and other "low types," originality only seems to be after all an attack on a degenerated ordinary. *Ordinary* and *original* therefore cannot be used as contradictory terms; or rather their use as such reveals the contradiction in their use.

The "direct communication" by which originality is to be transmitted reveals a further contradiction. Directness of communication means immediate ideal intelligibility. But since language has been degraded by its experiences, much of the originality will have to be employed in attacking the ordinary language of communication: direct communication, like the original type, will be able to go no farther than an earnest caricature of ordinary language, like the dialogue in Mr. Eliot's latest *Fragment of a Prologue*. But caricature is romantic. The poetry of Edith Sitwell is but one instance in contemporary poetry of the romantic caricature of language which contemporary classicism has fostered. Another aspect of the same general flaw is the incompatibility of the "things" which are supposed to be revealed in the direct communication ("things" in which apparently the first principle inheres) with the talent of the artist to see things "as no one else sees them." The barbaric absolute, the divine source of "things," wherever it has prevailed naturally, has always been marked by a penetrating obviousness. The Pyramids are penetratingly obvious: they nearly make absoluteness synonymous with obviousness.

124   *Laura Riding*

Creative originality can only be consistent with barbaric communism if it is not *superior* creative originality. The only kind of originality which can see "things" "as no one else sees them" for barbaric mass-humanity, for human ordinariness, is mass-originality: some mystical, large-scale process in which the artist is chosen as a seeing instrument without his ordinariness being destroyed. He may be regarded by his tribe as divinely inspired to communicate directly, but inspired in ordinariness. The ideal barbaric artist is superior in ordinariness rather than in originality. For a long time the new barbarism has been wasting itself on disguised romantics while Gertrude Stein quietly and patiently practised a coherent barbarism under its very nose without encouragement or recognition. Her only crime has been that she has followed directions and disciplined away discrepancies. She has been able to do this because she is completely without originality. Everybody is unable to understand her and thinks that this is because she is too original or is trying too hard to be original. But she is only divinely inspired in ordinariness. She uses language automatically to record pure, ultimate obviousness. She makes it capable of direct communication not by caricaturing language in its present stage—attacking decadence with decadence—but by purging it of its discredited experiences. None of the words Miss Stein uses have ever had any experience. They are no older than her use of them, and she is herself no older than her age conceived barbarically.

> Put it there in there there where they have it. Put it there in there there and they halve it.
> Put it there in there there and they have it. Put it there in there there and they halve it. ["Jean Cocteau"]

None of these words, it can be seen, has ever had any history before this. The design that Miss Stein makes of them is literally abstract and mathematical because they are etymologically transparent and commonplace, mechanical but not eccentric. If they possess originality it is the originality of gross automatism. Their author is a large-scale mystic, she is the darling priest of cultured infantilism to her age if her age but knew it.

> Nothing changes from generation to generation except the thing seen and that makes a composition. ["Composition as Explanation"]

Her admission that there are generations does not contradict her belief in a unvarying first principle. Time does not vary, only the sense of time.

> Automatically with the acceptance of the time-sense comes the recognition of the beauty and once the beauty is accepted the beauty never fails anyone. ["Composition as Explanation"]

Beauty has no history, time has no history; only the time-sense has history. When the time-sense acclaims a beauty which was not at first recognized, the finality of this beauty is at once established, it is as though it had never been denied. All beauty is equally final. The reason why the time-sense if realized reveals the finality or classicalness of beauty is that it is the feeling of beginning, of primitiveness and freshness which is each age's or generation's version of time.

> Beginning again and again and again explaining composition and time is a natural thing.
> It is understood by this time that everything is the same except composition and time, composition and the time of the composition and the time in the composition. ["Composition as Explanation"]

Originality of vision, then, is invented not by the artist but by the collective time-sense. The artist does not see "things" "as no one else sees them." He sees those objective "things" in which the absolute is repeatedly verified, personalized and represented by the age. He sees concretely and expressively what everyone else who is possessed of the time-sense has an unexpressed intuition of: the time-sense may not be generally and particularly universal; but this does not make the artist's vision, even his originality of vision, less collective or less universal.

> The composition is the thing seen by everyone living in the living they are doing, they are the composing of the composition that at the time they are living is the composition of the time in which are they are living. It is that that makes living a thing they are doing. Nothing else is different, of that almost any one can be certain. The time when and the time of and the time in that composition is the natural phenomena of that composition and of that perhaps every one can be certain. ["Composition as Explanation"]

All this Gertrude Stein has understood and executed logically because of the perfect simplicity of her mind. Believing implicitly in an absolute, she has not been bothered to doubt the bodily presence of a first principle in her own time. Since she is alive and everybody around her seems to be alive, why of course there is an acting first principle, there is composition. This acting first principle provides a "perfectly articulated given theme" because there is time, and everybody, and the beginning again and again and again, and composition. In her primitive good-humour she does not find it necessary to trouble to define the theme. The theme is to be inferred from the composition. The composition is clear because the language means nothing but what it means in her using of it. The composition is final because it is "a more and more continuous present including more and more using of everything and continuing more and more beginning and beginning and beginning." She creates this atmosphere of continuousness principally by her progressive use of the tenses of verbs, by an intense and unflagging repetitiousness and by an artificially assumed and regulated child-mentality: the child's time-sense is so vivid that an occurrence is always consecutive to itself, it goes on and on, it has been going on and on, it will be going on and on; a child does perhaps feel the passage of time, does to a certain extent feel itself older than it was yesterday because yesterday was already morrow even while it was being yesterday.

Laura Riding

Alfred as I was saying was in Gossols when he was a very young one and when he was a little an older one. Sometimes then later he saw a little sometimes of Olga the sister of the first governess the Herslands had had in their Gossols living staying with them. Sometimes the Wyman family made up to him. This is the way he had all these in him this that I am now beginning describing. This is now beginning to be a history of him, a history of Alfred Hersland of all the being and all the living in him. [*The Making of Americans*]

This is how Gertrude Stein wrote in 1906 and this is she was still writing in 1926. Writing by always beginning again and again and again keeps everything different and everything the same. It creates duration but makes it absolute by preventing anything from happening in the duration.

And after that what changes what changes after that, after that what changes and what changes after that and after that and what changes and after that and what changes after that. ["Composition as Explanation"]

The composition has *a* theme because it has no theme. The words are a self-pursuing, tail-swallowing series and are therefore thoroughly abstract. They achieve what Hulme called but could not properly envisage, a "perpendicular," an escape from the human horizontal plane. They contain no references, no meanings, no caricatures, no jokes, no despairs. They are so automatic that it is even inexact to speak of Miss Stein as their author: they create one another. The only possible explanation of lines like the following is that one word or combination of words creates the next.

As long as head as short as said as short as said as long as head. ["Jean Cocteau"]

A little away
And a little away.
Everything away.
Everything and away.
Everything and away.
Away and everything away. ["Jean Cocteau"]

This is repetition and continuousness and beginning again and again and again.

Nothing that has been said here should be understood as disrespectful to Gertrude Stein. What has been said has been said in praise and not contempt. She has courage, clarity, sincerity, simplicity. She has created a human mean in language, a mathematical equation of ordinariness which leaves one with a tender respect for that changing and unchanging slowness that is humanity and Gertrude Stein. Humanity—one learns this from Gertrude Stein but not from contemporary poetry—is fundamentally a nice person; and so is Gertrude Stein.

Having, in her recent essay "Composition As Explanation," explained composition and

The New Barbarism, and Gertrude Stein   127

composed explanation and made language serve critical and creative aims at the same time, she then proceeds to speak of romanticism as no other contemporary critic with a classical bias has been able to do; she speaks of it as a rôle which composition may play when it is being the same thing it is when it plays the rôle of classicism.

> Everything is the same except composition and as the composition is different and always going to be different everything is not the same. ["Composition as Explanation"]

We may draw from this a definition of classicism: it is the sameness of the differentness of composition. The definition of romanticism means only a shift of emphasis and Miss Stein does this for us.

> Romanticism is then when everything being alike everything is naturally simply different, and romanticism. ["Composition as Explanation"]

Romanticism is the differentness of the sameness of composition.

> After all this, there is that, there has been that that there is a composition and that nothing changes except composition the composition and the time of and the time in the composition. ["Composition as Explanation"]

The time in the composition is its sameness and its differentness, its classicism and its romanticism. If the composition is to have lastingness it must return to the sameness. If the composition is to have life it must begin again and again and again with the differentness. Such seems to be Miss Stein's philosophy of history in art. But as the composition is something which goes on and in on a continuous present and using of everything and beginning again and again and again, it does not seem to matter which comes first, romanticism or classicism, or whether a work or attitude is attributed to one or to the other or whether, indeed, it is ever necessary to refer to either.

Both, however, have a certain strategical usefulness. Classicism is a historical formula invented by criticism for any period of history whose art can be looked on as a whole. It is very strictly a term for the past and for the past only. However unique a work may seem, it cannot be properly called classical unless it can be associated with other things called classical. The word classical carries with it the weight of all works that have ever been called classical. The impressiveness of a "classic" is in the implication that it belongs in the company of other great works and, regardless of its time, really dates from long ago, from the time when the past was so solid that everything was classical. Everything up to a certain point, in history, the Renaissance says, was classical, even the late Greek, which has really only lost respectability because of its post-Renaissance influence. This is the ironical force of "a modern classic." Classicism is what Miss Stein means by "distribution and equilibration."

But when distribution and equilibration is urged or attempted while the composition is in process, when criticism recommends a contemporaneous classicism, then it is really being the criticism of the future, looking back on its own period (since classicism can only refer to the past) and attempting to order its own period backwards. This is why a division between modernist composition and modernist criticism is inevitable. The criticism is talking backwards. The composition, because its time is a continuous present, is talking forwards. Criticism drops a perpendicular at the point where the continuous horizontal of composition begins again with the contemporary time-sense. The point where the perpendicular meets the horizontal is unreal in the perpendicular, because past and therefore refuted by the presentness of the point on the horizontal.

Romanticism has a broader usefulness. Referring to differentness rather than sameness, it is a word for the present rather than for the past: the farther works are in the past the more same they seem, the nearer to the present, the more different. Romanticism is more useful if only by the greater of number of works to which it may refer, also because it characterizes without definitely classifying—"romanticism, which was not a confusion but an extrication" as Gertrude Stein says. Afterwards the distribution and equilibration, "there must be time that is distributed and equilibrated." Thus every period afterwards is in a way classical. But, while the composition is going on, it is not same, it is different, it is "an extrication." Contemporary composition which may be in sympathy with the classicism of its criticism must nevertheless in practice react against it; composition cannot go on if it is self-conscious about its sameness. It must be different if only because it must have different authors. Gertrude Stein, an ideal author for a one-man classical period, is nevertheless many different authors in one. She might seem more intelligible if it were possible to read her as many authors.

One way that the contemporary poet has of keeping romantically alive in classicism is by carefully avoiding theme. When Mr. Tate says, for instance, that Mr. Crane has not yet found a theme to match his poetic vision he is really explaining that Mr. Crane is preserving his vision from a theme, that his vision is reacting romantically against contemporary classicism.

Hart Crane's poems reveal many of the qualities peculiar to enforced romantics. It is noticeable that Mr. Tate joins him to other enforced romantics—Poe, Rimbaud, Edith Sitwell, T. S. Eliot, Wallace Stevens—although Mr. Crane has sufficient poetic dignity to be able to dispense with such literary boosting. Much of the intensity of his poetry—intensity which is often protracted into strain—is due to a conflict between discipline and originality, which may also be otherwise expressed as an attempt to identify the formality of accuracy with the finality of accuracy. The result is a compromise in the mysticism of rhetoric:

Bind us in time, O Seasons clear, and awe.
O minstrel galleons of Carib fire,
Bequeath us to no earthly shore until
Is answered in the vortex of our grave
The seal's wide spindrift gaze toward paradise. ["Voyages"]

This romantic mysticism of technique—romantic because discipline merges with originality rather than originality with discipline—results in a mysticism of geography (I shall not say of subject). The movements of his poems are the fluctuations of surfaces; they give a sea-sense of externality: the moon, the sea, frost, tropical horizons, the monotony of continuous exploration. Their formal direction is classical, that is, they tend to become mechanical by a sort of ecstasy of technical excellence:

> O, I have known metallic paradises
> Where cuckoos clucked to finches
> Above the deft catastrophes of drums.
> While titters hailed the groans of death
> Beneath gyrating awnings I have seen
> The incunabula of the divine grotesque.
> This music has a reassuring way. ["For the Marriage of Faustus and Helen"]

And here he would rest if he did not, in the extremes of restraint, have what he calls "fine collapses."

> We can evade you, and all else but the heart:
> What blame to us if the heart live on. ["Chaplinesque"]

By such tenderness and religiousness concealed in method and by such fine collapses, composition just manages to escape with its life—struggling to begin again and again and again in spite of its posthumous classicism.

Note

The text here is based on the *transition* publication; we have, however, silently emended typographic errors. As well, later in the essay, Riding cites a number of Stein texts and some poems by Hart Crane, and we have added the titles.

AN ACQUAINTANCE WITH DESCRIPTION

Gertrude Stein

Seizin Press, 1929

Mouths and Wood.

Queens and from a thousand to a hundred.

Description having succeeded deciding, studying description so that there is describing until it has been adjoined and is in a description. Studies in description until in attracting which is a building has been described as an in case of planting. And so studying in description not only but also is not finishing but understood as describing.

To describe it as at all through. Once more. To describe it as not as dew because it is in the trees. To describe it as it is new not because it has come to be for them if it lasts. At last to come to place it where it was not by that time in that way. And what is what is the name. Holly has very little red berries and so have very large fir trees but not at the same time even though in the same place. Not even in houses and gardens not even in woods and why, why because geraniums have one colour and to find it high, high and high up and a little like it was. Once more and more when it was once more and once more when more when it was. When one goes three go and when three go two go. She said she did not believe in there having there having been there having been there having been there before. Refusing to turn away.

A description refusing to turn away a description.

Two older and one very much younger do not make two older and one very much younger. Come again is easily said if they have if they have come back.

A description simply a description.

A sea gull looking at the grain as seen. And then remarkably farming and manufacturing they like wedding and still with horses and it does not matter if you ask they might there might be a choice. This makes that be what a little in the front and not at all what we see. Never having forgotten to be pleased.

What is the difference between not what is the difference between. What is the difference between not what is the difference between. An acquaintance with description or what is the difference between not what is the difference between not an acquaintance in description. An acquaintance in description. First a sea gull looking into the grain in order to look into the grain it must be flying as if it were looking at the grain. A sea gull looking at the grain. Second a sea gull looking into the grain. Any moment at once. Why is the grain that comes again paler so that it is not so high and after awhile there can be very many of a kind to know that kind. Next to find it coming up and down and not when it is directly through around. This comes to be a choice and we are the only choosers. This makes that be what a little in the front and not at all what we see. To have seen very many every time suspended. This can be in black and as grey and surprising. It is not early to be discouraged by their seating. Seating four to a colour.

Acquaintance with description if he holds it to him and it falls toward him.

Every little bit different and to ask did he might it be older might it be did it did it have it as suggested it might be older.

Very often not at all. An acquaintance with description and they might be if it were at all needed not by them fortunately. Fortunately is always understood. There is a difference between forests and the cultivation of cattle. In regard to either there is a choice in one a choice of trees in the other a choice.

An acquaintance with description if and acquaintance with description. Making an acquaintance with description does not begin new begin now. In acquaintance with description. Simply describe that they are married as they were married. They married. She the one and she the one and they and none and they and one and she and one and they they were nearly certain that their daughter had a friend who did not resemble either their daughter's father or their daughter's mother and this was not altogether why they had what they had they had it as if they might of if they had asked it of all of all. Meant to be not left to it as if it was not beside that it could be and best. Best and best can be delighted delighted delighted.

It is very inconvenient when there is that by this because because of this being that by then. An acquaintance with description has not been begun. An acquaintance with description to begin three.

Not it is not it is not it is not it is at all as it is. No one should remember anything if it did not make any difference it did not make any difference if it did not make any difference. No one should remember anything and it should not make any difference. No one should remember anything and it should not make any difference. Who makes this carefully. Who makes this carefully that it should not make any difference that not any one should remember anything. When two horses meet both being driven and they have not turned aside they turn aside. They both turn aside.

When it is not remarkable that it takes longer it does not make it more than they could do. It is not more remarkable that it takes longer than that it is more remarkable than that is what they have to do. It is not more remarkable that it takes longer than that it is they have it to do. It is not more remarkable. After this makes them prepare this. Very well she is very well. I will you will they will he will.

Not finally so much and change it.

They might like it as it is in the sun.

Naming everything every day, this is the way. Naming everything every day. Naming everything every day.

It is a great pleasure to watch it coming.

They might like it, as it is in the sun.

132   *Gertrude Stein*

It is a pleasure to watch it coming but it might that she could be unaccustomed to lie down without sleeping it might be that she could be unaccustomed to lie down without sleeping.

What is the difference between three and two in furniture. Three is the third of three and two is the second of two. This makes it as true as a description. And not satisfied. And what is the difference between being on the road and waiting very likely being very likely waiting, a road is connecting and as it is connecting it is intended to be keeping going and waiting everybody can understand puzzling. He said it nicely. This makes it as if they had not been intended and after all who is after all after all it is after all afterwards, as they have left there may be a difference between summer and winter. Everybody makes a part of it part of it and a part of it. If he comes to do it, if he comes to do it and if he comes to do it. He comes to do it. Anybody can be mistaken many times mistaken for it. Turkeys should never be brought any where they belong there where they are turkeys there and this reminds one at once. Acquainted with description is the same as acquainted with turkeys. Acquainted with description is the same as being acquainted with turkeys. Why when the sun is here and there is it here. Acquainted with the sun to be acquainted to be unacquainted and to be unacquainted and to be unacquainted and to be in the sun and to be acquainted to be acquainted with the sun. It can be there.

Look down and see a blue curtain and a white hall. A horse asleep lying surrounded by cows.

There is a great difference not only then but now.

After all after this afterwards it was not only that there had been more than there was differently but it was more often than not recognised there can be instances of difference between recognisable and between recognisable when they had been formidable and in the use of that notwithstanding. Having come along. And not being described as very likely to make it not belong to this at that time and very easily when they were delighted and might it be not only suggested and not only suggested as that could be while they came and after that by nearly very often having when it was that it should be decided. They might not only be very often not more nearly as if they could and should has returned. Not on that account.

Never to be left to add it too. Never to be left to add it to that.

Describing that that trees are as available as they were that trees were as available as they were. And to say that it is not to be more than understood very likely it is very likely to be. To be not only pleased but pleasing and to be not only pleased but to be not only pleased. An acquaintance with description.

What is the difference between a hedge and a tree. A hedge and a tree what is the difference between a hedge and a tree.

Next to that what is there to be more than if it was to be prepared.

In part.

Letting it be not what it is like.

The difference between a small pair and that colour and outside. If blue is pale and green is different how many trees are there in it.

Simply a description and sensibly a description and around and a description.

After all who might be who might be influenced by dahlias and roses, pinks and greens

An Acquaintance with Description 133

white and another colour. Who might be careful not to think just as well of what they had when they were there. And never having this by now. A plain description so that anyone would know that pears do grow very well on very good on the very best of pear trees. They made it be theirs yet. After a while they knew the difference after a while they knew that difference after a while they knew this difference after a while they knew the difference after a while they knew the difference after a while they knew the difference. Pleasing them with the description of a pear tree. Pleasing them with the description of a pear tree pleasing them with the description of a pear tree. Pleasing them with the description of a pear tree. And pleasing them by having it not made so much as much differently. They might have been and if by this at once.

Not after all.

An acquaintance with description the difference between by that time and why they went. We have left them now.

An acquaintance with description.

Mary Lake is a pretty name. Two five seven nine eleven. And I was to tell you what, about a window, what was it. She thought it was two four six nine eleven but it was not it was two five seven nine eleven. Mary Lake is a pretty name she said it was she said she thought it was she said she said it was. Mary Lake is a pretty name all the same she said she said it was. To change to poplar and trees. Mary Lake is a pretty name to change to poplars to change she said it was to change to she said she thought it was to change to she said she she said it was. Mary Lake is a pretty name to change to poplars and to change she said she said it was.

Now then they then they have to have what after all is a difference to be left alone. Nobody needs to be around and gathering the milk. If they have it here and nearly as if they also differently arranged chickens and to calve how do they need to be so sure sure and be certain that they have theirs there and the same. It is astonishing not to please.

Beginning with the poplars as seed. They grow fruit trees just as well. Beginning with the poplars as seed. Is there any difference between Nelson and a Brazilian admiral is there any difference between Nelson and a Brazilian admiral's son and where they chose it. Not as well as he did he is not only the eldest of five but the eldest of eight. In this way he absolutely has not only not but not gone. When they come to say they come and have spoken of an acquaintance with description in describing that there is no intention to distinguish between looking and looking. An acquaintance with description gives a very pleasant programme of fruit and some varieties of carnations. He quotes me. She does not like not only when but how. Not of him but of the time when there is no more relief from irresistible.

How can and how can he climb higher than a house if he can be at that time having had it be as much as that and certain. Never to mention more than never to mention more than that it was like a hat a cardinal can not have a stone hat not have a stone hat a hat and candlesticks of blue green when they are glass and small and a box made at all.

That pleases them and him.

Yes can be mentioned altogether.

Each one can be interested in at a time and added.

There is a difference between whether and leather there is more happening when no

134   *Gertrude Stein*

one needs to next to a need it for pansies. A watch kept in and there or all the time. Not a mother nor a step-mother but always after all when she did and after all when she did come to be called and they might if they came have it in three different kinds chickens ducks and geese.

Have it in three different kinds before that a sister and a brother and now when at first, at first makes it that they asked him and he said just farther it is a very fearful thing to cross the river Rhone when they might even when they might. They did the second time. The first time they did the second time. Might makes snuff might makes enough enough and snuff. It is very pleasant that a box a little box is just alike.

An acquaintance with description and and an acquaintance with description reconciled.

She is very happy and a farm. She is very happy and a farm. She is very happy and a farm. She is very happy and a farm. She is very happy and a farm.

In and sight if the once and before that could be a hearing heard at most. Might it be needed like it. He can be said if when it might that like it by now. Could he have had a had and have and had a hat. Very every time they were killed for their father. Their father might be their mother. Their mother might be that it might be in their and unison. Unison is not disturbed for their and for their and for their it can be that although they they might if she was here and he was there spoken to by that not alone by slow or snow not alone by snow or slow slowly and snow comes now not by having that it was different from a hollyhock by a chance. He did indeed indeed and might after all his aunt and if she were to be by by and by by and by with the one, they could very often need to select theirs in place. Let it be that his brother was killed altogether his father not his father his mother not his mother the children of his brother and he he was deafened by that and not altogether. He need he need he need he need he need to not to need to be what if it were differently Perrette and Perrine, that makes it said. Safe is when after all they could eat.

Thank you for a description and would have hesitated to ask.

Did you see him fall. Not at all.

If two and two and she likes it and dew was it that it could be not wishing to be left. Not to be respected as it was not to be respected as it was not why it was and she left them and he said I do too and she said do not bother exactly and around they met met if not likely to be nearly where as if looking. This makes it take a place.

Nicely and seated makes it left again left and right makes it regular and because it was not when they wished. They often know that. There is no difference between she not being comfortable and she comfortable. Never again to be signed and resigned and acquaintance with description. If it were not to use we would choose. If we were not Jews we would choose if it were not to use we would choose. They can be as small as that and there reliability there as counted. Never to like it smaller and a lavender colour. It might make it added one in green. Not fortunately an alignment. Repeat relate and change three and four to two. This makes it more difficult than fluttering. Not to be argued about. Noon is for nooning.

Do you leave it to be mine and nicely. Out of eight there was one how many are there when there are very many.

Seven and two and nearly awake because snuff is useful in little boxes where there are put metal clippers and no snuff. Anybody can be reasonably satisfied with that exactly.

An Acquaintance with Description 135

She liked my description of aunt Fanny, she liked my description of hazel nuts she liked my description of the resemblance between pheasants and peacocks she liked my description of how that would be what was wanted. She liked to have them hear it if it was good not only for theirs but for ours and she would not mind it if they could be what they had at that time and easily no one is ever allowed allowed and aroused around and not the difference between the distance between Brazil and France and the difference between whether they made it be what they liked. It might be changed. They might be not at all easily often all arranged so that they would prefer where it actually is and now as pleases it pleases her to please when it can be fortunately not at all as it might be if they were certain that shells and shells did and did make flowers did and did and easily having examined who they had and when they came they thanked. Now can it be two and Tuesday, leaving it alone.

Leaving it alone. From this time on to borrow to borrow is to reply and to reply is to be useful attentively and might as well as might and might as well as might, might it being the same come to be having it for this and that precisely. An interval between when they had this as well when they had this as well. She said and says that when a higher and not a high hill has it as their left and right how can it be told favourably. It can and will. An acquaintance with description or it can and will.

Will it be that they like when they see why it has not as if when it came leaving that in that round and settled so that if it is doubled they might be wrong. Not left to it only by what is after all why they like and had it here. This may be otherwise known. If they are sold as they are sold we might as well but not only really not at all reliably placing if it is as it as it is at all very well very well to do so. Yesterday to say.

Describing where they went. Describing when it was like it. They did put a clock face on the telegraph pole.

Eagerly enough they looked to see the difference between a horse and two oxen and they looked eagerly enough to see the difference between poplars at a distance and walnut trees.

Every little while they made it at that time. Not meaning to have lost it when when it had gone away. They saved it in order that it might be had when it was accepted as a large quantity. Not in order to be kind. They like it fancifully. Might they be placed where they could see. If they were left where they were sent and could be by it when it is fastened and to explain explained that it was that as that had had been theirs too and nearly not while it needed it for it to be arranged by the putting it side by side for them, at least as they had not been very liked and liking that as much as if it had been leaving it near them and coming to have the key put not as now underneath but nearly under all the top so that if when it is not only that he would be releasing sheep releasing sheep they might not only be two who have themselves seated there. Not while it did. Two who have themselves seated there not while it did not come to be four in renown and not be settled to become the next who near and needed did anybody know the difference between their fairly seated and leaving it as seen. Very nearly wrongly so and to be sure and next next can be why they went why they went to stay not as if it was when it is might it be changed changed every day to theirs having if they went and to cross. Back is not why they have called it. She knows what they mean. An acquaintance with description is not earlier and later than they say. They say that they have been as it is why they could. To like it better. I will always describe it where it is at its widest and it will be very well done.

Would it do it any good to be so where they went. To be sure to be so when they leave it to them. And they might have theirs half of the time which is why once and one they make it be that they did not take it then and take it take it apart. Not in this case and would leave it for them to see. Sit is as well as if on top they might have been to change not if it is where where can be separated from while and when it is the same they exchange pleasing it as if very likely when it had not as if she said been heard.

Like and it was if a guinea hen was wild they needed it as well when they had been liked as much if they had need be thought to come as well and it did not. Next to need not be well as well as said need to be seeing it where it is where there is leaving it as very likely well and they might be two having having leaving leaving let it not let it not is nearly around and it did not like that because it was salty because it was salty, not after a very long after a little while after it was there a little while after it was there a little while and might it be theirs for themselves it might. What was it as it said not so what is it as it said and this is why they could be nearly finally theirs in their being nearly when they had it. It need not be so very much. Here I can see it. If it was above and below they could be seen letting it be theirs to think of well why should they when they will be as they were in there and by this with it for the rest they do not need it leaving what it is because if they announced announced readily by the time that it is nearer than that which is very well. Letting it be not leaving it in this way and recommending what they need for it. Letting it be let it alone let it alone and like it. They would never like to let it leave. Continue. They make a mistake it was not that and coming back to it. There is a great difference and when they like it there is a great difference and when they like it. There is a great difference and when they like it. Not taking it away. This is one way to believe their pieces. Very like the water.

There is a difference between the middle and both sides.

They will not be themselves aloud they heard in that with it to leave not when and left, excuse me. If not they wish it.

How can it be left as it will when they know that each one is in some place as if it came to come and leave it likely that it is exactly there. Very often we looked for them. So many ways of forgetting that this is there there where if left to leave it.

Is it likely if it went that it went around it. Is it likely if it did not go and it was in it so that if it was not there it was placed would it be divided. They liked it to be said. Very likely not. It was very encouraging to hear them do it. Not at first it did not at first it did not at first seem to be very likely to be what they would do, to be what they would do it is reasonable that it is more intelligent to see it but not if all at all having not lost it altogether by this time theirs might be easily just as well as if it were. They can be divided between themselves and the others and if they are not only because both sides and pleases but actually when they are identical and left alone it really is too much in a crisis.

There is no difference between what between and at a distance as there is no difference between what between what and at a distance no difference between between and at a distance there is no difference between what between between and at a distance. Next. There is no difference between between and and between at a distance there is no difference

An Acquaintance with Description   137

between at a distance between and what between there is no difference between what between and at a distance. Next. There is no difference between where and where it is just before never before never between never before never at a distance before, leaving before at a distance between there is no difference between having decided upon thirty, thirty what and having decided upon using both using both how, using both habitably. That makes it different that it is not seen from there.

Example and precept, sitting if in sitting they are there they must as if in crossing two at a time and not bound not bound to be used to as in lead lead to it from their having this in use not to be reaching leaving it as well they might be theirs to connect having to indeed now and and turned around if it were to be prepared as if when this is when it is to be and back need and they need leaving it with a change changed to be could it be remembered and left that it might commandingly so not if as it was said come and across they might if they were third and altogether once more felt and after it was not in place but and beside and a little change and this is if if it was when it was to study study could be could be should it have it round and as could be when there is little to be left when separated not all through when it is shorter than it could and and could not be used as so and it was not to be not when it was that length at length and never yet after all when when is doubtfully repeated in this letting it be as much as if could it be heard coming not in shawl and not in all and after very much after longer not very much shorter and held not very much as held to be coming how often has there been a white one where they could not think to see. It. It is not needing blue having artificially leaves and connecting as stems it is never theirs by right by right winding it later might make not so nearly nearly white and white and white which is just as naturally as every letter. This makes them say delighted. This makes them say delighted. To be liking liked like it like if like like to like like and often often where where is it. It is there just there where I am looking. Very clearly expressed.

Not to leave it be alone and looks like in the way and when it is not left to be themselves have it to say they made it come as if it would be leaving it as fast nicely. One this is to be that it is not here leave it for them by this with whom it is to nicely handle it with what is meant when it is not to be changed what I notice. It is not very nearly that it is not at all it when it is that in the leaving it leave it in not around they might have had it sent it not to come to be theirs when they leave and it was very likely that it had been in that first when it needs to mention how could there in there not so much as that when to be leading it not when it is in front and kept to be sure to be sure. Would it be almost what it is leaving leaving never needs it left because not white it is certainly better than here better than here there.

She would be there if it was very well said that it would be it is would be unsatisfactory it is would be it is would be unsatisfactory and find it from the things as it is done done has been has been it would as it would be is it as it would be unsatisfactory. Find it as it would be unsatisfactory. She said and as it would it it is as it would be as it is in that from this and as it is in this to be and is to be and is to be and is to be unsatisfactory. She said it would be as it is to be unsatisfactory. It is very easily certain that it could happen happen and to be would be would be and to be would be unsatisfactory. Even every thing like in and like and that. In every even like and thing and like and even in and every even in and like and that. There is no difference at all between paper and basket, this has nothing to do with fruit and soap, this has nothing to do with places and head this has nothing to do with their arrangements. Not to be with it in theirs in hand and now. Now it is open open and liked liked and to-morrow to-morrow when then, the Saone.

Would it be nearly as certain that they would like to have theirs be as much as if when they did by this time if they did make it. Not to mention what it was when they were altogether part of it because because allowing because allowing it to be for this reason leaving it aloud and much of it and never to be what it was when it was opened and very nearly very little ones and as much more as when it was to be sure to be sure erected erected to make islands having it not only that it was sold once and they made it be because of that over and under over and under makes it be nearly that if spoken to spoken of spoken of birds birds and very nearly grass in their and to be sure leaving it as an announcement and readily readily makes it be in tufts and when there are two and when there are two and once more it was necessary to buy a piece of ground in order to plant upon it one hundred poplars and to precisely understand plant upon it one hundred poplars and to precisely understand moreover not to be exactly and precisely dated when it is not only to be purchased but also to be purchased planted and very certainly absolutely designed as one hundred poplars when in any event not only having been attached to that but very often very favourably needed needed and needing using using is never adaptable using had advanced as by and by developed because indeed they might and they might not, because once at once and as this was to be new it was also very nearly needed now. One more observation. It does not need need and necessarily and necessarily and very well understood. And now leave it to be what was as much interrupted like why is it to be looked looked for it now when it is not altogether where it was where is it. An acquaintance with description and not very good. They planted theirs and have it as it might so that if they and many wider many wider and as if it could not be as a mistake to be in certain certain certain certain that then there there is as not as a mound not as a not as a not as a failing failing that if all at once at once at least and remaining not in right in right in right as if with that and sound sound in a leaf a leaf to be who can be nearly where it was when it was not which needed while it did, telling it as sound as soundly as not by that time to be and when to copy copy which copy which is which is what they could if it could not be in change in change for this at once at once is never nearly why they did not let it be at best at best is what is not when it was change and changed to rest, rest at most thank you. Not an acquaintance with not only with and only with description and only with with it. Is it and and an account of it.

Always wait along never wait so long always wait along always wait along never wait so long never wait as long always wait along always wait along never wait so long never wait so long always wait along always wait as long always wait along never wait so long always wait along. Not to believe it because not to believe it because not to believe that it is here. Come over here now. Left and right white and red and never to be along at all not at all when it is to be nearly left as it was by the time when it shall be so well so well allowed allowed and allowed and leaving it all to that when it is might have been not a little never and a little at all by the time that it is where there is leave it too long have it. Having left it there until there was what seemed to be a little at once like the rest like the rest fairly well finally to be in and in might it have that in change leaving not it not it at last at last differs from the leaving having having never can there not by this about in the way from never there in is they used find it can there is looking at in in comes to let and very well it was not why they did consider it not at all one way.

To find it there yes put it there yes to put it there if to put it there by which not it not it now to see it as it and very adapted to partly leave it there to partly not to partly not put it there it might if a little bit when it is in a corner for the morning so that not to allow allowable around when it is separately not separate to the shore, can a river have a shore or can a little little more before can it be interrupted and not once or twice when too might two be only left to throw it away away from that which was outlined, it was and if wish to wish to a paving it with that. Now to have it in their way when they have it as they will be that they do not mind it.

Why and why often and why often when it is not by the time that there is much much as much as said as said as will because of this and thinning of it out and in this is this that the left is sent by this around and ground and not to leave it in this might it be the change of that to theirs theirs have this leave it very nearly place and might it if it not in this pleased if this when is it in their leave as not all of it can be in this in theirs and interchange in also not to change and china can be sought in this in places in this and places places from this two and uneasy which is why that it must be shown as that in the next never asked to as coming in delight and relight when this is that in theirs left it to be not for this in change near neighbour coming in the last and finding it as can it be that it is right and left so that it is for this and with theirs obligation nearly by this in the instance that it is arranged for that in the most and believe in half and kindly kindly give it to them and away and can it be in theirs and for remaining can and can not left to be in so much as it is in theirs and added not by this which is relieved by none and none to add it more than is not for this openly so seen can in and likely leaving it so nearly with it in this case can find bequeath and needed in regularly to that in those and called and layer of that this below which send sent to the are there why is it as addressed left it as when as or that come to the last which is for that not finally incased but surely where as there is that in an allowed now this and here there most come to be supplied with the whole and share and this and leaves and why and could and some and nestles and no much and come come in and that beside the noise and leave and trust and how to. Following it altogether. She it might be come. Not how is it.

I understand that you do not do much in winter with your land.

Leaving it out when this is seen in the nearest afternoon to there having had left there that is not to do that which is might and might it be and for this as their even left it to be at namely why this is for them considerably liking and like then when it could be after letting and distributed. Now again named whenever it is to that beside by and by can if in the central and why it is not alone nor should it come to theirs be advised leave when shall it reduce to this coming can leave where in the not to be altogether where it is placed to be divided between fish and moths. There to be divided there to be divided divided between find and find out find it in nearly to be sure and more easily if named. When one is what is what is it then it is easier when it is when it is in their name. Leaving out having had it now. They might be while they can if it is can it and they no doubt can leave it leave it at

140   *Gertrude Stein*

that. There is every day every day every day to be sure to be sure that they can go and have to have very well I thank you. Leave out and account leave it out and account account not to be always to be said that it was there that it was there that it was in there not in there but like in there as it not in there when it was begun begun to be left and left not in that allowance but in that in spite of it being that it was what they could in arrange like it and some to some to some some who have not best at all why not as much as after a while not theirs very well. Remembering everything as seen to like it only is it that it should should come to be what is it when it is no longer theirs at all. To know why we why can it be leave it to be three. There can always be a difference.

If she works then he works but if she reads then he pleads.

If she does knit and he does count how many are then in it. Five in each but unverified and beside beside unverified too and a market two and well left beside the pressure pressure of an earring.

Never deriding anything and then it was not only at a distance but in the distance that it can be many makes it come to be so now. That is not to what it does not have it so to speak that is and said consider it to be theirs aloud.

When it was left. Water was running as large as two fists eighteen. What is when it is of that to be not green and wheat but green and why and green and it can have it to be that it is a third the next of that which when the come for it too leave why which where they announce amuse leave it for in that way come should it have the never changing most now and then in as not have seen the having thought of three as two to be sure from that where they they might could it be curtain and hat not as much as net not only if it were to be wrapped in and for the which it was by this to come to that it is now known. Excuse me.

To change from what was what to that.

Everything that must be as a bed or hedge must when it is to be had where it was must be what is left to be theirs as they wish come to be left when it is found and further could be decided that it was not nearly an arrangement that they had if this was theirs as if it were to be not at least and negligent and so to say so to find it naturally where it was to be if there it was does it really have as much when it is not as much and coming to be not at all nearer nearer than it is to it. Thank you for having been so kind.

There he said he had said that it was where there it was and after all nobody should touch it.

Not more than seldom not more than winning not any having this as that and for it in leaving that is what is when it is at the end of the house which is when it is not an end and it does not look differently because they have seen it otherwise it would look differently because I had seen it otherwise it would look otherwise it would be it would be it would be otherwise it otherwise if it is not not what is it every little one larger larger and so much smaller when there is no difference between a white carnation and a white lily both are white when they are here when they are here when they are when they are here in this case not as well not as well long as well charcoal as well water as well leaving as well lambs as well why and when with as well leave as well but as but as well why as well a while as well with what as well the piece as well as if as well three more to four as well and as well as well as as well as well as well when if in as and well and see in to be some to cause could in there be from the one that

An Acquaintance with Description   141

can be in there by the coming to this to be that it is by that in there with it for in in could leave no more this by for it come to be not while it is shall be come to this if it can leave it in this coming talking be as well as the kind at first should left that it was all could can it as rest the rest of it to be that it is not there theirs as it is should the stand fall at once what is it.

That is one way of that to be new nicely see and seen come come to be alike. We are very grateful that it is so large.

Would anybody be allowed would anybody be allowed to come to ask to have it sent in winter.

This is not theirs to be to be to be to be very much very much left as if as if very well knew and known that it should not be again and again and in again and in again and again and again and in again. Peaches should always be eaten over more over as if strawberries as if papers as if printed papers as printed and papers as if printed and papers as if printed and papers and wool as if printed and papers and peaches as if printed and papers and wool as if printed and papers peaches should always be eaten as if as if papers as if printed and papers as if strawberries as if as if peaches and papers as if as if as if as if papers as if peaches and papers as if printed papers and wool and strawberries and peaches as if papers as if printed papers as if.

Always the same.

Not as to delight.

An acquaintance with description.

If it is to have the leaving as an obligation to be there and come to to the rest that if there is if there is the next to have it leave to to be in that way four three one leaving it around as it might indeed have it that they not as if it were in opposite around let it might and might be considered as two three three there many there how many there how many three two one leaving it as much behind behind to mind letting letting all in theirs for that most when makes what is why it was as much as much for the having having to be interrupted shall it shall it have the name when there is that in two made which is much the more than theirs for that now leaving it in this to be to be sure let it coming coming to have it given given in place of theirs to have it can it be and fairly well at most in that which which when where and light and come to last last and might and might it be in this and change get it is it not what in their might it come to have it in this place it could it be that it is when it when it is in theirs to place and to say need it and it was not only why it came to left and calling this is in the way of any other one which is not only why they left they did not have it to fit in when it was that the two were two were to make four places and a little below to say so if it must be just their in that complete why is it only when it is not only is it is in that increase. There can be no difference between a circus a mason and a mechanic between a horse and cooking a blacksmith and his brother and his places altogether and an electrician. In every other way I am disappointed. Yes when it is not only this and having been not prepared to be so much and wonder they had it and they changed it and they made it be very nearly might it be what is it when it is not after all very little of a having not seen it when it came.

It is not well placed if before they had it there and now they put it there and will they place it there and could it be what it was when it might. It is very nearly intended to be a basket made over.

142   *Gertrude Stein*

They might do.

If it after all was not what was it when it came and it might do. When could it leave it in this way and say it for this was to be and like it all thank you to say. They went to see it.

Again Albert again write to Albert again basket again changed to have it again have it basket again again as again as a change again basket again basket again it is again as a change again as a basket again at again larger again as many again as a basket again have it a basket again larger again is it again it is it again a basket again as larger again a basket again get it again is it again a basket again it is.

It is is it. A basket.

Basket it is is it.

Very nearly fairly pleased.

Which is why it is that it is looking is it in it as it it is as it is is it as it is there.

There it is.

There is always some difference between nine o'clock and eight o'clock.

An acquaintance with description.

There is an arrangement as berries. There is also an arrangement as loop holes. There is also an arrangement as distance. There is also an arrangement as by the way. There is also an arrangement as at first. There is also an arrangement as to be. There is also an arrangement as disappointed. There is also an arrangement as why and let. There is also an arrangement of poplars that give a great deal of pleasure. There is also an arrangement that it can be twice chosen. There is also an arrangement which is advantageous.

Never be left to be that it can have to be if it could leave it all let it be mine while it came shall it have that to see come again like it while it is much to be relied upon as yet and while and awhile and while and it is not that but what if it is by the breaking of it in the place of that nearly by changing that to make it have it be nearly coming as if there is not more than it could be theirs so much not by that time there is between needing needing not by that and if it is in let it let it in light and might it be very well said that if a cloud is light one could read by it. What can be after all the difference between candles and electricity, they go out one after the other they come one one after the other they go on together. Let it be known. It is.

Not to think of anything which is not what is at least when poplars come to have to be a very little bridge to see at any way if not before when it is well to have a rain bow let alone a wire place and met it. Not easily there chance. After all and met it not easily there chance. An instance of it as a distance from the come to come and have it had and with it with and leave it let leave it as it must be while then for this as it is not for this for this come to be in their choice come to be this is in an angle if it comes come let it with some not perch come left that not as a very good half to help let it let is is let to be there singular relieve it with it for the not there when why cinnamon and come to have it that it is as a district describe while white not so much as if at first a lake as come to come to pride where fair that it is not so have it from the end to end alright.

Six is more than four how many to a door, who can be so late to see if they wait to be to see if it can to have to meet if it does which is as were and left to right and with it as if when it fell so that he was where it could be and in that as could it by the trace of left and right

An Acquaintance with Description   143

come to the having as and stands that is as bale that is as hay that is as then that is as if letting be it so much care this to then if for and in case fasten and in most fasten and very likely why it was when it was if they had not had it come to be remembering that to run up hill that to run up hill that to run up hill for the heard it come to be. An actual reasonable time. No one must be very lively about it. It is not at all necessary that it is after this so much as much as much way much for much to much in much left much then much there much those this that the under left might join come leaf and left as if it were not not not not not white.

Anybody could be one. One one one one.

This time not uneasily.

An acquaintance with description above all an acquaintance with description above an acquaintance with description above all an acquaintance with description above an acquaintance with description and above and above an acquaintance with description and an acquaintance with description. Please and an acquaintance with description please an acquaintance with description please an acquaintance with description.

They must be as well as ever to be had to be it when they can if it must as well as if and that is what it can be now that it is if in plainly as much as if what is not come to be had if when it is not that if it is not to have to own and then there scare and scarce and this that in that might which can for most where with in much come to be that this with it left to make to me to mention to the same let if that which in candied let it mean that if then where there this is not that now which is when it is left come to this there come have to be not reconsidered. It meant that it was not kept up.

If if and this is wild from this to the neatness of there being larger left and with it could it might if it not if it as lead it lead it there and incorrectly which is at this time. Once more if refused. Make make it left it with with with not with there may may may not be there though though though if left and the same not only had but will have once more having let it fall altogether.

If in way that should left come by it it not must can near to naturally why do it because it is a pleasure.

What you want to do.

What you want to do.

What you want to do.

Left it what you want to do.

Left it what you want to do.

The regular if all much not could lean well settled plus return more than be lighter for that here.

Very well not in might to ran made with it coat for is need banding when is it sense and send not is it come can for this sure that it change makes it always have the had it could must lean leaning as mine there are in are plain plan must it be trees with be find not lying for this time in and a middle while it is very likely there it is what when not come to this walnut tree if you know that walnut can grow. Say so.

The next which and which to say is how many trees are there in it and what are their ages and their sizes. Who has been counting at a distance. An acquaintance with description is to be used again and again.

144   *Gertrude Stein*

And acquaintance with description is to be used again and again. And acquaintance with description is to be used again and again. Always begin an acquaintance with description to be used again and again.

A once in a way makes it at once in a way makes it at once makes it at once once in away makes it at once in a way makes it at once in away. After this it is left that if it is as wide as less than that as it is as wide as less than that it is as wide as less than that. Never happen to have been in even evenly never to have been in even never to have been in even never even to have happen never to have happen to even to have even have been never even to have happen to have been even as for the point let should not been more as it caught is not the name very easily.

How can there very well be a bell as bell upon as hunting upon as hunting had as there is upon a hunting dog there is.

Pass paper pass please pass pass trees pass trees please pass please pass please pass please as paper as pass as trees. Very likely very nearly likely nearly likely very. Nearly likely very. Nearly very. It is very easy to like to like to pass very likely it is very near nearly to like to pass grass. Farmers or do it. Farmers or do it no one should mix what is heard with what is seen. No one should mix seen and heard. In this way. In this way. Leaves leave it. In this way. Leaves in this way leaves leave it in this way leaves in this way leaves in this way. Not at all to like as alike not at all as this way not trouble some in this way not in this way in this way to have and did it in this way. Different, after having seen one having seen some having seen some. Having seen some. Not having between not having between as long as a field not having between not having seen between as long as a field not having between.

The right was down on the side of the road and the left was on the road. The left was on the road and the right was down on the side of the road. The right was down at the side of the road and the left was on the road. The left was on the road and the right was down by the side of the road.

Let it be for them to know.

Not as much as they could say.

When it is where they have been.

Not to be too much to see that it is so.

There when did it leave to have to come to have given, how did it leave it come to there there there more no. No and acknowledge.

Oh yes of course below.

Because she is because she is Julia because she is Julia because she is and English Julia and Julia Ford.

Never to have been a two one one two one one never to have been a two one one.

To not be surprised if it should rain.

They are to not be surprised if it should rain.

They are to not be surprised if it should rain. There is a difference between rain wind and paper. What is the difference between rain wind and paper. There is a difference between rain wind and paper.

After a little while there is a difference between rain and wind. After a little while there is a difference between wind rain and wind rain and paper and between rain wind and

An Acquaintance with Description   145

paper and there is after a while there is a difference between rain wind and paper. Thank you very much as much as very much thank you very much as very much as much there is thank you very much there is a difference after a while there is a difference between rain wind and paper thank you very much there is a difference between rain wind and paper thank you very much thank you as much. Let it be that they came there. It was quite as if it was not only not to be not only not to be satisfactory but to be perfectly satisfactory satisfactory satisfactory.

Very well to do it to it to it very well to do it to it to it very well to do it to it very well to do it to it very well to do it to it very well. Why do very small very small marshes very small marshes give pleasure very small marshes give pleasure very small marshes.

Little pieces of that have been where that has made while that is there need it as it can be said to be more and more and more and more and more to be sure come to be what is it for the next and to be sure more and as it is as when they need to be their with their to their be there like might it be come to be mine come to be next when if if it is not might when for spare and let in that come to come with as need it for the have to be nicely near if they consider an acre an acre an acre an acre like much seem when if this let in sign and side two sent which which is a relief if it is sure sure sure surely now how there is a difference in climbing a hill with or without climbing a hill with or without climbing a hill.

Could be a little marsh.

Promise not to be so yet if this is so and this is more and when it is as it was for them if it can and is to be left it alone so that it can if when if it is by that who in that case and can and it is as if it is as if it is as it was to them to them to them to if it was as if it was to them to them and let it come to this for this for this let it as if as if in spite and mean to share let it be come to be beside with them in that in that and could and have and did and like and like and why and in and must and do in do and do leave do leave do leave not without that with with come come come to to to be sure where if if when is when is it when is it all not this to be there and sent when if should have come to be spoken like like like it is alike alike for it is because it is used to it.

There made a mistake.

Do be like it for that which is why when it is not as if in their being made for that in their being to being made to be what is it not as like as if they had had to be when is it that if they could have it be which is as well. He is very certain to be sure to be sure to be sure to be sure not to be sure not to be sure not to be sure to not to be sure to be sure to be sure not to be sure not to be sure not to be sure not to be sure to be sure. Not to be sure. Let it be when it is mine to be sure let it be when it is mine when it is mine let it be to be sure when it is mine to be sure let it be let it be let it be to be sure let it be to be sure when it is mine to be sure let it to be sure when it is mine let it be to be sure let it be to be sure to be sure let it be to be sure let it be to be sure let it be to be sure let it be to be sure to be sure let it be to be sure let it be to be sure let it be to be sure let it be mine to be sure let it be to be sure to be mine to be sure to be mine to be sure to be mine let it be to be mine let it be to be sure to be mine to be sure let it be to be mine let it be to be sure let it be to be sure to be sure let it to be sure mine to be sure let it be mine to let it be to be sure to let it be mine when to be sure when to be sure to let it to be sure to be mine.

146   *Gertrude Stein*

Well there there there very well very well there there there there well there well there there well there and easily counted there there counted easily there there there counted there there there there. Everybody knows everybody knows everybody knows that there there they are easily counted there there there there they are easily there there they are easily counted. Not easily counted as easily seen in between as easily counted not as easily seen counted easily seen there there there easily counted in between as easily seen there. There is no use explaining that melons can be used when melons can be used when melons can be used yellow melons can be used. That if as it might be left to be that if they are as corn as many as corn as many as many as corn as seen as many as corn as seen. There has come a decision that everything and named.

Much as much as if to to be remember that it is to be remember much as much as if to be as much as much as if to be remember that as much as much as if to be remember that as much as much as much as much as if to be remember that as much as much as much as much as much as much as if to be remember that as much as much as much as much as much as much as much as if to be remember that as if to be as much as much as much as much as much as if to remember that as if to be to be as if to remember that as if to be as much as if to be as much as to remember as much as if to be as much as remember as much as if to be as if to be remember as if as much with wide with wide as much as if to be remember if as much as if as to be as if as much as if to be as much as if as wide as much as if to be to remember as if to be to remember as much to remember as if as much to be as wide as if to be as much. Very naturally they can be if is when last in for be by beside made is in can for that in light and need and made made why can fit this in this and that there leave come easily need why make it be once again to that which is why they can have both grapes and apples and pears. That is might it if when is it in and at a time by which by which by which by which it is very much inclined inclined to inclination which is seized that makes it naturally believe be like and to have it faster than at first. We thought not at all. Go might it be all coming which is why which is why which is which is which is which is which is a very nearly certain certainly letting and let it much as it does when the moon rises. It is very pleasant to see the moon in daylight.

It was easy to be sure that it looked so far away pansy as the let it be as much which is when it is might be so much as much further which which very wide very well and very not and mount. Pansy. Not having counted the pansies it is impossible to say just how many pansies are in it. Very much let it be last which having it be worn and where can it be if it can be that there is no difference between ridges and between ridges. There is a difference between ridges and between ridges and between there is a difference between there there and ridges between there there there and ridges there is a difference between there there there there and ridges there is a difference between no difference between pansies and there between pansies and there between not between not telling between not telling the difference between ridges there there there pansies there there there difference there between difference distance there there between distance difference ridges there there there there distance between and very place as much as place as much as place as much how many trees are there place as much as nectarines nectarines is a mixture of vineyard peaches and counted plums and careful very careful very careful of pears. This makes pansies one time

An Acquaintance with Description   147

at one time at one time pansies not pansies at one time let it at one time two rosy on two rosy in two in two rosy in at one time in and it is true the little pieces are where they are and those that are are a pair a pair of all around it.

An acquaintance with description asking an acquaintance with description asking for an acquaintance with description. All around it asking for an acquaintance with description.

It is very remarkable. Not that. It is very remarkable that that this is after it has been not only that it is when would it be laughed laughed at and about about to do about to do so and about about what where it is by whom by whose after all by whose having had which it for this as this is in a stream a stream can wash celery celery to be sure there there to be certain to be certain there there cultivate to be most to be most and very to be most most which is moistened by their their arranging wool wool which when very much in the meantime greatly greatly influenced by as much as if in this case in each case and arrangement. Let it be not for this when when is it it is not fortunately that they were understood that the same renting relenting buying rebuying referring referring which is it that is not why then and very much an advantage. The situation in respect to what is seen when there is letting it be carefully to-day. It was not not likely that that it was was to be left to them to decide. Let us unify four things principally and pansies, very reasonably and rightly, come to be as much theirs as it was, and left to be not only thirty but thirty trees.

Do not do not what climb the hills hills which are hills and hills which are hills which are strawberry plants and strawberry plants and in and in that when there is none noon there is should shall and might might be an eraser. Very nearly what they did to-day. Should shall be in case of and never be by this this that leave not with this look again.

Find as much.

Not as to bird this year. Let to this why not if it is not as where that is undoubtedly not from to be that this now touch when leaving leaving lay lane much at behold behold for let this inches inches make make please why they can. What happened was this a bee a wasp which tried when there believe behind make that not before when in this into a bank which is made of shrubs which do not grow in California.

Like this.

Once two three.

Once two three again two three two three.

How do you do happily happily with that happily with that. There is a difference between twice one one and leaving it be chosen that they do not any of them always like that. Not only if this is theirs too to have it be that it can send and consent and finally letting letting that if when after that it should be not only recalled but estimated not in case and care for that to be as much as much as much to be sure leaving leaving it for this at once nearly by all. All of it at one time easily.

Might it be that it can be that it can be might it be that it can be that it can be might it be that that it can be might it be that might it be that it can be might it be that it can be might it be that it can be might it be that it can be might it be that that it can be might it be that it can be might it be might it be that might it that it might be might it be that it can be. Very many who have come very many who have come very many who have come who have come very many who have come very many who have come very many who have come. There is to be

148   *Gertrude Stein*

sure what is there to be sure what there is to be sure that there is what is what is there to be sure there is what there is to be sure. They might be not might be be seated might be not might not might be not might not might be seated not might be not might be not might be not be seated not be seated not might be not might be seated might be not might not might not might not be seated might be. Leading theirs to this and sown sown makes which when when then an indicative nearly an indirectly as satisfied for that as immediately near and lessen too be what is never with it as in minding fairly should it be the carefully resting and left which is it that that let it have it to be fall of the year how is it if the minding minding to be heard let it alone after much leaving so very much to them to them in this how to be sure surely nearly very very well welcome and for that for that. Any one can know that a house which when when it it was was placed having having having at that distance distance was not not by that which is what is what is it let it be while at one time. In this way a very large house looks small and so that is true two roofs that is true, not two to three that that is true that is true not why not why not why not why that is true not why that is true it is why must it be what must it be after this is heard heard heard, the daughters can cannot go.

Nevertheless if there is distress and they planted two hundred more when it was certainly not what was needed trees not what what was needed vines not what was needed places and not what was needed and now not what was needed and nearly not what was needed and not what was needed and so not what was needed very well in exchange. Did her brother if he was twenty-five years old was he did he like to leave it here. If her sister who was seventeen years old did she need to be left to be here need to be left to be here need to be left need to be left to be here and if her mother who had been sixteen years or a widow need to be left to be here and if she needed to be left to be here and it was not to be undoubtedly that it was not to be undoubtedly that it was not to be not to be needed to be left to be here. It is certainly very much better that if that would that to be that when and might and make it and this that and that to be with to be with that to be with that to be with to be with that to be with that to be with to be with that very much as if when not and nearly to be nearly which with that there are might to be not for this not because not not because this this and water with with and fruit in in as much and left let it be carried. They might be indifferent. Need it to be left to be their own. With it for them in as much as while while at last neither with nor by and when it is in no way as an estimation which can which can place pleases and colouring collected could it be that they had been waiting. She was very nearly easily seated. Like and like it. Not can it with much left to them now. That which is suited to irresistible irresistibly be very likely need needing needless and needed needed and needed and needed and needed and needed now and now and now and needed needed there is there is there is there is there is there there there will they will they will they hearing made easily made made made come to be making to be made very who is under very well very well. We said the elder he said who is under very well the who is very well who is very well who is very well very well who is under the very who is under the very well the elder who is very well the under the very well. Having five white roses and one having three white roses and very likely two of them were mislaid. Not is to be mean to be to be to be very necessarily that after that after that then and not as well as October after November. Even a wind can be must be could be that and were were not not to come let it be what is not as to a place

An Acquaintance with Description 149

have this. It never could be nearly when to be when to be when to be would they care to see this now as candles. This now as candles this now as fruit and this now as this now as this now as this now as this now as this.

There to be like alike in here to be like it thank you very much as when do not when do not do more than it is prepare for this and and come to this to the let it shall for this come to this not as much as if letting in in to not nor can it have to be nearly in this come to be in considerable, if it was not for this at that time come to be sure to will and leave and leave and in as if and in are to be come to be in liking let it not when can this and call seen for his and surely to compare it let it not to be near than nearer than this is now what is it come in to when it is not left and left and fairly not to be in when come to be mine. There is when it can to be sure which is left in liking when nearly near come with it welcome for this use and used and very well should it be letting it come to this this this this half of it half of the time they know and now can it be left to them bread and chance to be which is with pears and not to let it come that is when if not coming to in them shut if not as it must at all come to be did it not not to not only left it there. Having watched a further than it is beside. This makes it not which is it nearly nearly never had to be left to them how do they know the difference between bulls and vines and pears and houses and leaves and hares and houses and theirs and by the time it was to be near nearly nearly there there there there can it there there there was it that it was not only in as much as much as not as not at all. It is very easy easily to know to know to do so do so to so so to wish wish wish leave it to need need in case of this which one two cows one two sheep one two ducks one two trees one two not one two not one two not one two not one two not not at once one two one one two not one two one one one two. One two.

Description from the way to have been at the time if not to be certain that it is left to be fallen down there and if it had been then the terrace and it is not by reason of their not only allowed but nevertheless changing not because their nearly having it be like after all shall and by this time. Very readily see see that from the terrace if there is a flooring flooring fixed fixed it so nearly at a while from distance come to be with it in hand. Looking at it last have hand and share. Three plans not three not found there not not much at a time it is easier to rent than to buy than to rent than to buy.

One at a time a meadow at a time a distance at a time and half a house a house at a time and and at a time and then at a time and there there at a time. Who has who had who has who held held it in pieces of theirs beside.

Let leave leant learn line let it make it be it have have have here and might might it try try it try not it as come to be in where they might do it too mix which come there leave and allowance allowance handle handle they make which is it as as likely very likely to be or sure and feeling and faintly faintly there make a mistake useful need a glance shall it be near them the same at once.

There is a great difference between people and places.

Once again have them too all the time might and while to be sure plainly as will not can for this as be shall kind and there. When is it.

When is it that they might see them.

One at a time and a peculiarity of interchanging need it be this to-day to-day clearly which is might it be when if reasonable and liking meaning fortunately exchange by wishes left alone nearly and coming very well to prepare bread.

Bread.

Come to that come to that come to that come to that.

Might it be around. Come to that. Full and feel this place eight days fourteen days really days why will days for the days it need it needed it needed braid it needed braid it needed it is not sound it needed it needed if it needed soldered it needed with it it needed could if it needed with with it with it with it with it with it it with it which is if the difference if this which soldered which which if be and bear and break and be and bear and be and share it find and not at all either not much not as much feel it white make it last.

It is very easy to cook bread in a communal oven. Why because it is prepared in a basket and easily being fluid it remains in place on a pale and the oven being very nearly stone it is longer heated than it was. An hour two an hour too and hour an hour and a half not as very not by the way in standing. Not an acquaintance not an acquaintance with not an acquaintance with description not an acquaintance with with description not an acquaintance with not an acquaintance with description.

Now be by the way. Ellis now be now be by now be by the way Ellis now need now be now be now be now by the way Ellis now be now be now need now be now by now be now be now by the way.

Now Ellis.

Now be now by the way.

To know.

What is there in difference which is what is when it is there most. Like it like it like it for them to them like it very much by which they went.

Fellow follow for fell feel for likely by a stretch of time time to be mostly and usual usually they make make which in strangely let it very likely be which is when there is in January to be there. Who makes might it mountains.

An acquaintance with then with description and leaving which it matters matters very much to them. An acquaintance with description. With then.

Ellis with then.

An acquaintance with their an acquaintance with description which may be which may be pleased and pressed as planted planted makes it be nearly there as choosing choosing and losing who knows. Can we be see. An acquaintance with description nearly very nearly.

Let it be not nearly five which follow cows which follow cows sheep which follow cows let it be not nearly which follow cows sheep. That is one thing. Let it be which when when not for this is like that to theirs allow come satisfaction remount and more over let this come to be to see might it have should it now come this let it for them must it for near now nearly. This is at one time. There is just as much letting it be when is it not to have been nicely recommenced and a lake. Very frequently there is no sunshine very frequently even then it is not very cold even then. Now and now and now roses. Very white and roses very pretty very pretty very pretty large very pretty large very pretty large very pretty roses very pretty very pretty very pretty very pretty very pretty as very pretty roses very pretty large very pretty very pretty very pretty large very pretty. Some some some he did not like to hear it said to him some some some some he did not like to hear it said to him that in place of then to then to then and as in place twenty as in place now could it after which is letting letting letting. A fish where hare where straw where apples where there there any day a way away and kindly. She preferred to have it named after he had he had he had she must five is five so often as often as often one as often, having half and nearly Jenny too, too two two. Jenny is a drop. This is clear clearly. You do leave it here here here here Chambery.

Look up look her up look her up look her up look her look her look her look her up and down. Mr. Pernollet does not supply it yet Mrs. Press does not express lady fingers which are here she was very likely to be really two at most Mr. Baird Mr. Baird makes it better to do so if he likes it which is what what is it it is what very much makes theirs start to finish Mrs. Father has a daughter they do they know they know they do they do they do. Mrs. Middle has a husband really two and two really freshly really freshly freshly really she really very really very very come too, Mr. Bourg is now at peace if he goes if he goes if he goes, can two one of them older and the sister of his mother which is why his wife was is leave it to him, not now that is why liking by it soon. Never to tell well.

What is the difference between a park and a field.

When is a meadow under water when it is a marsh and after which is higher there is always something not might not after this very which is that.

Has it been to be.

If it is when she.

Let it can it be.

If you can and three.

If you see the mountain clearly it means that it will be rainy if you see the mountain it means that it will not be rainy if you see the mountain clearly if you can see the mountain clearly it means that it will not be rainy if you can see the mountain clearly it means it will be rainy if you see the mountain clearly it means that it will be rainy. After this they went to be nearly four nearly five nearly after this they went to be nearly five nearly five nearly four nearly, after this they went away nearly five nearly after this they went away.

Having stopped to gather butter butter can be made to fruiten fruiten can be made to butter having nearly having made to butter having made to fruiten having made to butter fruiten having made to nearly having made to butter fruiten.

Leave which is mine nearly always after it has been the contrary the country nearly which is mine which has been the country which has been the contrary nearly which has been nearly which is mine the country. Leaves which is mine.

Needless to say that it is very needless to say that it is in every way a pleasant month of October as to weather.

There can be flower too flour too flower too there can be corn flour too when there is this and more. There can be this and too when there is corn and too there can be flour too corn flour and this and too. What is the difference between them and grapes grapes are sweeter, what is not what is not ivy what not and ivy which is join and Paulette. Paul and Paulette which is elder older white and next older elder which is left to be now. Does anybody suggest suggest that he can find can find a house with that with that when could eight brothers and their sisters work harder and how. How and how. Could they work harder and

152   *Gertrude Stein*

how how and how. They kneel knee can it be and see see sat which which is when is this every in the can there make which is why this will this cake if eggs are purchased. Leave it for them to them with them in them and then then like it for its use when this can be nicely left to come to which very little which is not their likely why can it be claimed at once. To like it. Therese can be compared to Therese can be compared to Therese can be compared, very likely very likely which is why it is with that. It is very well very well well enough come to this. Helen has rounder sounder found her found her found her. Think then could it be trout. Trout how. Very likely. Not now not all.

It must be in this little way of placing everything that they believe them it must be as if it is when that it is not as when as when believe it for this which makes nicely not in with and for them this with and for them to be certainly let it be not for this in instance. First they made what is what is let it let it need to be what is meant and unexpectedly have them be theirs. Let us imagine what they do spy what they do spy what they do do what they do with with with spy with spy with with with in what they do. A place which makes when it is not only as high as which can be two see, under like it make and for which is which is why they have to be in pleasing let it be nicely that four houses are mentioned. Four houses are mentioned. Four houses are mentioned. Four houses are mentioned. One for one for one for one for one after that three which may be and not needing it now they cannot them and not needing it now they cannot them and two at once two at once two at once more two at once more more more more two two two more two at once and one to one and to one one and to one to one to one one, have can have one which when a duck two cries makes cannot cannot one can cannot can one can one one, two two which two and one which one. Georgie would like a letter. Not about it. But rather for pleasure. To be sure to be having could it leave it for this might a lieutenant be what is after after all after all small small small after all nicely in decide decide train and nearly which, after this while needs to needs to to needs to needs needs to this next fall as if if water flowing flowing with no flow flowing with no flow flowing need cows cows be fruit and fruit be mentioned mentioned moon as likely as if to intend let it not have it have it in this come it come it and committee and after all never having returned an answer as to the name of that that let it be not to be when to be then to be Xenobie. It is very surprising that a young girl about to be certain that one preparation is better than another is named Marie.

An Acquaintance with Description   153

154   *Gertrude Stein*

WORKS CITED

Primary Sources

Correspondence of Gertrude Stein, 1929 to 1946, 1952. Papers of Robert Graves: Correspondence (arranged by correspondent). St John's College Library, University of Oxford. GB 473 RG/J/STEIN.

Laura (Riding) Jackson and Schuyler B. Jackson collection, #4608. Division of Rare and Manuscript Collections, Cornell University Library.

Gertrude Stein and Alice B. Toklas Papers, Yale Collection of American Literature. Beinecke Rare Book and Manuscript Library, Yale University.

Secondary Sources

Baker, Deborah. *In Extremis: The Life of Laura Riding*. Grove Press, 1993.

Burns, Edward, editor. *The Letters of Gertrude Stein and Carl Van Vechten, 1913–1946*. Columbia University Press, 1986. 2 vols.

Dean, Gabrielle. "Make It Plain: Stein and Toklas Publish the Plain Edition." *Primary Stein: Returning to the Writing of Gertrude Stein*, edited by Janet Boyd and Sharon J. Kirsch, Lexington Books, 2014, pp. 13–35.

Dydo, Ulla E. *Gertrude Stein: The Language That Rises, 1923–1934*. With William Rice. Northwestern University Press, 2003.

Eliot, T. S. "Charleston, Hey! Hey!" *The Nation and Athenaeum*, 29 Jan. 1927, p. 595.

———"Tradition and the Individual Talent." 1919. *The Sacred Wood*, Methuen & Co., 1920, pp. 42–53.

Esdale, Logan. "Gertrude Stein, Laura Riding and The Space of Letters." *Journal of Modern Literature*, vol. 29, no. 4, summer 2006, pp. 99–123.

Fletcher, John Gould. "Recent Books." *The Monthly Criterion*, vol. 6, no. 2, August 1927, pp. 168–172.

Ford, Hugh. *Published in Paris: American and British Writers, Printers, and Publishers in Paris, 1920–1939*. Macmillan, 1975.

Foster, Stephen C., editor. *Hans Richter: Activism, Modernism, and the Avant-Garde*. MIT Press, 1998.

Friedmann, Elizabeth. *A Mannered Grace: The Life of Laura (Riding) Jackson*. Persea Books, 2005.

Gallup, Donald, editor. *The Flowers of Friendship: Letters Written to Gertrude Stein*. Alfred A. Knopf, 1953.

Graves, Robert. "Correspondence." *The Monthly Criterion*, vol. 6, no. 4, October 1927, pp. 357–359.

———. *Good-bye to All That*. 1929. Edited by Frank Brearton. Penguin, 2014.

Hammer, Langdon, and Brom Weber, editors. *O My Land, My Friends: The Selected Letters of Hart Crane*. Four Walls Eight Windows, 1997.

Heffernan, Laura, and Jane Malcolm. "We Must Be Barbaric: An Introduction to *Contemporaries and Snobs*." *Contemporaries and Snobs*, by Laura Riding, University of Alabama Press, 2014, pp. ix–xxiii.

Holbrook, Susan, and Thomas Dilworth, editors. *The Letters of Gertrude Stein and Virgil Thomson: Composition as Collaboration*. Oxford University Press, 2010.

Horrocks, Roger. *Len Lye: A Biography*. Auckland University Press, 2001.

Jackson, Laura (Riding). "The Word-Play of Gertrude Stein." *Critical Essays on Gertrude Stein*, edited by Michael J. Hoffman, G. K. Hall, 1986, pp. 240–60.

Jackson, Laura (Riding), and Schuyler B. Jackson. *Rational Meaning: A New Foundation for the Definition of Words*. University Press of Virginia, 1997.

Jessop, Anett. "Geopoetics and Historical Modernism: Gertrude Stein, Laura Riding, and Robert Graves in Mallorca, 1912–1936." *Mediterranean Modernism: Intercultural Exchange and Aesthetic Development*, edited by Adam J. Goldwyn and Renée M. Silverman, Palgrave Macmillan, 2016, pp. 123–48.

Liston, Mauren R. *Gertrude Stein: An Annotated Critical Bibliography*. Kent State University Press, 1979.

Loy, Mina. "Gertrude Stein." *The Transatlantic Review*, vol. 2, no. 4, Oct. 1924, pp. 427–30.

Meyer, Steven. "'An Ill-Matched Correspondence': Laura Riding's Gertrude Stein." *Raritan*, vol. 19, no. 4, spring 2000, pp. 159–70.

O'Prey, Paul, editor. *In Broken Images: Selected Letters of Robert Graves, 1914–1946*. Hutchinson, 1982.

Paul, Elliot. "Gertrude Stein." 1927. *The Left Bank Revisited: Selections from the Paris Tribune 1917–1934*, edited by Hugh Ford, Pennsylvania State University Press, 1972, pp. 265–67.

Riding, Laura. *Anarchism Is Not Enough*. 1928. Edited by Lisa Samuels, University of California Press, 2001.

———, editor. *Everybody's Letters*. Arthur Barker, 1933.

———. *Four Letters to Catherine*. 1930. Persea Books, 1993.

Riding, Laura, and George Ellidge. *14A*. Arthur Barker, 1934.

Root, Waverley Lewis. "Season's Most Brilliant Book Is Gertrude Stein's Biography." 1933. *The Left Bank Revisited: Selections from the Paris Tribune 1917–1934*, edited by Hugh Ford, Pennsylvania State University Press, 1972, pp. 277–80.

Samuels, Lisa. E-mail to the editors. 19 July 2021.

Sitwell, Edith. *Poetry and Criticism*. Hogarth Press, 1925.

Stein, Gertrude. *At Present*. 1930. *Operas and Plays*, Station Hill Press, 1987, pp. 315–24.

———. *How to Write*. 1931. Sun & Moon Press, 1995.

———. *The Autobiography of Alice B. Toklas*. 1933. Vintage, 1990.

———. "Why Do Americans Live in Europe?" *transition*, no. 14, fall 1928, pp. 97–98.

Toklas, Alice B. *The Alice B. Toklas Cook Book*. 1954. Harper Perennial, 1984.

Wagner-Martin, Linda. *"Favored Strangers": Gertrude Stein and Her Family*. Rutgers University Press, 1995.

Wexler, Joyce Piell. *Laura Riding: A Bibliography*. Garland, 1981.

Wilson, Jean Moorcroft. *Robert Graves: From Great War Poet to* Good-bye to All That *(1895–1929)*. Bloomsbury Continuum, 2018.

Woolf, Virginia. *A Room of One's Own*. 1929. Harcourt, 1989.

INDEX

Aldridge, John, 37n, 76, 78n, 80, 80n, 87n

Anderson, Margaret, 19n6, 63n; *My Thirty Years' War*, 63n

Anderson, Sherwood, 4, 18n6, 21n19, 33n

Arthur Barker (publisher), 79n, 103n

Baker, Deborah, 15

Barney, Natalie Clifford, 63n; *Aventures de l'esprit*, 63n

Basket (poodle), 72, 73n, 74, 76, 78, 90, 104

Beinecke Rare Book and Manuscript Library (or Yale University Library), 14, 21n24, 22n27

Bookstaver, May, 9

Boyle, Kay, 27, 28n

Brewer, Joseph, 33n

Bryher (Annie Winifred Ellerman), 4, 18n3, 19n6

Cameron, Norman, 37n

Canellun, 14, 74n

Cézanne, Paul, 2, 108n

Charterhouse School, 85, 85n

Chicago Tribune, 5, 28n

Church, Ralph, 41, 44n; *A Study in the Philosophy of Malebranche*, 44n

Clarke, John Henry, 63, 64n

Close Up, 19n6

Collins, Wilkie, 73, 74n

composition, 7–8, 17 ("the hand is accidental not composition"), 26n ("creating the possibility of poetic thought to come"), 31 ("if we did all our own composition"), 31n, 32 ("a thing I am doing about grammar and in description"), 34 ("I am writing pretty well"), 61 ("writing my autobiography"), 62n, 63 ("I have just begun writing"), 65 ("I am getting my sentences"), 68–69 ("Laura's writing is becoming"), 69 ("thrown me back to grammar for words"), 71 ("the hand is accidental not composition"), 78 ("I'm making a Compendium"), 85 ("I am busy on the word"), 85 ("We are bringing our press out"), 86 ("I am writing poems about certainty"), 90 ("I am writing and Alice is tapestrying"), 102 ("I am writing a poem called Laura and Francisca"), 107 ("What is said in letters is of course always better left unsaid"), 125–29 (Riding offers a close reading of Stein's "Composition as Explanation")

Cone, Claribel, 79n

Cone, Etta, 79n

Constable (publisher), 104n

Contact Editions, 12, 19n6; *Contact Collection of Contemporary Writers*, 79n

Cook, William, 75n, 76–77, 79n, 80–81, 81n, 86, 90, 93, 102, 104

Cooper, Katherine ("Kanty"), 76, 78n, 82n, 83n, 84, 85n, 87n, 89, 90, 91

Criterion, The, 3, 4, 18n4

Cullen, Countee, 90n

Cunard, Nancy, 80, 80n, 83n, 89, 95, 100, 102

Crane, Hart, 2, 45–46, 46n, 53, 53n, 63, 98, 99n, 122, 129–30

Daily Herald, The, 76

Daniel-Rops, Henri, 21n23

Dean, Gabrielle, 12

Dial, The, 5, 19n6, 19n8, 52

Draper, Muriel, 63n; *Music at Midnight*, 63n

Duncan, Irma, 74n, *Isadora Duncan's Russian Days and Her Last Years in France*, 74n

Duncan, Isadora, 73, 74n
Dydo, Ulla, 5, 7, 15, 20n16, 26n

Éditions de la Montagne, 12, 96, 96n, 99, 100n, 100
Eliot, T. S., 4, 5, 18n4, 19n10, 122, 123, 124, 129
Ellidge, George, 13, 103n
enclosures, 1, 6–7, 11–12, 17, 25 (book), 26 (book), 27 (newspaper clipping), 30 (proofs), 32 ("list of the few mistakes"), 36 (prospectus), 40 (book, textile), 41 (shawls, letter), 45 (labels, binding), 46 (labels), 47n (shawl), 50 (copies of *An Acquaintance with Description*, shawl), 65 (two poems), 66 (Lye's "Still July," Thompson's poem, drawing, book), 68 (found text), 71 (drawings), 78 (book), 89 (book), 90 (verse letter, books), 94 (pebbles), 96 ("the inclosed"), 98 (cheque), 100 (postcards, card), 101 (letter), 102 ("a sheet of our printing")
Esdale, Logan, 22n29

Fletcher, John Gould, 18n4
Footprints Studio, 39n
Ford, Ford Madox, 63, 74, 75n; *Return to Yesterday*, 63n
Friedmann, Elizabeth, 15–16, 22n29, 55n, 71n
Fugitive, The, 3, 32n

Gallup, Donald, 14, 22n27; *The Flowers of Friendship*, 14
gardens, 12, 72, 72n, 73, 96, 98, 104, 131
Gerald Howe (publisher), 78n
Le Goff, Marcel, 2–3
Gottschalk, Louis, 29n
Gordon, Taylor, 87n, 90n
Graves, Beryl, 14
Graves, Robert, *But It Still Goes On*, 101; *Contemporary Techniques of Poetry*, 19n9; *The Feather Bed*, 19n9; *Good-bye to All That*, 9, 14, 20n13, 61, 62n, 63, 63n, 66,

73–76, 73n, 75n, 76n, 80, 85, 89, 90n; *I, Claudius*, 79n; *Impenetrability*, 19n9; *Lawrence and the Arabs*, 6, 20n13; *Mock Beggar Hall*, 19n9; *Poems (1914–1926)*, 18n4; *Poems (1914–1927)*, 14, 26, 26n, 30, 110; *Poems 1929*, 23n, 31, 32n, 35n, 66, 67n, 68, 68n; *A Survey of Modernist Poetry*, with Laura Riding, 3, 24n, 106n; *Ten Poems More*, 83n, 98, 105n; "To Be Less Philosophical," 26n, 109–10; *To Whom Else?*, 104n
Graves, Rosaleen, 54n

H. D. (Hilda Doolittle), 18n3
Hawthorne, Nathaniel, 5
Heap, Jane, 4, 19n6, 21n19
Heffernan, Laura, 19n11
Hemingway, Ernest, 4, 18n6, 21n19, 84, 85n, 108n
Herbert, A. P., 37n
Hernandez, Mariana, 77, 78n, 79n, 90
Hoffman, Michael J., 22n26
Hogarth Press, 3, 4, 5, 12, 19n9, 40n, 47n; *Hogarth Essays*, 19n9
Horwood, Harry, 20n18
Hugnet, Georges, 12, 20n17, 21n19, 96n, 100n
Hunt, Sidney, 80, 80n

illness, 8, 10, 23, 33, 33n, 44, 49, 50n, 50, 55, 63–64, 66, 84, 102, 103n, 106, 107

Jackson, Schuyler, 13, 29n
James, William, 20n16
Jewishness, 3, 14, 21n 22, 73, 74n, 102, 103n, 119–20
Jolas, Eugene, 4, 27–28n, 37, 39
Jonathan Cape (publisher), 24n, 26n, 62n, 69n, 69n, 75, 89, 91
Joseph Horne (department store), 81n
Joyce, James, 5, 123, 124

Kelly, Eleanor Mercein, 77, 78n
Kennington, Celandine, 37n
Kennington, Eric, 37n

Ladies Home Journal, 39, 44n
Lawrence, D. H., 93, 93n
Lawrence, T. E., 20n13
Leman, Ulrich, 78n
lesbianism, 102, 104n
Little Review, The, 19n6
London Film Society, 80, 81n
Loy, Mina, 4, 19n6, 21n19, 106n
Luhan, Mabel Dodge, 4, 18n6, 20–21n19,
    63n; *Intimate Memories,* 63n
Lye, Len, 2, 7, 9, 11, 13, 37–47, 50–51,
    53, 55, 60n, 64, 66, 67n, 68, 69, 70n,
    74n, 76, 78n, 79, 80n, 80–87, 89–96,
    98, 108; "Laura Riding Shawl," 37,
    38 (fig. 6), 39, 47n; *No Trouble,*
    22n28, 35n, 41n, 66, 67n, 102, 103n,
    115n; "Still July," 66, 67n, 113–14;
    Tusalava, 37, 45–46, 46n, 50, 64, 71,
    72n, 81, 81–82n, 83n, 86, 89
Lyle, Marius (Una Maud Lyle Smyth), 77, 78n

Macdougall, Allan Ross, 74n; *Isadora
    Duncan's Russian Days and Her Last
    Years in France,* 74n
Macpherson, Kenneth, 18n3
Malcolm, Jane, 19n11
Man Ray (Emmanuel Radnitzky), 83, 84s
Marsh, Edward, 62n, 64, 64n
Mayers, Isabel Reichenthal, 80, 80n
Mayers, Richard, 80, 80n
McAlmon, Robert, 19n6, 21n19
McBride, Henry, 4
McGuinness, Norah, 21n20, 47n
Means, Gaston, 106n; *The Strange Death
    of Warren Harding,* 105, 106n
Mellow, James R., 15
Meyer, Steven, 22n29
Moallic, Jeanne, 75n
modernism, xi, 1–5, 7, 12, 18n3, 18n4
    19n10, 19n11, 41, 63n, 77, 86, 105,
    106n, 123–24, 128–29
Montagu, Ivor, 82n
Moore, Marianne, 4, 18n4, 19n6
Moore, Merrill, 80, 80n
Myrga, Laurence (Marcelle Marie
    Clémence Tulle), 83, 84n

Nation (or *The Nation and Athenaeum*),
    The, 52
Neale, Russell, 78, 79n; *Hobby House,* 78,
    79n
New Republic, The, 52
New York Herald (Paris edition), *The,* 27,
    27n, 27n, 28 (figs. 3 and 4), 30n, 34n
Nicholson, Nancy, 2, 3, 27, 29n, 30n,
    37n, 47n, 48n, 48, 48n, 50, 54–57,
    58n, 59, 67n, 70, 105, 106n
Nicholson, William, 105, 106n, 107–8

Observer, The, 52
Omega Workshops, 39n
O'Prey, Paul, 21n21

Pagany, 20n17
Paul, Elliot, 4, 5, 21n19, 28n
Payson and Clarke, 33, 34
pebbles, 11–12, 86, 94, 94n, 95, 95n, 96,
    96n
Phibbs, Geoffrey, 13, 47–50, 47n, 48n,
    48n, 49n, 54–59, 54n, 56n, 58n, 58n,
    67n, 70, 71n, 78, 85, 85n, 87n; *It Was
    Not Jones,* 47n; *The Withering of the
    Fig Leaf,* 47n
Picasso, Pablo, 2, 12, 104n
Plain Edition, 12, 20n17, 32n, 100n
Po, Li (or Li Bai), 5
Poe, Edgar Allan, 129
postcards, 10, 15–16, 21n25, 53n, 81,
    87, 87n, 94, 95n, 96, 97n, 101n, 105,
    105n
Pound, Ezra, 5, 123

Ransom, John Crowe, 3, 18n4
Richards, Vyvyan, 80, 80n
Richter, Hans, 81, 82n
Riding, Laura, Cornell archive, 14–15,
    16, 21n25, 22n28; *14A,* with George
    Ellidge, 13, 21n20, 103n; *Anarchism
    Is Not Enough,* 6, 25, 26n, 26n, 47n;
    The Close Chaplet, 2, 3, 4, 18n4, 40n;
    The Collected Poems of Laura Riding,
    111; *Contemporaries and Snobs,*
    19–20n11, 24n; "Death as Death,"

Riding, Laura (*continued*)
24n; *Everybody's Letters*, 22n28, 78, 79n, 86, 87n, 101, 101n; *Experts Are Puzzled*, 12–13, 62n, 69n, 77–78, 101, 107, 120; "Fine Fellow Son of a Poor Fellow," 8, 40–41, 110–11; *Focus*, 22n28; *Four Unposted Letters to Catherine*, 22n28, 83n, 91n, 103n, 103n, 105n, 108n; "If This Reminds," 24n; *Laura and Francisca*, 102, 104n; *Love as Love, Death as Death*, 7, 14, 23n, 35n, 40–41, 40n, 62n, 111; "The Lullaby," 111; "The New Barbarism, and Gertrude Stein," 4, 5, 15, 19n10, 19n11, 22n26, 22n29, 24n, 121–30; "One," 18n4; "Other, who have tasted the true water," 65, 67n, 112–13; *Poems: A Joking Word*, 67n, 69n, 77, 79n, 91, 96, 98, 105n, 107; *A Survey of Modernist Poetry*, with Robert Graves, 3, 24n, 106n; *Rational Meaning*, 20n15; "Sea-Ghost," 24n; "This," 65, 67n, 111–12, 113; *Though Gently*, 13, 103n, 103n, 107; *Twenty Poems Less*, 83n, 89, 89n, 91n, 93 (fig. 15), 105n; *Voltaire*, 2, 40n; *The World and Ourselves*, 22n28; "The Word-Play of Gertrude Stein," 15, 22n26, 103n
Rimbaud, Arthur, 129
Root, Waverley Lewis, 10

Sage, Robert, 27, 28n
Samuels, Lisa, 26n
Sanders, Frank J. H., 80, 80n
Sassoon, Siegfried, 3, 75, 75n, 76, 76n, 86, 87n, 89–91, 91n, 105
Saturday Evening Post, The, 44, 73, 77, 78n
Saturday Review, The, 52
Schneider, Isidor, 46n
Scudder, Janet, 63n; *Modeling My Life*, 63n
Seizin Press, 2, 3, 5–6, 7, 9, 12, 19n9, 20n13, 21n24, 23n, 31n, 34–35, 35n, 39, 40, 53n, 67n, 80n, 85n, 100n, 103–4n
shawls (by Len Lye), 7, 11, 37, 37n,

38–39, 39n, 40–41, 41n, 42–44, 44n, 47, 47n, 50–51, 53n, 53, 53n, 66, 74n, 81, 138
Sitwell, Edith, 3–4, 18n5, 21n19, 76n, 124, 129; *Poetry and Criticism*, 18n5
Somerville, Mary ("Maisie"), 80, 80n
Steele, Alan, 95, 95n, 96
Stein, Gertrude, *An Acquaintance with Description*, 2, 3, 5, 6, 7, 8, 9, 10, 11, 12, 21n24, 22n29, 23n, 24, 30–31, 31n, 31n, 34–37, 35n, 39, 44–46, 47 (fig. 9), 49n, 50–53, 52 (fig. 11), 86, 96–100, 100n, 131–53; "Arthur A Grammar," 32n; "As a Wife Has a Cow A Love Story," 24n; *At Present*, 32n; *The Autobiography of Alice B. Toklas*, 4, 10, 11, 12, 20n18, 63n, 75n, 81n, 89n; "Basket," 51n; *Before the Flowers of Friendship Faded Friendship Faded*, 20n17, 100n; "Composition as Explanation," 4, 5, 23n, 31n, 76n, 98n, 125–29; *Composition as Explanation*, 2, 19n9; "Constance Fletcher," 76n; *Dix Portraits*, 89, 90n, 96, 96n, 101, 102n, 103n, 103n; *Everybody's Autobiography*, 81n; "Film: deux soeurs qui ne sont pas soeurs," 51n, 79n; "Five Words in a Line," 51n; *Four Saints in Three Acts*, 25n; *Geography and Plays*, 2, 18n6, 33n, 76n; *How to Write*, 8, 22n29, 32n, 65, 68, 69, 100n; "Idem the Same. A Valentine to Sherwood Anderson," 33n; "If I Told Him. A Completed Portrait of Picasso," 102, 103n; "Jean Cocteau," 4, 125, 127; *Lucy Church Amiably*, 12, 99, 100n, 104n; *The Making of Americans*, 2, 18–19n6, 75n, 96n, 127; *Matisse Picasso and Gertrude Stein*, 100n; "Melanctha," 32n; *Morceaux choisis de la fabrication des américains*, 96n; *Operas and Plays*, 12, 100n; *Picasso*, 36n; "Poem Pritten on Pfances of George Hugnet," 20n17; "Preciosilla," 4; "Regular Regularly in Narrative," 32n; *A Saint in Seven*, 4; "Sentences," 32n, 51n; "Sitwell Edith Sitwell," 4;

Tender Buttons, 2, 4, 18n6, 37n; *Three Lives*, 2, 32n; "Two Women," 79n; *Useful Knowledge*, 7, 33n, 33n, 34, 44; "Van or Twenty Years After. A Second Portrait of Carl Van Vechten," 33n; "Why Do Americans Live in Europe?", 37n; *The World Is Round*, 21n21

Stevens, Wallace, 129

Stokes, Henry Paine, 74n; *A Short History of the Jews in England*, 74n

Studio des Ursulines, 82n, 83, 84n

suicide, 7–9, 11–13 54, 54n, 55, 55n, 59–60, 60n, 61–63, 62n, 64–65 ("permanentest cut to liberty"), 85, 115–18

Tate, Allen, 3, 82, 84, 85n, 98, 122–23, 129

telegrams, 8, 16, 47–48, 48n, 49–50, 54

Thompson, Jane, 60, 60n, 64, 66, 67n, 76, 78n, 80–83, 80n, 86, 87n, 89, 90, 94–96, 95n, 98, 114–15

Thomson, Virgil, 2, 6, 20n17, 21n19, 25n, 27, 71–72n, 96n, 104n, 106n, 108

Times Literary Supplement, 52

Toklas, Alice, 2, 7, 9, 11, 12, 21n21, 25n, 27, 28n, 56n, 70n, 72–74, 72n, 74n, 75n, 76, 78, 81n, 82n, 85–90, 87n, 88 (fig. 14), 89n, 94, 96n, 99, 100n, 101, 105n; *The Alice B. Toklas Cook Book*, 21n21

Transatlantic Review, The, 18–19n6, 75n

transition, 4–5, 7, 24, 24n, 24 (fig. 2), 27–28n, 37, 37n, 38 (figs. 5 and 6), 39n, 39, 39n, 44n, 46n, 47n, 95, 102, 103n

Van Leyden, Ernst, 97–98, 98n

Van Vechten, Carl, 4, 18n6, 21n19, 21n24, 33n, 87n, 89, 90n, 104n

von Ranke, Hubert, 13, 14, 21n21

Wagner-Martin, Linda, 15

Wexler, Joyce Piell, 18n2

Wilder, Thornton, 14, 21n24

Willets-Burnham, Anita, 100–101, 101n, 104

William Jackson Ltd., 95, 98–100, 101n

Wilson, Edmund, 5

Wilson, Jean Moorcroft, 71n, 75n

Wood, Clement, 74n; *A Short History of the Jews*, 74n

Woolf, Leonard, 3, 19n9, 80; *Two Stories*, 19n9

Woolf, Virginia, 3, 19n7, 19n9; *A Room of One's Own*, 19n7; *Two Stories*, 19n9

Woolston, Jane, 22n27

www.ingramcontent.com/pod-product-compliance
Lightning Source LLC
Chambersburg PA
CBHW031819100825
30844CB00002B/80